Victoria Glendinning

ELIZABETH BOWEN

Victoria Glendinning was born in the north of England and read French and Spanish at Oxford. Her first book was *A Suppressed Cry*, a family memoir about her Quaker great-aunt. She has written biographies of Edith Sitwell (which won the James Tait Black Award and the Duff Cooper Prize), Vita Sackville-West (Whitbread Prize for Biography), Rebecca West, Anthony Trollope (Whitbread Prize for Biography), Jonathan Swift, and Leonard Woolf. She coedited *Mothers and Sons* with her son Matthew Glendinning, and has published three novels, *The Grown-Ups*, *Electricity*, and *Flight*. She reviews books for national newspapers and journals, has been a judge of the W. H. Smith Prize and other literary awards, and chair of the judges of the Booker Prize. From 2000–2003 she was president of English PEN. She is an Honorary Fellow of Somerville College, Oxford, and was awarded a CBE in 1998.

ELIZABETH BOWEN

Elizabeth BOWEN

by Victoria Glendinning

Anchor Books

A Division of Random House, Inc.

New York

FIRST ANCHOR BOOKS EDITION, DECEMBER 2006

The Library of Congress has cataloged the Knopf edition as follows:
Glendinning, Victoria.
Elizabeth Bowen / by Victoria Glendinning.—1st American ed.
Bibliography: p. Includes index.
1. Bowen, Elizabeth, 1899–1973—Biography.
2. Novelists, English—20th century—Biography.
PR6003.O6757 Z65 1978
823'.9'12
77-10604

Anchor ISBN-10: 0-307-27740-2
Anchor ISBN-13: 978-0-307-27740-4

www.anchorbooks.com

Printed in the United States of America
10 9 8 7 6 5 4 3 2 1

For my mother,
EVE SEEBOHM

CONTENTS

ILLUSTRATIONS

Sean O'Faolain with Elizabeth
(courtesy of Noreen Butler)

Elizabeth opening the door of 2 Clarence Terrace
(courtesy of Alfred A. Knopf)

Charles Ritchie in the 1940s
(courtesy of Charles Ritchie)

Elizabeth with Howard Moss
(courtesy of Howard Moss)

Alan Cameron studying the map

In the kitchen at Bowen's Court
(courtesy of Noreen Butler)

Settling the annual account with Mrs. Cleary
(courtesy of Noreen Butler)

Elizabeth with gardener Eddie Flynn

Parties at Bowen's Court with Lady Ursula Vernon,
Jim Egan, Mary Delamere, Stephen Vernon,
Iris Murdoch . . . and with Maurice Craig,
Irish Murdoch, Eddy Sackville-West, Hubert Butler
(both courtesy of Noreen Butler)

A studio portrait, 1950
(© Angus McBean)

In the country with a friend

With Cyril Connolly outside her last house in Hythe
(courtesy of Deirdre Connolly)

In Regent's Park, 1946
(courtesy of Alfred A. Knopf)

Elizabeth at Bowen's Court
(courtesy of Noreen Butler)

At the Knopf home in Purchase, New York
(*courtesy of Alfred A. Knopf*)

In America in 1963
(*courtesy of Alfred A. Knopf*)

Elizabeth at 2 Clarence Terrace
(© *Bill Brandt*)

One of the last photographs of Elizabeth Bowen
(© *Angus McBean*)

ACKNOWLEDGEMENTS

I SHOULD LIKE TO THANK first of all the literary executors of the late Elizabeth Bowen for permission to use copyright material and for support and help of every kind. I owe particular thanks, too, to Audrey Fiennes, Charles Ritchie, and Noreen and Gilbert Butler, who were more than generous to me in the research for this biography.

I am also very grateful to the Humanities Research Center, the University of Texas at Austin, for allowing me to use material from their impressive Elizabeth Bowen holdings, and especially for the help there of David Farmer and Ellen S. Dunlap; to Sir Rupert Hart-Davis and the University Librarian, the University of Durham, for permission to use Elizabeth Bowen's letters to William Plomer; and to the University Librarian, the University of Sussex, for her letters to Virginia Woolf.

My gratitude also to the following, who have helped in a great variety of ways, including the giving of information, permission to look at and quote from manuscript sources and unpublished letters, and the loan of photographs; and who have in many cases generously given their time to talk to me about Elizabeth Bowen. If any have been inadvertently omitted, I hope that they, too, will accept my thanks, and apologies:

Constance Babington Smith; Georgina Battiscombe; Nina Bawden; Professor Theophilus E. M. Bell; Sir Isaiah and Lady Berlin; Jean and Barry Black; Hilary C. J. Boyle; Neville Braybrooke; The British Council; the Honourable William Buchan; Hubert Butler; Lord David Cecil; Mrs. L. Chapple; Mrs. John Clay; Esmé Colley; Finlay Colley; Deirdre Connolly; Maurice Craig; Josephine Egan; Felicity Elphinstone; Patience

Acknowledgements

Erskine; Lady Fairfax-Lucy; Roy Foster; A. W. Gates; Eric Gillett; Michael Gilmour; Nigel Glendinning; Livia Gollancz; F. L. T. Graham-Harrison; Graham Greene; John Gross; John Guest; Stuart Hampshire; Ruth Harris; Sir Rupert Hart-Davis; Sir William and Lady Hayter; Derek Hill; Jacqueline Hope-Wallace; Thomas Hyde; Julian Jebb; Elizabeth Jenkins; Professor Harold Jenkins; Molly Keane; Francis King; Eardley Knollys (Edward Sackville-West's literary executor); Alfred A. Knopf; William A. Koshland; Celia Lanyon; Rosamond Lehmann; Caroline Lippincott; William Maxwell; Nelly McLaren; John Morley; Raymond Mortimer; Howard Moss; Iris Murdoch; Nigel Nicolson; Diana Oakeley (John Hayward's executor); Molly O'Brien; Sean O'Faolain; Iris Origo; Joan Osiakovski; the Reverend Oliver Peare; Eileen Pembroke; John Perry; Frances E. Popplewell; Norah Preece; Goronwy and Margaret Rees; Laurance and Isabel Roberts; Eileen Ross-Williamson; Jean Rowntree; J'nan M. Sellery; Francis Scarfe; Desmond Shawe-Taylor; Gerard Shiels; the Most Reverend George Simms, Archbishop of Armagh; Stephen and Natasha Spender; Oliver Stallybrass; Stephen Tennant; Herbert van Thal; Colin Thubron; Philip Toynbee; Susan, Lady Tweedsmuir; Major Stephen and the Lady Ursula Vernon; Julian Vinogradoff (Lady Ottoline Morrell's literary executor); Dame Veronica Wedgwood; G. P. Wells (H. G. Wells's literary executor); Terence de Vere White; W. W. Winkworth; Francis Wyndham.

FOREWORD

WHY A LIFE OF ELIZABETH BOWEN? She was born in 1899 and died in 1973; it is too soon to assess precisely her place among twentieth-century novelists. At this close remove, her position is a little obscured by the established reputations of writers who preceded her and by the impact of contemporary writing. But she is a major writer; her name should appear in any responsible list of the ten most important fiction writers in English on this side of the Atlantic in this century. She is to be spoken of in the same breath as Virginia Woolf, on whom much more breath has been expended. She shares much of Virginia Woolf's perception and sensibility: but Elizabeth Bowen's perception and sensibility are more incisive, less confined, more at home in the world as well as in worlds elsewhere.

Her best-known and most widely read novels are probably *The Death of the Heart* (1938*) and *The Heat of the Day* (1949); these, for different reasons, have a universal appeal. But if I were to pick the novels essential to illustrate both the quality of her writing and its development, they would be *The Last September* (1929), *The House in Paris* (1935), *A World of Love* (1955), and her last novel, *Eva Trout* (1968). Elizabeth Bowen had an active writing life of half a century. She is what happened after Bloomsbury; she is the link that connects Virginia Woolf with Iris Murdoch and Muriel Spark. She changed with the century in approach and technique without losing her original inimitable voice.

She made the short story particularly her own. In the

* The dates given are for the earliest publication of any work, whether in England or in America.

stories—which were, she said, "a matter of vision rather than of feeling"—she achieved a mastery that gives the best of them a perfection and a unity that the sustained narrative and shifting emphases of a novel do not attempt. It may be that posterity will judge the best of her stories over the novels: and the best Bowen stories, for me, are "The Disinherited", "Summer Night", "Mysterious Kôr", "The Happy Autumn Fields", "Ivy Gripped the Steps", "A Day in the Dark".

She can be compared with Colette in her evocation of colour, texture, flowers, landscape, neighbourhoods, rooms, furniture; but her style, her characteristic and essential rhythms, are utterly her own, as is her evocation of light, space, mood, shifts in time. She suggests—and suggests only, never describes —the fantasies, fears, and manipulations that underlie social behaviour. Her writing is full of tension even when her plots are tenuous. She was herself both a romantic and a woman of the world, and she wrote on, and of, the tightrope between innocence and disillusion. As Spencer Curtis Brown has written, "What she saw was an Eden in the seconds after the apple has been eaten, when Evil was known, immanent and unavoidable but while there was still awareness of what Innocence had been".[1] But Elizabeth Bowen, from her first book to her last, also shared with the reader her inexhaustible capacity for amusement. She combines an emotional intensity second to none with a humour that ranges from the subtlest social comedy to Dickensian burlesque. She entertains in her books because she herself found life entertaining.

In life, too, she entertained. Elizabeth Bowen had an overwhelming personality. She was vital, indefatigable, sociable, independent, extremely hard-working, brave, kind-hearted, perceptive. A respecter of the conventions, she was not a conventional person. She was sometimes formidable. She had a talent for friendship, and a large and unusually heterogeneous group of friends.

She was also Anglo-Irish. This is of significance in the

history of European literature, as when she died the Anglo-Irish literary tradition died with her. When she was growing up, all Ireland was still part of Great Britain. She lived between Ireland and England all her life. Since the twenty-six counties of the Republic of Ireland became a separate nation, the Anglo-Irish have lost their peculiar position and their cultural identity. There is no Anglo-Irish writer of Elizabeth Bowen's generation of the same stature, and hers was the last generation in which Anglo-Ireland, in its strict sense, existed. Her sense of comedy and social nuance has the same roots as Maria Edgeworth's and George Moore's; her apprehension of the supernatural is akin to that of Sheridan Le Fanu. She belonged to the old untenable Protestant Ascendancy, and her perceptions were formed in an Irish country house built by her ancestors; she was reared in a precarious world in which grace, charm, courtesy, and respect for tradition were valued. She never reneged on these personal values, which are the ones invoked by Ireland's greatest poet, W. B. Yeats, in "A Prayer for my Daughter":

> And may her bridegroom bring her to a house
> Where all's accustomed, ceremonious;
> For arrogance and hatred are the wares
> Peddled in the thoroughfares.
> How but in custom and in ceremony
> Are innocence and beauty born?
> Ceremony's a name for the rich horn
> And custom for the spreading laurel tree.

ELIZABETH BOWEN

CHAPTER I

Bowen's Court

I N LATE 1959 Cornelius O'Keefe bought Bowen's Court, near Kildorrery, County Cork, from Elizabeth Bowen, the last of the direct line, at a relatively modest price. She hoped that he and his family would inhabit and look after the house. The next year Derek Hill, the painter, asked by Elizabeth to do a painting of Bowen's Court to hang in her new home in England, drove over from Edward Sackville-West's house in County Tipperary. Parking his car by Farahy church, he looked north towards the familiar façade and saw that the roof was off Bowen's Court. By the end of the summer the whole house was demolished.

One can still approach what was Bowen's Court along what was the Lower Avenue. The woods and fine trees around the house are gone; the avenue is rutted by tractors. It may take the stranger a little while to identify the site of the house; it seems strangely small, covered with grass, scrubby bushes, and wild flowers. A line of stable buildings still stands. Walking north from the house-space towards the Ballyhoura mountains, through what was once rockery and laurel-lined woodland, you see that the walls of the three-acre walled garden, too, are still there. Elizabeth wrote of this garden:

> A box-edged path runs all the way round, and two
> paths cross at the sundial in the middle; inside the
> flower borders, backed by espaliers, are the plots of

3

fruit trees and vegetables, and the glasshouse backs on
the sunniest wall. . . . The flowers are, on the whole,
old-fashioned—jonquils, polyanthus, parrot tulips, lily
o' the valley (grown in cindery beds), voluminous white
and crimson peonies, moss roses, mauve-pink cabbage
roses, white-pink Celestial roses, borage, sweet pea,
snapdragon. . . .[1]

To go to the garden, walk around in it, select flowers for the
house, talk to the gardener, could fill most of a morning for
any lady of Bowen's Court. Once Elizabeth's father went there
looking for his wife; both vague and dreamy people, they
missed each other, and she left, locking the door in the wall,
and Henry Bowen was shut in. The walls of the garden enclose
nothing at all now.

The third Henry Bowen made Bowen's Court, completing
it in 1775. "Since then", wrote Elizabeth, "with a rather alarming sureness, Bowen's Court has made all the succeeding
Bowens". After the house was gone, she said that one could
not say that the space on which it had stood was empty: "more,
as it was—with no house there". And it was, as she said, a
clean end.

The little church of the hamlet of Farahy and its glebe
lands are carved out of the Bowen's Court demesne. The church
is now no longer used. In the little churchyard, against the stone
wall that faces where the house was, are the graves of Henry
Bowen, his sister Sarah, Elizabeth, his only child, and her
husband, Alan Cameron. Not much traffic passes on the
Mallow-to-Mitchelstown road, which bounds churchyard and
demesne on the south side. It is very quiet. "The churchyard is
elegiac", wrote Elizabeth about Farahy. "Trees surrounding it
shadow or drip over the graves and evergreens. Catholics as
well as Protestants bury here; their dead lie side by side in
indisputable peace". From the Bowen's Court side of the
churchyard wall a straggling shrub dangles its branches over on

to Elizabeth's grave. As late as mid-November it manages a few pink flowers.

Elizabeth inherited Bowen's Court on her father's death in 1930. The house, despite its many perfections, was not comfortable in the modern sense until, after the success of *The Heat of the Day* in 1949, Elizabeth spent some money on it and put in bathrooms. A little later, planning to live permanently at Bowen's Court instead of being based in England, she did more; the big drawing-room was embellished with curtains made, incredibly, of pink corset-satin: "A very good pink that goes beautifully", C. V. Wedgwood wrote to Jacqueline Hope-Wallace in December, 1953, "the kind of satin that grand shops make corsets and belts of; some local director of Debenhams found they had bales and bales of it left over— actually you would never think of it, but once you have been told you can think of nothing else!"

But even in earlier, more spartan days, Bowen's Court, when Elizabeth was there, was full of people and talk and life. The summer of 1936, for example. On September 25th of that year, Elizabeth wrote to describe her summer to the critic and editor John Hayward, who had written to her from London that "my little world turns very slowly in your absence". Early in August, Lord David Cecil and his wife, Rachel, had been to stay for ten days. "I like Rachel so particularly much, and David's really my oldest, securest friend". The three of them had talked non-stop, she said, "without fatigue, suspicion, exhibitionism, strain, unseemly curiosity or desire to impress". And after the Cecils left more came—the house had been full, which created a problem because although there was lots of space there was not much furniture:

> Beds, and even a room in a neighbour's house were borrowed, washstands, blankets (we really did need some new ones), cans, scratchy local bath-towels and four small new teapots bought. Then they all arrived:

Roger [Senhouse] and Rosamond [Lehmann] one morning from England, Shaya [Isaiah] Berlin and two student friends [Stuart Hampshire and Con O'Neill] from Killarney that evening, John Summerson, of the Nash book, the morning after, Goronwy Rees two days later. My cousin Noreen Colley was also here. . . . I think of all the guests Roger was really the nicest—in fact I know it—he is so sort of participating, such a support, and makes one feel he really cares for a place itself apart from just the sensation of being there. Shaya was also an angel: I'm very fond of him. . . . Rosamond looked quite lovely, was sweet and I think enjoyed herself. After most of the party had gone, a few other odd people came—one Michael Gilmour, and a nice Irish don who often visits All Souls: Myles Dillon from Dublin.[2]

When the contents of Bowen's Court were sold at auction in Cork—a two-day sale in April, 1960—the accumulation of many Bowen lifetimes was on offer. As always when old family houses are sold up, the lots ranged from collectors' items to pathetic collections of junk; from gilt mirrors carved with eagles and lions and important pieces in eighteenth-century walnut and mahogany down to waste-paper baskets, lampshades, broken garden tables and "Ewbank carpet cleaner and 2 Hand Bags" (Lot 303). Among it all were "4 China Teapots" sold on the first day with a lustre hot-water jug as Lot 12: perhaps the four teapots bought specially for the 1936 house-party. And the end of the second day saw the end of the pink drawing-room curtains as Lot 353, promoted for the occasion from corset-satin to "silk damask".

In the beginning, the Bowens were Welsh—ap Owen—from the Gower Peninsula. A Henry Bowen took up arms for the

King's party in the Civil War, then switched sides and went to Ireland as a lieutenant-colonel in Cromwell's army. He was a professional soldier, an atheist, a hard man, and was married three times: from the second marriage came the Bowen's Court Bowens.

There was a family myth about the way in which Henry Bowen acquired his property in County Cork. Hawking was his one pleasure, and he had brought with him from Gower a pair of hawks. His sport was disapproved of by the Cromwellians as frivolous and ungodly, but Henry cared for no one, except maybe his hawks. Once when Cromwell sent for him, he turned up with a hawk on his wrist, and played with it while Cromwell was speaking. Cromwell, infuriated, wrung the hawk's neck, and the two men parted in anger. But either Henry turned over a new leaf or Cromwell was impressed by his spirit, for the next thing was that Cromwell proposed to give him as much Irish land as the other hawk could fly over before it came down.

This story was invalidated for Elizabeth by the Buchan family, who told her that a hawk flies straight up and hangs until it drops on its prey. Be that as it may, the story is that "standing near the foot of the Ballyhouras, Colonel Bowen released his hawk, which flew south". And a hawk remained the family crest.

The land over which the hawk had allegedly flown comprised over eight hundred acres, fifty-five of which were designated "unprofitable"—in the terms of the deed of 1653, "Mountain and Bogg". Colonel Bowen made his home in a small half-ruined castle near the Farahy stream, where he was joined by his eldest son, John, from Wales.

Colonel Bowen's great-grandson married rich Jane Cole, and the Bowens absorbed not only her lands but, in all succeeding generations, her name: Elizabeth was Elizabeth Dorothea Cole Bowen. And Colonel Bowen's great-great-grandson, a third Henry, was the builder of Bowen's Court. The architect is not known, and no plans or drawings seem to have survived. The house was ten years in the building, was dated 1775, and the family moved in the following year. The money ran out before everything was finished; the Italian plasterers from Cork (trailing plaster roses and basket-work in the drawing-room) were paid off before they had decorated the well ceiling of the great Long Room, which ran the length of the top storey of the house. The north-east corner of the intended square never got built, and the makeshift staircase that joined the first floor with the Long Room remained the only one. Furniture, glass, and silverware Henry had made specially in Cork; so far as design and craftsmanship were concerned, he could not have placed his orders at a better period.

Elizabeth imagined the third Henry and his wife surveying their new home in the moonlight, its newly glazed windows "giving the house the glitter of a superb maniac". Henry said he would like to beget a child to look out of every window in Bowen's Court: in the south façade there were twenty. The Bowens had fourteen children (and seven who did not survive). The third Henry, with insoluble financial and legal problems— the Bowens were compulsive litigants—was the first Bowen, but not the last, nervously to pace the Long Room up and down, up and down.

The year of the United Irishmen's rising, 1798, brought drama to Bowen's Court. A rumour reached the Farahy rectory that the house was going to be attacked. Running across the field, the incumbent warned the Bowens. The household defended itself, and the house, built like a fortress, helped. Shots were fired from inside and out, and in the morning a dead man was found in a pear tree. On this night, a shot was fired into the dining-room. At the house-party in 1936, conversation at dinner one evening about this was shushed by Elizabeth, as one of the maids in the room was from a family that might have been involved in the 1798 raid. (The topic was a mistaken

8

one not because it might reawaken antagonism but because it lacked delicacy.)

During the potato famines of the late 1840s, the current and fifth Mrs. Henry Bowen, a widow, fed the sick and starving from the house; she opened a soup-kitchen in the big stone-walled room that in Elizabeth's day was the laundry. Some died on the way up the grass track from the Farahy gate; a famine pit was dug in a corner of little Farahy churchyard.

Her son Robert Cole Bowen was the first "high-voltage" man, the first big Bowen, in Elizabeth's words, since the house-building Henry. When he took over the run-down and impoverished estate, Bowen's Court became a business. Rents and wages came in and went out more regularly than ever before, and the woman he married, Elizabeth Clarke, had both money and gumption. They were Elizabeth's grandparents, though she never knew them.

Robert, a true Victorian, obliterated what Elizabeth called the "unemotional plainness" of Bowen's Court. He filled the house with the glossy, ornate furniture of the 1860s and '70s. The drawing-room was redecorated, and the white, grey, and gold wallpaper he chose remained on its walls afterwards, growing ever more faded, for as long as those walls stood. And he brought in gilt mirrors, gilt pelmets, satin-striped beetle-green curtains, a patterned carpet. His most revolutionary creation was the Tower, at the back of the house (containing two W.C.s, topped by a tank), which was approached by the back stairs.

Robert Cole Bowen's W.C.s remained the only ones until Elizabeth's improvements in 1949; this was something that visitors such as Blanche Knopf, her American publisher, had to get used to. For Mrs. Knopf—exquisite, Americanly addicted to cleanliness, warmth, and comfort—a stay at bathless Bowen's Court was quite an experience, to which she did her gallant best to respond; she wrote to Elizabeth in August, 1938:

9

I cannot even begin to tell you what staying at Bowen's Court has meant to me. I have never seen anything quite like it of course, but I never realized how living that way could possibly be.

Possibly, on occasion, it could be rather uncomfortable. Nine years later, Elizabeth told Blanche that the house was in considerably better order since she was there, "though the upstairs rooms are still rather Chas. Addams-ish—I often remind myself of his hostess showing in a guest: 'This is your room. . . . If you want anything, just scream'."

To return to Robert Cole Bowen: he planted screens—thin strips of woodland—to protect the fields, and made the Lower Avenue down to Farahy, to balance the third Henry's Upper Avenue, which ran from the front steps westward to come out on the road to Mallow. And Robert and Elizabeth's eldest child, born in 1862, was Henry Charles Cole Bowen, Elizabeth's father.

He and his eight surviving brothers and sisters had a thin childhood in that overfurnished great house. They were thin children; their nursery diet was thin; they grew tall very fast (Elizabeth's father was six feet two inches) and lived "keyed-up": they suffered, Elizabeth thought, from inanition. "Their child life, congested and isolated, their life as Bowens together made a drama from which, as grown-up people, some of them found it hard to emerge. This was Personal Life at its most intense". And they were afraid of their father.

But if Robert Cole Bowen lived at high pressure, his household ran smoothly. The Bowen's Court housekeeper who was still in office in Elizabeth's day, Sarah Barry, came as a very young kitchen maid from Nenagh in those early days (fetched by Robert in a dogcart), and told Elizabeth that "downstairs" life was so harmonious that "you would hardly know who was a Protestant". (The butler was, for one.)

Elizabeth's father did not fit into the role ascribed to him as Robert Cole Bowen's eldest son and heir. He was absent-minded and courteous—"If he saw men as trees walking", wrote his daughter, "he bowed to the trees". High-principled and obstinate, he mentally rejected his father's success ethic. He took against horses, menservants, social discrimination, farming, and display of all kinds. But he loved Bowen's Court, he knew about rocks and trees, and he was able to talk to his mother. He was sent to St. Columba's—the Eton of Ireland—and then went to Trinity College, Dublin, where he remained peaceably isolated, enjoying things in his impersonal way; "He in no sense coveted life, and frustrated covetousness is, I suppose, at the root of most people's conscious unhappiness".

Between school and university, during a trip to Europe, Henry caught smallpox and arrived home already ill. His father immediately took off the rest of the family, most of the servants, and himself. Henry's mother stayed to nurse him. Now it was she who walked up and down, alone, in the Long Room. Henry recovered. But she caught the smallpox from him, and she died while only the convalescent boy was with her.

Sarah, the sister next in age to Henry, took over at seventeen the running of Bowen's Court. A year later their father married again, but his wife, "poor Georgina" Mansergh, was never accepted by the larger brood of highly strung young Bowens, and Robert was becoming increasingly more difficult and mentally unstable. "He became incapable—if he had ever been capable—of an unspoilt relation with anyone". Poor Georgina died after only four years of fraught marriage.

At Trinity young Henry distinguished himself in classics and ethics, then decided to read law and take up a profession. Robert was violently unsympathetic: "the father cared for success, the son for accomplishment". It became a constitutional crisis between father and son. Robert saw all he had worked for—political and social position in the county, his smooth-running farms, the new modern machinery in the yard—being neglected and going to waste in the years to come. In his despair he composed a will that made the decline of Bowen's Court even more likely, and began to fell the timber that he himself had planted, until Henry took out an injunction to stop him. In 1888, the year after Henry was called to the Irish bar, unhappy Robert died "in the throes of a violent mania".[3] Henry continued to travel between his work in Dublin and Bowen's Court, and he and his sister Sarah now ruled the young household.

Family history is hard to absorb; but it is important in that it was important to Elizabeth. She was intensely aware of her Bowen heritage—both the spiritual and the material heritage. It is not altogether a happy family history, and it cast its shadow. Bowens tended towards strong will, obsessiveness, and fantasy. The obsessions and the fantasies were generally to do with land, and Bowen's Court, latterly, was at the centre of them. Elizabeth knew herself to be part of this:

> What runs on most through a family living in one place is a continuous, semi-physical dream. Above this dream-level successive lives show their tips, their little conscious formations of will and thought. With the end of each generation, the lives that submerged here were absorbed again. With each death, the air of the place had thickened: it had been added to. The dead do not need to visit Bowen's Court rooms—as I said, we had no ghosts in that house—because they already permeated them. . . . The land outside Bowen's Court windows left prints on my ancestors' eyes that looked out: perhaps their eyes left, also, prints on the scene? If so, those prints were part of the scene for me.

Elizabeth's heritage was classic Anglo-Irish, in spite of Welsh, not English, origins. The term would apply to a family of the ruling Ascendancy class, after several generations, whether of Norman, Scottish, Welsh, English, or any other descent, and even when intermarried with the real Irish. Generalisations about national characteristics are dubious, and the Anglo-Irish do not even constitute a discrete nationality: Elizabeth used to say that they were really only at home in mid-crossing between Holyhead and Dun Laoghaire. While by no means all Anglo-Irish are Protestant, Brendan Behan's definition of an Anglo-Irishman as "a Protestant on a horse" is near enough some broad truth to have become a cliché. One would be more chary about characterising the Anglo-Irish were it not for the fact that they themselves have not been in the least chary about it. There is no need to go beyond their own observations.

Elizabeth herself put great stress on the effect of the isolated existence in country houses, not only on herself, but on all her class, though these families would normally have spent some of their time in London or Dublin. But in the country, they lived "in psychological closeness to one another and under the strong rule of the family myth". Each demesne is an island, and sometimes the family may not leave it for days at a time. "English people, or people from cities, ask what such families 'do' all day. . . . The preoccupation of Irish country people with their own affairs may be found either mystical or irritating". The isolation is more than geographical: it is, for these people who are still in some sense "settlers" after generations, an affair of origin. Their lives, Elizabeth wrote, "like those of only children, are singular, independent and secretive". (Elizabeth was both Anglo-Irish and an only child.) Elsewhere, and less emotionally, she described an Irish estate as "something between a *raison d'être* and a predicament".

Melancholy tinged with self-irony comes up in Cyril Connolly, in *Enemies of Promise*: "I have just enough Irish blood to be afraid of the Irish temperament. The literary form it takes, known as the 'Celtic twilight', consists of an addiction to melancholy and to an exaggerated use of words, and such good Irish writers as there have been exorcise the demon by disciplining themselves to an alien and stricter culture".

For the geniuses among the Anglo-Irish are generally "prime examples for export", according to Terence de Vere White in his *The Anglo-Irish* (1972). In spite of the gifted ones who do stay, it is on the whole "a hearty, horsey, rather than a literary society". This hearty horsiness is just as typical as the melancholy. When the real Irish think of the Anglo-Irish, says Terence de Vere White, "they have in mind loud-voiced, confident people with English accents, wearing tweeds, heading for sales of work in aid of disabled soldiers or parading in the rings at the Horse Show". Elizabeth, while she didn't much like horses, was not out of place in this group: she recognised her own physical type among its women, she lent Bowen's Court for Protestant Whist Drives, British soldiers always attracted her indulgence and hospitality, and she was unmistakably "a lady".

Yet there is something more vital and attractive in Anglo-Ireland than either the melancholy stereotype or the horsey one would suggest, and outsiders are very conscious of it. "To English and American ears", writes Terence de Vere White, " 'Anglo-Irish' has an encouraging sound. It means wit, elegant writing, Georgian architecture, aristocracy picturesquely decayed. . . . The Anglo-Irish say things like, 'Come into the garden, I want my roses to see you' " (as Sheridan is said to have done). Mr. White is ironic; but the fact remains that as a class they have great style, and a verbal fluency that leaves the rest of these islands nowhere. This stylishness and this verbal fluency Elizabeth had in full measure. At its lowest it can become, in some people and especially in Dublin, what Susan Mitchell (in her book on George Moore) called "a most futile and diverting cleverness". At its best, it produces Sheridan, Burke, Swift, Maria Edgeworth, George Moore, Oscar Wilde, Somerville and Ross—and Elizabeth Bowen.

Elizabeth found herself—and all the Anglo-Irish—

belligerent, always game for a fight, for which the duelling tradition and the tradition of daredevil riding were ideal outlets. But talking and writing can express the same vitality:

> To [writing] we have taken like ducks to water. Accommodating ourselves to a tamer day, we interchanged sword-play for word-play. Repartee, with its thrusts, opened alternative possibilities of mastery. . . . Bravado characterises much Irish, all Anglo-Irish writing: gloriously it is sublimated by Yeats. Nationally, we have an undertow to the showy. It follows that primarily we have produced dramatists, the novel being too life-like, humdrum, to do us justice. We do not do badly with the short story. . . . To most of the rest of the world we are semi-strangers, for whom existence has something of the trance-like quality of a spectacle. As beings, we are at once brilliant and limited; our unbeatables, up to now, accordingly, have been those who best profited by that: Goldsmith, Sheridan, Wilde, Shaw, Beckett. Art is for us inseparable from artifice: of that, the theatre is the home.
>
> Possibly, it was England made me a novelist.[4]

There are not many literary Anglo-Irish in Ireland any more. The "settlers" no longer call the cultural tune. Most leave, in the end. "The literary Anglo-Irish have fled, like the Wild Geese", wrote Terence de Vere White. "When Elizabeth Bowen took wing Ireland saw the last of them".

The Anglo-Irish attitude to the English is ambivalent. Historically their interests have lain in the connection with the country by whose authority they held what position they had. From the time that improved transport made it feasible, Anglo-Irish children tended to go to school in England; younger sons went into the Army. Yet in Elizabeth's childhood, no less than today, to say that something or someone was "very English" was most unlikely to be a compliment. Cyril Connolly said that his Anglo-Irish cousins teased him about being English, which he gathered meant having "a combination of snobbery, stupidity and lack of humour and was a deadly insult". The Anglo-Irish, he inferred, were a superior people: "Better born, but less snobbish; cleverer than the English and fonder of horses; they were poorer no doubt but with a poverty that brought into relief their natural aristocracy".[5]

In general the Irish and the Anglo-Irish, within the context of an enormous communicativeness, have a tact and sensitivity that are sometimes taken to a baroque point where they almost become something else. Elizabeth herself was extremely reticent about personal matters, and this is a characteristic of her "race" and class. When she and her mother went to live in England, her mother, she said, liked the English but found them "impertinent". And Elizabeth in *The Last September*, at the tea-party, describes Mrs. Carey fearing that she detects in Mrs. Vermont "a tendency, common to most English people, to talk about her inside". English directness often seems like crudeness in Ireland; and English casualness like rudeness; and English self-containedness like lack of feeling.

There is one Anglo-Irish characteristic, deriving more from the real Irish in them, that Elizabeth fully shared: a natural warmth and gregariousness that lead to a great sense of hospitality and a liking for celebrations of all kinds. Elizabeth's English friends often, at the beginning, wondered whether she could really like them and enjoy their company *quite* as much as she seemed to. This warmth and gift for friendship, this ability to live in the present and make a good time, did much to offset the more uncertain, nervous Bowen heritage. She inherited it in large part from her mother's family, the Colleys.

The Colleys were very different from the Bowens. They lived in a house called Mount Temple at Clontarf, which is on the road running north-east from Dublin to Howth Head round the edge of Dublin Bay. It was a Victorian house with gables, and views over the bay. The young Bowens were motherless: the Colleys were anything but. Mrs. Colley—born Elizabeth Isabella Wingfield—was a dominant, dynamic, anti-intellectual, confident lady: "a very good woman", wrote Elizabeth, "with all those gifts through which wicked women most often succeed". Her children were Bessie, Maud, Florence (who was to marry Henry Bowen), George, Laura, Wingfield, Gerald, Constance, Gertrude, and Edward. There was also her husband, Henry Fitz-George Colley, who was something of an invalid.

The Colleys had a flair for family life. "In their love of the present, and their power of storing up memories, they were ruled by an innocent sensuousness". Unlike the Bowens, they were not conditioned by any special place; they were not "inhibited by proud fine-strung place-bound nervousness", as the Bowens were. They were very well connected.

Mr. Colley's father had been a Pomeroy, and had changed his name in order to inherit property. His maternal grandmother, Mary, wife of Arthur Pomeroy, the first Lord Harberton, had been a daughter of Henry Colley of Castle Carbery, County Kildare. The Colleys first appear as Cowleys: Walter Cowley was solicitor-general for Ireland in 1537 and later surveyor-general. His son and heir, a captain in the Elizabethan army, was "of Castle Carbery". Four generations later, an Elizabeth Colley married Garrett Wesley—or Wellesley—of County Meath. Garrett Wesley's son left his property to his cousin Richard Colley, provided Richard changed his surname to Wesley. In 1746, this Richard became Baron Mornington. His son became Viscount Wellesley and first Earl of Mornington, and *his* third son, Arthur, was none other than the great first Duke of Wellington. So one lot of Colleys had become Wellesley, and the other, through the marriage of the heiress Mary, had become Pomeroy. That is why Henry Fitz-George's father became Colley, to continue the name and identify it with the family property at Castle Carbery (which had long ago, needless to say, since this is an Irish story, fallen into ruin and become uninhabitable).

The Colleys were rather grander and much more cheerful than the Bowens. Mrs. Colley was firm about the few social distinctions she made. The Church and the Army were all right as professions. She would countenance wine-merchants (from old wine families) but not brewers; barristers, but not solicitors. Happily, Henry Bowen was a barrister. Nevertheless Mrs. Colley submitted the Bowens to minute examination before permitting Florence's engagement to Henry.

Henry was unworldly, introspective, and scholarly. And Florence Colley? Florence, as a girl at home, was difficult; and "to be a rebel in an unhappy home might be comparatively straightforward, but Florence was, rather, a misfit in surroundings recognised as idyllic". She was successively reflective, stormy, ecstatic. She "found herself difficult". Her daughter thought perhaps she suffered from a sort of family-claustrophobia. She was liable to accesses of penitence, worship, or love; she could be maddening, but not tiresome; she was funny, and full of ideas. Most often, she took refuge in vagueness. She was very pretty, with a pointed little face, and bronze hair coiled on the top of her head.

Henry Bowen fell in love with her. Perhaps her vagueness, their daughter thought, "established a quiet bay in which she and Henry met without alarm". Florence told one of her sisters that she loved him for his "nobility and great mind". They were both unusual people, and "they continued to love one another on the plane on which they had first met, a plane of innocence and nobility".

Mrs. Colley's anxieties about the match concerned the newness of Henry's practice, the size and isolation of Bowen's Court, and the fact that it was still full of Henry's brothers and sisters; nor did she find the family history of inbreeding and

instability at all encouraging. These things having been overcome, Mrs. Colley and Florence's sister Laura (Laura, not
Florence, because Henry did not want his bride to "come down
and be looked at") went on a highly successful visit to Bowen's
Court. Laura was touched to notice the furniture carefully
disposed to hide the worn patches in the drawing-room carpet;
and Mrs. Colley was no doubt reassured by the cast-iron bust of
the Duke of Wellington, her husband's kinsman, on the side-
board in the hall.

Henry and Florence were married at Clontarf on the tenth
of April, 1890; he was twenty-nine, she was twenty-four. On
the honeymoon he began to teach her Greek. When he brought
her home to Bowen's Court, it was night-time, and the tenants
were waiting in the dark outside the big gates; they took the
horses out of the shafts and pulled the carriage up to the house
themselves. "Ireland is a great country to die or be married in",
wrote Elizabeth.

CHAPTER II

Bitha

Elizabeth was not born at Bowen's Court, but in Dublin. Bowen's Court did, however, become Henry and Florence's home; the brothers and sisters moved out, the eldest sister Sarah settling close by in a house in Mitchelstown; Florence was a little overawed by them all, especially by Sarah. Florence disinterred the original furniture from the basement of Bowen's Court, and banished some of Robert Cole Bowen's heavier contributions, and she cleaned the portraits. She was a very haphazard housekeeper—they had in those early years some shocking cooks—but she and Henry were happy. Because of his practice, they could not live all the time at Bowen's Court, and acquired a house in Dublin as well—15 Herbert Place, a brown brick Georgian house with steps up to the hall door, facing the canal. Now, for the first time since it was built, Bowen's Court was not lived in continuously.

Nine years passed before Elizabeth was born. Florence saw her much younger sister Gertrude—married to Alberic Fiennes—producing a family before her and without difficulty. So it was with particular triumph that she announced her own pregnancy. The baby—who was going to be another Robert—was four weeks overdue. When finally Florence gave birth, in a back drawing-room at Herbert Place, on the seventh of June, 1899, it was not to "Robert", but to Elizabeth.

When Elizabeth was six weeks old, she was taken down to Bowen's Court to the nursery over the drawing-room, which was to be her room until she married. For her first seven years, life was divided into two parts. At the end of May every year, she and Florence would go down to Bowen's Court (Henry following later, when Trinity term ended), and in mid-October they returned to Dublin. So it was always summer, in County Cork. When Elizabeth was told she was born in Dublin, she said, "But how? My birthdays are always at Bowen's Court".

In Dublin, she went for walks along the canal with her governess, on Sunday afternoons went on the tram with her parents to see the Colleys at Mount Temple; and she led as social a life as an under-seven well can. She went in white muslin to dancing classes in the Molesworth Hall. Writing about the Dublin half of her childhood in a short book, *Seven Winters* (1942), she remembered being "a crack polka-dancer", but not so good at the waltz. Her preferred partner was a red-haired little boy called Fergus; but "with implacable male snobbishness—a snobbishness I would hate to see decline", he would not dance with her until she had mastered the waltz. The dancing-teacher was Continental and demanding, and her pupils were not good material—another "racial" characteristic, according to Elizabeth:

> I would say that, in general, the Anglo-Irish do not make good dancers; they are too spritely and conscious; they are incapable of one kind of trance or of being sensuously impersonal. And, for the formal, pure dance they lack the formality: about their stylishness (for they have stylishness) there is something impromptu, slightly disorderly. As pupils one saw what she thought of us. . . .[1]

On Sunday mornings there was church. The Bowens went to St. Stephen's, the focus of the perfect vista along Upper Mount Street from Merrion Square. The church was packed, in the early 1900s, with prosperous Dublin Protestants.

Elizabeth had no sense of belonging to the minority culture, the minority religion. She knew very few Roman Catholics; and "as to the difference between the two religions, I was too discreet to ask questions—if I wanted to know. This appeared to share a delicate, awkward area with those two other differences, sex and class". She had, she repeats, "an almost sexual shyness" on the subject of Roman Catholics. On Sundays, of course, everyone went to church, and all kinds of church-bells rang. But on weekdays, only those "other" bells rang. This alien disposition to frequent prayer suggested "some incontinence of the soul".

Both in County Cork and in Dublin there were children's parties, given and attended with a splendour and ceremony that today's children do not know. Florence insisted that Bitha —as she was called—must not be shy. Florence could not bear children to "burrow when they were introduced". It sounds a bit of an ordeal, but Bitha did not see it so. Before she was seven, she was launched on a career as party-goer and party-giver that she was to enjoy for a lifetime. "I pity people who do not care for Society", she wrote. "They are poorer for the oblation they do not make". In County Cork the distance between houses made the parties and visits even more passionately anticipated: "At Bowen's Court one used to jump on the steps with excitement as a vibration throughout the silent country developed into a rumble of carriage wheels—the little So-and-Sos coming to tea". The opening sentence of *The Last September* (written over ten years before the recollection in *Bowen's Court*) re-creates this exactly:

> About six o'clock the sound of a motor, collected out
> of the wide country and narrowed under the trees of
> the avenue, brought the household out in excitement on
> to the steps. . . .

And here, the actual moment of arrival, before hosts or guests have spoken, is the "moment of happiness, of perfection".

Vague Florence was not altogether vague as a mother. She gave her daughter what Elizabeth regarded as the best possible start in life: "the radiant, confident feeling of being loved".[2] The relationship between the two of them was very intense. "She was so much desolated that she unnerved me when anything went wrong between her and me". It was also intermittent, not only owing to vagueness. Florence told Bitha that she kept a governess so as not to have to scold her herself. And, having arranged Bitha's day so that this buffer was almost always between them, "she thought of me constantly, and planned ways in which we could meet and be alone". Florence's most intense moments had always been solitary; and after the nine childless years, motherhood was experienced with "a rapture of incredulity".

About some aspects of Bitha's upbringing Florence had very strong opinions. Bitha must drink lots of milk, never over-tire herself, must wear gloves so as not to get freckles on her hands—Bowens always got freckled hands—and she was not allowed to learn to read until she was seven: Bowens over-worked their brains. Bitha never connected these gentle strictures with their true origins, which lay in Colley apprehensions about the Bowen temperament.

Florence and Henry saw to it that their daughter led an intense juvenile social life. But this in no way mirrored theirs; they lived pretty much in a world of their own. As a young couple in the 1890s, they had had no contact with the theatrical or literary Dublin of Yeats and Æ: Elizabeth had never even heard about the Irish literary revival until she was a teenager at boarding-school in England. If the Bowens went to the theatre, it was to the Gaiety, not the Abbey; if they dined out, it was with family or Henry's colleagues. In Dublin Horse Show Week, the social climax for Anglo-Irish society, they were always down at Bowen's Court. And Henry was working very hard.

He worked too hard. When Elizabeth was five, a little girl

called Gerry Bridgeford, whose parents were in India, came to stay with them for a year. That was the year things began to go wrong, though Elizabeth didn't know. Henry had left the bar for the Irish Land Commission, which dealt with the sales of estates to the government and their allocation to tenants. The examination of landlords' titles—Henry was an examiner of titles—was a tedious and intricate job, as most estates were heavily encumbered with mortgages and family charges. The end product was an Allocation Schedule, setting out the claims of all parties to the estate. The schedule had to be settled by the examiner with the solicitors of all claimants present, adding their own claims for costs (and the land agents') to the schedule.

Henry had to work under high pressure, in an office, far from the chatty life of the Law Library. He was also beset by worry about a relatively unimportant financial failure of his own. He had a nervous breakdown—or so we would say now. Then, the unconcerned said he had "gone off his head"; the doctors called it anaemia of the brain. On one occasion during the settling of a schedule, he courteously asked one of the company to open a window. Then he gathered up the mass of legal documents, and tipped the whole lot out into Merrion Street.

Florence was not well equipped to deal with the situation. For some time, before Henry's illness took a dramatic turn, she did not notice that anything was wrong. She was not particularly observant. Within her parents' marriage, Elizabeth wrote, "each ruled their private kindom of thought"; and she, in her turn, an only child, began to set up her own. "My parents did not always communicate with each other, and I did not always communicate with them". She described the home atmosphere, with hindsight, as "unique and intensive, gently phenomenal". Henry and Florence were accustomed to living together in long phases of happy absence of mind, punctuated by moments of impetuous communication. Florence was enchanting, and had many of the qualities necessary for Henry Bowen's mate; but she was emphatically not the capable, mothering sort of wife.

So as Henry became more and more black and withdrawn, it was outsiders, and not Florence, who saw that he was in trouble; and it was hard for friends and family to speak bluntly in the face of her gentle detachment. But in that summer of 1905, Henry was persuaded to go to England for treatment. Florence was left to the unaccustomed worry of administering the family's practical affairs. Meanwhile, Bitha, Gerry, and the governess stayed at Bowen's Court, carrying on "that sort of miniature drama that forms between two girl children and an emotional woman cut off from everyone else". (The governess wrote to Florence, "I am SO SORRY about Mr. Bowen, isn't it disappointing, when he seems so much better and then goes back again. . . . I must tell you, Bitha told me yesterday that I am uncommonly picturesque and would do for an act. I can't think where she gets her words from . . .".)[3]

That winter all three Bowens were back at Herbert Place, but Henry wasn't better. All through the first stage of his illness, however hard he found the rest of the world, he had wanted to spend time with Bitha; now, in an excitable phase, he wanted to be with her and to take her for walks constantly. Florence was supported by her brother George (who was stone-deaf from a childhood illness) and by her sister Laura. And Bitha, aged six, built up her own defences: she pursued her "campaign of not noticing".[4]

During this winter, the doctors told Florence that she and Bitha ought to leave Henry, for his good. They went to England to stay with the Fiennes cousins, and then to Bowen's Court (where Bitha at last was taught to read), and then made a last attempt to return to Henry in Dublin. This time it was worse than ever. Henry became violent. Late one night, after a day of alarms, Bitha was woken up by her governess and taken in a cab to the house of cousins, where Florence later joined them.

Bitha had left Herbert Place for ever, without knowing it. Henry, certified by his own wish, went to a mental hospital outside Dublin.

It would be deceptively easy, extrapolating from these happenings, to see Elizabeth the child as irrevocably scarred. This would not be quite right. What did happen was that she to some extent insulated herself from what was happening, and insulated herself, too, from her own emotions; she lived in the moment. Her "campaign of not noticing" was pretty successful. Because of the affectionate vagueness of the household, she had been thrown a good deal upon herself, and to this she attributed the greater significance that things and places had for her, as a child, than did people. All her life, places were as important to her as people. She also attributed to the dream atmosphere which she shared the fact that she seemed, later, to have fewer *early* memories than anyone she knew. Both these things could also have come from an early necessity to "not notice".

In any case, she did not come out of all this as a "nervous" child. For all Florence's anxieties about her constitution, Elizabeth was tough; physically, she was as strong as a horse, and indefatigable. Serious illness apart (and most illness she did her best not to acknowledge), this was so for her whole life. ("Like an animal", her husband used to say.) She was not a particularly easy child: "I was demonstrative and excitable: an extrovert". The demonstrativeness was satisfied in her relationship with Florence, which, away from Henry, grew ever closer. There was only one permanent and perceptible scar: "I had come out of the tension and mystery of my father's illness, the apprehensive silence or chaotic shoutings . . . with nothing more disastrous than a stammer".[5]

Elizabeth's stammer, though it caused her agony as a girl, became very much part of her as a woman. It was a stammer, not a stutter—she was very particular about the distinction: stutterers were an altogether different class of person. Elizabeth's stammer was a pronounced hesitation, a complete stalling on certain words. She would help herself out by gestures with her hands, and by substituting a different word. The severity of it varied; it was worse when she was tired, and sometimes almost non-existent when she spoke in public or on television. It did not indicate any lack of confidence in what she was saying; and was often found by others to be an additional charm in her.

Once a rich friend paid for her to go to an Austrian psychiatrist to have it cured; after several visits, the psychiatrist had laid bare before her his own personal anguishes, both private and professional; Elizabeth, fascinated, had characteristically laid bare nothing, and the treatment was abandoned. The stammer remained.

The nature of Elizabeth's stammer is illustrated by an exchange of internal memos within the British Council. After Elizabeth had completed several successful lecture tours for them after the war (their man in Zurich, reporting in 1950 to the British Council in London, mentioned her stammer as "not at all disturbing, but if I may say so, 'endearing' rather than distracting"), there was some question as to her suitability for further lecturing, on account of the stammer. Back came an answering memo: "She is a *most* successful lecturer with a *most* successful stammer".

They should leave Henry, the doctors said, not only for his sake but for Bitha's. So the year she was seven, mother and daughter went to England, where they were taken over by a network of Anglo-Irish relatives; just as well, for the "suspiciously lovely-looking" Florence, unwidowed and with a child, was a vulnerable figure. The most powerful relatives were Cousin Isabel Chenevix Trench, who lived in Folkestone, and Cousin Lilla Chichester, in Sandgate. Florence and Bitha settled on the Kent coast.

Though "settled" is hardly the word. They moved constantly in the next five years, between Folkestone and Lyminge
and Seabrook and Hythe, according to the state of Florence's
finances and the vagaries of her temperament. Both of them
adored the Victorian and newer Edwardian seaside villas,
which had sprung up all around. The Georgian houses of fault-
less proportions in which Elizabeth and all her relations lived
in Ireland seemed to the child sad and unadventurous in comparison. Florence and Bitha were intoxicated by "white bal-
conies, ornate porches, verandahs festooned with Dorothy
Perkins roses, bow windows protuberant as balloons . . .
sublimated ivory-fretwork inglenooks inset with jujubes of
tinted glass, built-in overmantels with flight upon flight of
brackets round oval mirrors. . . ."[6] They became connoisseurs
of villas, adept at extracting keys from house agents and then
getting rid of the agent. And of each rented villa in which they
lived, each fantasy home, they made a "pavilion of love".
Elizabeth did not consciously miss Ireland, or her father. "Perhaps", she wrote thirty years later, "children are sterner than
grown-up people in their refusal to suffer, in their refusal, even,
to feel at all".[7]

Her senses were stirred not only by the villas but by the
landscape. Ireland was the norm: here everything was roman-
tically different, and she throve on the difference as she throve
on all—nearly all—subsequent changes, chances, and dislocations. There is one particular road going up from Seabrook to
where Hythe's railway station used to be, with the sea down
below on one side and steep ridges inland on the other. She
never played there alone, always preferring to be with boon
companions. ("I know where there's a wood with a dead sheep
in it", says Sheikie in *The Little Girls*. It was by this road that
Bitha saw her dead sheep.)

She registered the beauty of the scene, out of the corner
of her eye, with unwilling love: and here, she thought at the
end of her life, "was the beginning of a career of withstood

emotion". Not quite the beginning, an outsider might think; rather its confirmation. She went on to say, "Sensation, I have never fought shy of, or done anything to restrain".[8]

England also gave her the sensation of history, from the Romans onwards. (History tended to be played down, in Anglo-Ireland.) In Kent, she lived a non-stop historical novel in her head, a continuous daydream of a heroic past, which has everything to do with her becoming a writer:

> As a novelist, I cannot occupy myself with "characters", or at any rate central ones, who lack panache, in one or another sense, who would be incapable of a major action or a major passion, or who have not a touch of the ambiguity, the ultimate unaccountability, the enlarging mistiness of persons "in history". History, as more austerely I now know it, is not romantic. But I am.[9]

The romantic daydream was not solitary; Bitha never was, if she could help it. With Audrey Fiennes, her cousin, who came to stay at Hythe (or wherever they were) twice a year, she kept up a continuous game of imaginary families that they would take up where they left off last time. The girls acted it all out, themselves being the mothers—eighteenth-century ladies—Bitha using immensely long words, often wrongly. Bitha drew the families, too, and their clothes, filling book after book. With Hilary, a child living next door during the last summer in Hythe, she wrote alternate chapters of a novel about Bonnie Prince Charlie; and they drank their cocoa over the flowers in the middle of the table to the King over the Water, sometimes, confusingly, a German princeling called Rupert.

Her schooling was varied and intermittent. She liked Lindum, the day-school she went to in Folkestone, which was ordinary, cheerful, and noisy—a large, crude theatre of action from which Florence withdrew her from time to time in her anxiety not to "tire her brain". She was less happy, and less successful, sharing a governess with the Seabrook rectory children—the idyllically normal family life was just too much for her. She was used to her Fiennes cousins, who fought among themselves when she was with them: she stirred things up. The Colley aunts told Florence that Bitha was bumptious.

But Audrey Fiennes loved staying at Hythe, where Florence let them run wild in a way that made other mothers raise their eyebrows. For Florence did not fuss, or mind what people thought, and though she had acute financial problems, she transcended them by thinking it was comically vulgar to be rich. And Florence and Bitha together were demonstrative in a way that most people then were not. It was contagious. Audrey wept when she went back to London, and surprised her mother by embracing her and calling her "darling", as was the custom in the temporary pavilion of love she had left.

Everything was temporary. Away in Ireland, Henry had been gradually recovering. By the time Bitha was twelve, he had resumed his practice and was coming over to his wife and daughter in Hythe for the vacations. He had convalesced at Bowen's Court, mostly alone. Nelly Gates, seven years older than Bitha, whose mother was Florence's close friend in Kildorrery and whose brother Jim was to be a great friend of Bitha's all her life, remembered Henry Bowen in those days as

> a big gentle giant of a man who walked everywhere, muttering to himself and continuously clasping and unclasping his hands behind his back—even in church (we sat in the pew just behind the Bowen's Court pew). Despite these mannerisms, which scared us a little, we liked his kindliness and gentleness.

In Hythe, Hilary from next door also found him dreamy, unreal, but kindly. He came upon Hilary and Bitha eating dog biscuits (Bitha's idea), being overcome by hunger between meals. He took them out and bought them great hot doughnuts oozing jam. He and Florence discussed the move back to Ireland; but it was only discussion. Florence was happier, more tranquil, in Hythe than she had ever been; Ireland was clouded for her now by memories of trouble.

There was another reason why plans could now only ever be plans. Florence had cancer. When the three of them went over to Ireland in the summer of 1912, she had an operation and was told she had six months to live. In the event she had less. Her brother George and his wife, Edie, were staying at Bowen's Court, and Florence told Edie: "I have good news, now I'm going to see what Heaven's like". In the late summer the Bowens were back in Hythe; Florence's sister Laura came to look after her. Florence and Henry were closer than they had been for years, and Florence, sentenced to death, seemed perfectly happy. She died in her room with its peacock-blue walls and views over the Channel, near the end of September, 1912, and was buried in Saltwood churchyard, just inland from Hythe.

And Elizabeth? She, towards the end, had been sent to stay with Hilary next door. It was her Aunt Gertrude who came over the evening her mother died, to break the news. Elizabeth was sharing a bedroom with Hilary; that night they also shared a bed, and cried themselves to sleep. But next day everything went on as usual; and Hilary was told not to talk to Bitha about her mother. Hilary, whose family was of a different persuasion, thought it odd that Bitha was not taken to see her mother's body and to say goodbye. On the day of the funeral the two children were sent to their governess's house on the other side of the town: "Bitha gave way to an excess of high spirits", recalls Hilary, "which I found hard to understand, though I do now. It would have been better I think to have let her mourn naturally. . . ." Perhaps it would. In *Bowen's Court,* Elizabeth described the death of her father's grandmother; the elder grandchildren were brought downstairs to say goodbye and be there when she died: "The scene, which they always remembered, seemed to the three of them natural, intimate, mystical. . . ."

For Elizabeth the pattern was established differently. Shortly afterwards, staying with the Fiennes, she shared a room with Audrey. Audrey heard her sobbing in the night. But she could never talk about it, or about her mother, and so Audrey couldn't either. Other children were perhaps both braver and crueller. In Elizabeth's novel *The House in Paris*, Leopold (aged nine) asks Henrietta (aged eleven) about her feelings for her dead mother. "There is no end", wrote Elizabeth here, "to the violations committed by children on children quietly talking alone".

Elizabeth was thirteen when her mother died and, in Audrey's opinion, she never really got over it. One of the words at which her stammer consistently baulked her was "mother".

The remainder of Elizabeth's upbringing was taken over by a committee of aunts. Florence had arranged things with Laura before she died; and Laura duly took Elizabeth to Harpenden, in Hertfordshire, where she kept house for her brother William Wingfield Colley (Uncle Wink, to Bitha), curate in charge of St. John's. Laura was a sweet, anxious spinster, and Wingfield a shy and easily embarrassed bachelor. The absorption of a bereaved thirteen-year-old into the household was not altogether easy for any of the three. The Colleys had had a bad year in 1912: in March, Constance, who had become a doctor, had died of consumption; in April, the youngest brother, Eddy, had gone down with the *Titanic*. And then, in September, Florence.

Aunt Laura had chief care of Elizabeth but there were others with plenty to say. Aunt Maud was a disciplinarian, much taken up with the conversion of the Jews and other unspeakable good causes. Elizabeth thought she was like "a very nasty looking-glass that made you look horrid". Even when she and her cousins were quite grown-up, they would wipe off their make-up before going in to Aunt Maud. The most potent aunt, however, was Edie, the wife of kind dear George Colley. Their daughter Noreen, though much younger than Elizabeth, was, with Audrey Fiennes, the cousin closest to her heart. Edie reigned at Corkagh House, in Clondalkin, County Dublin, a household that often included Gerald Colley and his pretty wife, Dorothy; it was Dorothy to whom Elizabeth and Audrey turned for ideas about clothes in their adolescence. The atmosphere at Corkagh was cheerful, astringent, and ultra-Colley; Elizabeth as a teenager came in for a certain amount of criticism disguised as humour here. But it was the family centre; and Aunt Edie was Henry Bowen's confidante as well as everyone else's.

But to start with, Elizabeth's base-camp was Harpenden. She channelled her emotions and enthusiasms not so much into the neat semi-detached world of South View but into her new school, Harpenden Hall, which she entered at mid-term in a state of shock. "I had what I see can go with total bereavement, a sense of disfigurement, mortification, disgrace". Part of her wanted more than anything to be with strangers who knew nothing, who could not pity her. Yet she insisted on wearing a black tie with her new brown uniform. Her "black" was the last she had of her mother—once that was left off, it was as though she had gone for ever. For Elizabeth "could not remember her, think of her, speak of her or suffer to hear her spoken of".[10]

Not surprisingly, she did not star academically at Harpenden; but socially she did. She became the leader in initiating school crazes. Though St. Agatha's in *The Little Girls* is placed in Kent, it was at Harpenden that the burying ritual—the core of that book—actually took place. The actuality was less im-

pressive than the second ritual imagined half a century later—
the original of the "coffer" was a small biscuit tin containing
some cryptic writing and two or three broken knick-knacks.

The Harpenden crazes included a passion for witchcraft
and the occult. Bitha and her companions learnt all they could
about cursing and possession, and pored over Marjory
Bowen's *Black Magic*. They brewed potions and moaned in-
cantations. This came to an end when the girls began to get
nervous, and Bitha to have qualms about Uncle Wink.

In the Christmas holidays Hilary from Hythe came to
stay; at a fancy-dress party Bitha was Spring in a pale green
dress with flowers sewn on. (She was not really a pretty child;
much her best feature was her wavy fair hair.) The girls went
tobogganing, and had their toboggan stolen when they left it
under a bush at lunchtime; that would never have happened in
Ireland, said Bitha loyally—and correctly. That summer she
and Henry went abroad with Aunt Laura and Uncle Wink. On
a Rhine steamer they heard German schoolboys singing. The
grown-ups were touched by the beautiful sound. But Bitha,
still protecting herself against feeling too much, "stayed hostile to the emotion that made those children sing".[11]

Most summers of remaining childhood were spent at
Bowen's Court with her father and her cousin Audrey, chap-
eroned by Aunt Sarah from Mitchelstown—by now a stately
person with yellow-white hair. Elizabeth and Audrey were
quite uncontrolled and largely unsupervised. They spent their
time making dollhouse furniture, and impossible cotton frocks
from material bought locally, and eating huge quantities of
soft fruit from the garden; Bowen's Court was famous for its
outsize raspberries.

They were at Bowen's Court in August, 1914, and on
their way to a garden party at Mitchelstown Castle, when
Henry Bowen stopped to buy a newspaper and told the girls
that England had declared war on Germany. That garden
party was one of the last great Anglo-Irish reunions in County

Cork; the war changed everything, and was followed by Ireland's own war. Many of the houses from which the guests in their summer finery came that day were to be burnt to the ground in the next few years.

All Elizabeth had wanted to know, when her father read the news from the paper, was "Then can't we go to the garden party?" Like all young people, she was self-centred. She is harder on herself than that: "If at ten or twelve I had been precocious, at fifteen I was virtually idiotic".[12] The inevitable silliness of girlhood was something it gave Elizabeth no pleasure to look back on. In later years she and Audrey, who had shared much silliness, had an unspoken conspiracy to forget that phase.

In spite of her way of life, pillar-to-post between aunts, Elizabeth was insistent that her adolescence was not a painful process. She felt that the usual agonies bypassed her:

> Towering periods of silliness, oh yes. And I made vile scenes with unfortunate Aunt Laura, but those were, rather, instances of protracted childhood, which a furious selfishness reinforced. At around sixteen I dabbled in introspection, but hardly more. Tormenting nameless disturbances, conflicts, cravings were not experienced by me. I had never heard of them.[13]

Even taking into account a bravado that revised her own history, "protracted childhood" is the key here. For her complexity as a grown woman had more in common with the state of being a child than, as with many (maddening) women, a state of unrelinquished adolescence. The way she looked forward passionately to treats, outings, happenings; the way she suffered and rebelled if these fell through—these were a child's reactions, not an adolescent's. She was not moody, but she could be recalcitrant. Her vanity was the vanity of a child. And her approach to children, as an adult, was on equal terms. If she failed to get on with a child, it was on her own argumentative, bickering level she met him. And the child in Elizabeth—the child who in Hythe had daydreamed the history of England—is there in the writer. Writing (she said in a B.B.C. interview in 1959) was "an extension . . . of the imaginative play thing a child has—that life isn't amusing enough, so you build it up with imagination of your own".

This appears to contradict what she wrote in the introduction to a 1949 reissue of her earliest stories.[14] There she said, in essence, that she wrote in order to prove that she was grown-up. "All through my youth I lived with a submerged fear that *I* might fail to establish grown-up status. . . . A writer and a grown-up, it appeared to me, could not but be synonymous. . . . I was anxious at once to approximate to the grown-ups and to demolish them". With that "and to demolish them" the contradiction evaporates. (It would not invalidate anything if the contradiction had crystallised; Elizabeth contradicted herself continually, and in all self-respecting contradictions both sides are true.) Writers, she wrote in an article of 1952 (later published in *Afterthought*), were not secretive so much as shy: "The fact is, they are of a childishness which could seem incredible, and which is more than half incredible to their thinking selves".

Her reading as a child was voracious, although her late start in learning to read for herself left her with a cosy taste for being read to. Her governesses had read aloud to her the story of Perseus and *Jungle Jinks* and most things in between. Once she read for herself, she had a passion for George Macdonald: his Curdie was one of her heroes. She loved Baroness Orczy's *Scarlet Pimpernel*, and E. Nesbit's books. She read Dickens exhaustively as a child and, as a result, could not read him as a young adult: "There is no more oxygen left, for me, anywhere in the atmosphere of his writing".[15] But Dickens is one author—Jane Austen is another—whose influence on her as a novelist she was always eager to acknowledge. And she went back to him for her book *English Novelists* (1942), where it is the child in him that she recognises and celebrates:

> He gives a child's value—a poor child's—to the enjoyment of sheer physical bliss. . . . At the same time, he keeps a child's apprehensiveness of the weird, the unknown, the unsubstantially threatening. He gives loneliness, sense of loss or sense of betrayal all the frightful force they have as a child.

In a B.B.C. talk of 1947 about the book that had most influenced her early years, she chose to talk about Rider Haggard's *She*; she came upon it at the age of twelve, "when I was finding the world too small". The descriptions of Kôr, the great derelict city, caught her imagination. She "saw" Kôr before she ever saw London: "Inevitably, the Thames Embankment was a disappointment".[16]

Elizabeth described her childhood reading as "sensuous"; real life was overlapped and haunted by layers of synthetic experience. Her frequent use of the words "sensuous" and "sensuousness" in this kind of connection is to be taken literally; it has nothing to do with implications of sexuality. In an introduction to a 1946 reprint of Sheridan Le Fanu's *Uncle Silas*, she wrote of the "sensuousness" of the girl Maud, and characterised this sensuousness as un-English; the novel as a whole, she wrote, was Irish in two ways: it showed a sublimated infantilism, and it was sexless. The emotional climate of sensuality was "Irish" as the climate of sexuality was not. ("Talking of being virginal", says a clever Oxford undergraduate in an Irish country house in *The Last September*, "do you ever notice this country? Doesn't sex seem irrelevant?")

Elizabeth was the very opposite of the studious reader; a child like herself, she thought, had more in common with an outdoor child, and what they had in common was the life of sensation. And sensationalists, of whatever kind, band together in a conspiracy of their own. Books introduced her to desire and to danger. She acquired a need for mystery, "a feeling for the dark horse": "I can trace in all people whom I have loved a succession from book characters—not from one only, from a fusion of many". Places, too: a real place that was first known in a story was known in a private and special way: "I had a line on them".[17] Lillie Road, where she first lived in London as a young woman, was more than itself for having been mentioned in Compton Mackenzie's *Sinister Street*.

Criticism and conscious literary appreciation destroy the Eden of pure sensation. The only above-board children's stories for grown-ups, she thought, were detective stories, and those she read for pure pleasure all her life. No one can remain at the magical level of the child-reader. Elizabeth expressed this in a much-quoted sentence, the essence of which has been taken to convey the overriding theme of her own fiction:

> No, it is not only our fate but our business to lose innocence, and once we have lost that it is futile to attempt a picnic in Eden.[18]

Yet Elizabeth in life may not have felt the attempt to be entirely futile—not if the company was congenial, and not if there was good wine in the picnic basket, for wine "raises agreeability to poetry", as she wrote in *A Time in Rome*.

It is hard to say whether Downe House, the girls' boarding-school near Orpington, in Kent, where Elizabeth was sent in September, 1914, would qualify as Eden. The school is now at Cold Ash, but in Elizabeth's time it was at Downe itself, Charles Darwin's old house; his study was the common room. It was—is—a square, solid, charming house, extended by peculiar outbuildings built by odd-job "man" Miss Nickel, who stomped about in a brown monk-like robe smelling of engine oil. The chapel was a whitewashed ex-bedroom on the top floor. Everything was slightly irregular and amateurish. The girls wore brown stockings for games and black ones in the afternoon, green djibbahs and purple tweed coats. One lingers over the original Downe House, and over Elizabeth at Downe, because it was a very powerful institution with a very powerful headmistress. Olive Willis, ex-Somerville College, Oxford, had started the school in 1907 in partnership with Alice Carver, international hockey player. Miss Willis's personality pervaded everything. On Elizabeth's first evening, she told the assembled girls that it did not matter if they were happy, so long as they were good. (The headmistress at Harpenden had said just the opposite.) With her girls she was speculative and ironic. It was not so much "Don't" as "Need you?" She taught that all was transient, especially school-days; Elizabeth was grateful that never once in three years did she hear the expression *esprit de corps*, nor were they ever addressed as future mothers. And it was at Downe that Elizabeth developed her phobia about "silliness"—for silliness, to Miss Willis, was the most dreary, the most mortifying crime of which anyone could be accused. Miss Willis believed in self-control and disliked bad language—Patience Erskine was nearly expelled for saying "damn" when she fell off a haystack. At the beginning and end of each term, Miss Willis would have a confidential session with each girl in turn: these little discussions were known as "jaws".

Every Downe person of decent vintage—and sixty years before the Sex Discrimination Act, one was a Downe "person", not "girl"—talks a very great deal. (Elizabeth did.) For conversation was highly valued. At the beginning of each term, tables for meals were "picked" like teams; the object of each team was to make as much conversation as possible, so chattiness, tact, and resource were at a premium. The mistress in charge of each table expected to be continuously entertained. To be able to keep up a stream of amusing talk was a matter of prestige. To be dumb was to be a poor fish. The

result was, as Elizabeth said, that "many of us have turned
out to be good hostesses".[19] It also made some of them compulsive nervous chatterers and bad endurers of normal silences.
As one Downe person wrote: "To this day, the briefest lull at
a luncheon or a dinner party is instantly filled by me with
remarks of an inanity which startles even my children".[20] But
this skill—the talent to amuse—was sympathetic to Elizabeth's
temperament and became part of her self-confidence as an
adult.

When a person is habitually idolised, there is a perverse
interest in hearing the other side. Here is a version of Miss
Willis by a Downe person who was at the school some fifteen
years after Elizabeth:

> She was a great personality and was considered the
> quintessence of charm, and all parents, specially fathers,
> and nearly all her pupils through the years, came under
> the spell. She was a woman of great culture and wide
> interests. Though there were nearly a hundred girls at
> Downe in my time, she kissed each one of us goodnight,
> looking deeply into our eyes, while her horrid Samoyed
> dogs drank the water out of our washstand jugs. She
> preached in chapel every Sunday. . . . *I* wouldn't have
> been surprised to see her administering both chalice
> and paten. We were, nearly all of us, blissfully happy
> at Downe, and she *was* the school. She was original and
> broadminded. Why then does the memory of her coming
> down the icy corridors swathed in chiffon scarves still
> fill me with vague dislike and distrust?[21]

Elizabeth felt nothing of that distrust. She settled easily
enough at Downe: she was by now nothing if not adaptable.
A contemporary remembers the new arrival as a quiet girl, not
so much shy as self-contained. Downe was strong on theatricals,
and in her very first term Elizabeth, in spite of her stammer,

was persuaded to take a part. But for most of her time there she was more active in writing and producing revues than in acting in them. She didn't play games well, being very short-sighted. Her short sight was partially responsible for the "impressionistic" quality of her writing. What she saw and responded to was the general effect of light, colour, and form; and she fully focussed only on nearby detail, which thus acquired a disproportionate significance. She preferred not to wear her glasses, whatever the inconvenience. In middle life, walking in the garden at dusk at Angus Wilson's house in Suffolk, she walked straight into a hedge, talking hard, and unconcernedly backed out, "like a bus" (according to Stuart Hampshire), still talking hard.

Elizabeth in her teens already had the traits that characterised her as an adult, in her friends' eyes: the same school friend who found her initially quiet also found her observant and analytical, sympathetic and understanding of other people, and with a great feeling for what was funny, with that "awareness of the knife-edge which divides the comic from the tragic and sometimes doesn't even divide them".

Elizabeth took to what she called the "curious, quick, characteristic psychological pace" of Downe. Originality in some form was expected, and one tended to caricature one's own foibles: "it seemed fatal not to be at least one thing to excess. . . . Personality came out in patches, like damp through a wall". Doggedly, in retrospect, she insisted on her toughness as a new girl, though her relative vulnerability was—as everyone's mercifully is—apparent to others. She did concede that her vanity would at that time have been mortified wherever she was; and that her heart was all over the place anyway.

Downe produced its crop of emotional friendships and intimate talks—mainly held in dressing-gowns, leaning on the radiator next to the tap where they filled their hot-water bottles. But the girls, Elizabeth thought later, were not highly sexed, and attachments had an "aesthetic, snobbish, self-interested tinge". They did not discuss men much—perhaps because of the war, and people's brothers at the front, which gave the whole sex a morbid, quasi-religious association. The war cast a moral seriousness on all their undertakings: Miss Willis instilled in them a horror of being *bouches inutiles*, and although there was no food shortage, one felt there ought to be. This austerity was softened by the Kentish countryside around the school—"the beautiful superabundant sillinesses of nature", in Elizabeth's phrase—epitomised by the cuckoos in spring, "too near, too many, making themselves cheap".[22]

Elizabeth worked hard for the lessons she liked, and instead of preparation for the ones she didn't like she read poetry, the Bible, and checked out the facts of life in the encyclopaedia. She seemed quite clever to the others, but not outstanding; as Patience Erskine dryly said, "There were a lot of bright girls at Downe". In the spring term of 1916, measles and mumps broke out together; Elizabeth and Audrey Richards brought out a magazine called *The Meamper* to divert the sick. And Miss Willis ran a small literary society of six or seven persons, of whom Elizabeth was one. She paid tribute to Miss Willis for teaching her "how not to write".[23] They used to read to each other what they had written each week. Joan (Druce) Osiakovski, who belonged to the group at the same time, remarks that Elizabeth's recognisable style, often assumed to be a "mannered" later development, was very much hers right from these beginnings: "Her style was simply herself". Readers of her very first published stories will find this easy to believe.

One other thing Elizabeth learnt at Downe, if she did not know it already, was to be a perfect gentleman. The girls cultivated a great sense of honour—there was even no talking after lights-out. She regretted in retrospect the loss of their "sense of delinquency". Hers, in fact, was never really lost. As for the problem of being happy and/or good, posed on her first evening, happiness for her, at Downe and after, was experienced as "a kind of inner irrational exaltation having little to do with morals one way or the other".[24]

She left Downe House in the summer of 1917, and began her adult life.

E   B

CHAPTER III

Encounters

ELIZABETH'S FATHER CONTINUED TO BE WELL. The Easter Rising of 1916 found him on holiday with Elizabeth in England. He took the next boat home only to be greeted by Cousin Georgina—Mrs. Bowen-Colthurst—looking for help for her son John, who was in trouble of a horrifyingly serious kind. Henry was indeed a lawyer, but not the right sort of lawyer for this; he referred his cousin's case to others.

Captain Bowen-Colthurst, with sixteen years' service behind him, was stationed at Portobello barracks in Dublin. In the searches, interrogations of suspected Republicans, round-ups, and general horror of the days after the Rising, he arrested Francis Sheehy Skeffington, a sympathiser with the Republican cause but a known pacifist, a writer and editor, who had no involvement in the events of that week other than making an attempt to stop looting and vandalism. Either because Skeffington had witnessed the gratuitous shooting of a boy on Bowen-Colthurst's orders, or just because the captain was, as his senior officer later said, "a neurotic bigot", Bowen-Colthurst had Skeffington shot. This murder shocked even a city that was becoming all too familiar with violence. Bowen-Colthurst at the court-martial was found insane. But this was not revealed, for why then was an "insane" man promoted, as he was, shortly after committing an insane act? He was only arrested after his senior officer, Major Sir Francis Vane, went to London to report the incident in person. But the British Army, like all the professions, looks after its own.

Bowen-Colthurst was sent to Broadmoor, released in less than two years, and went to Canada. Hanna Sheehy Skeffington, the murdered man's widow, rallied support for the Republican cause, her husband's memory, and anti-militaristic ideals with a passionate lecture given in America, later published on both sides of the Atlantic under the resounding title *British Militarism As I Have Known It*. "Captain Colthurst", she said, "like Cromwell, was a very religious man". John Bowen-Colthurst identified with Ireland's most notorious oppressor did no good to the image or credibility of the British Army in Ireland. Fuel to an already well-kindled fire. None of this—the court-martial or the subsequent Commission of Inquiry—impinged much on Elizabeth, back at Downe House for the summer term. But it became another peripheral Bowen burden.

The increased presence of the British Army in garrisons up and down Ireland in the uneasy months and years following the Rising meant something quite different to the girls—and their mothers—in the Anglo-Irish country houses. It meant more young officers to be entertained, and endless tennis parties, dances, and ephemeral flirtations conducted sitting on the wide front steps of houses like Bowen's Court in the long Irish summer twilights. If the young men had to take their turn on patrol, if soldiers shot Sinn Feiners and Sinn Feiners shot soldiers, these things were not discussed with the girls. Elizabeth, when she left school, was still based, when in England, with Aunt Laura at Harpenden. (Uncle Wink had now become rector of Blisworth, in Northamptonshire, and had got married.) But when Elizabeth was in Ireland, she took her place as *jeune fille en fleur* at Bowen's Court. What is more, in September, 1918, her father remarried—it was a sensible, affectionate match, and Elizabeth's Aunt Edie approved, which was important. He married Mary Gwynn, daughter of old Dr. Gwynn of Clontarf, sister of Stephen, Lucius, and Edward Gwynn, all old friends of Henry's. Everyone was pleased, though some of the Gwynns were apprehensive on Mary's behalf. Elizabeth liked Mary very much, and life at Bowen's Court became less haphazard.

Elizabeth, for all her strictures on the Anglo-Irish as dancers, was keen on and good at dancing. She had learnt at Downe and, in spite of being practically tone-deaf when it came to singing, had a strong sense of rhythm. She and her cousin Audrey, on holidays at Bowen's Court, practised those "poised totterings, hesitations and smooth rushes forward" of the "modern" dancing she described in *The Hotel*. They managed to get themselves invited to garrison and country-house dances anywhere within reach. Once they drove in an open governess cart forty miles over the mountains to a dance in County Tipperary; and once returned in an outside car at three o'clock in the morning from a dance in Fermoy, to see Mary's face peering anxiously down at them over the banisters. They paid little heed to her. In 1920 they even gave a ball themselves, of a somewhat improvised kind. There were no drinks provided—the gentlemen must have brought their own. Elizabeth and Audrey spent the morning banging nails into the drawing-room walls, through Robert Cole Bowen's grey, gold, and white wallpaper, to stick candles on. No one stopped them. Henry was benevolent, Mary impotent. Foxtrots, quicksteps, tangos, and waltzes: that year, they danced to the bodeful strains of "Destiny" and Rubinstein's "Melody in F". Elizabeth enjoyed herself. She was more self-contained and more apparently grown-up than Audrey. They exchanged no intimate confidences. Elizabeth's emotions were vivid but inward. Some of them were discharged at Corkagh, and dealt with by Aunt Edie. Like Theodora (aged fifteen) in *Friends and Relations*, "her personality was still too much for her, like a punt-pole".

Elizabeth was never the stereotype of the pretty, social

Anglo-Irish débutante. She wasn't pretty enough, silly enough, or secure enough ever to be quite that. The little Bowen family, oddly circumstanced as it was, was poorly equipped for the larger social productions. Elizabeth, though passionately gregarious, had and always retained an instinctive reticence. Sean O'Faolain, thirty-five years later, was to say of her writing: "One hears from behind her civil façade that kind of *farouche* note which one associates with teenage delinquents about to break prison—that is, about to leave home".[1] There is a sort of pent-up feeling about her as a girl, a potential wildness. She was no delinquent in the ordinary sense; Downe House had indeed seen to that. But as both a person and a writer, her strength and her fascination lay in this underlying, almost vulgar gypsy romanticism which was just as much a part of her as her perfect, ladylike demeanour and beautiful manners. She was not specially pleased with O'Faolain's essay in which this note was sounded—for one thing, she did not think friends should write about friends. But she had in fact used the word "*farouche*" of herself in print years before his piece appeared. One reason for writing, she said (*Why Do I Write?*, 1948), was to work off "the sense of being solitary and *farouche*. Solitary and *farouche* people don't have relationships: they are quite unrelatable. If you and I [to V. S. Pritchett] were capable of being altogether house-trained and made jolly, we should be nicer people, but not writers".

She was not "unrelatable"—she got on like a house on fire with the young officers, and was to have a *tendre* for soldiers young and old all her life—and, motherless, she was fond of attractive older women. Elizabeth in fact became more "civilised", more house-trained, than most people ever are; with growing confidence, her *farouche* side developed in parallel. It was reflected in the way she dressed: she always had a penchant for large earrings, necklaces of false pearls or great glass bobbles, and flashy fake jewellery that on her looked neither flashy nor fake.

The year after the Bowen's Court ball, she was in love. The chosen one was, inevitably, in the British Army. Lieutenant John Anderson was about five years older than she. He was a solid, ordinarily handsome young man, with a moustache and brushed-back hair, a little earnest, good with children. Major Brutt in *The Death of the Heart*—always longing, always contingent, an unsuitable port in a storm—was perhaps a projection of what John Anderson might have become. Aunt Edie was in a hotel in Bordighera, in Italy, for a four-month stay with her children. Elizabeth joined them, in a considerably heightened state, and announced she was engaged. Aunt Edie was sceptical. John Anderson, too, came out to Italy. Nothing worked out. Audrey, also in Bordighera, went back to England before Elizabeth; Elizabeth gave her a little parcel to post in London. It was the engagement ring. She was as heartbroken as anyone in that situation is; and as anyone at that age does, she got over it. It wouldn't have done. At home in Ireland, houses, relationships, and lives were being destroyed. British and Irish troops' reprisals and counter-reprisals escalated hopelessly. In one spring night of 1921, three Anglo-Irish houses in the immediate neighbourhood of Bowen's Court were burnt by the Irish. The British answered by burning the farms of putative Sinn Feiners, some even nearer home. Henry Bowen wrote to Elizabeth in Italy to prepare her for the worst: "I am afraid that, as things are now, there can only be one other development. You must be prepared for the next news, and be brave. I will write at once".[2] Elizabeth, then beside Lake Como, taught herself to imagine Bowen's Court in flames. But Bowen's Court was not burned.

She wrote years later that her girlhood at Bowen's Court was, "though accented from time to time by aspiration, passing romance or pleasure, mainly a period of impatience, frivolity, lassitude or boredom. I endlessly asked myself *what* I should be, and when?"[3] Surreptitiously, her work-life was already developing. As a child, Elizabeth had been fonder of drawing than of writing. She had said she was going to be "an artist". On the strength of this, when she was twenty, she went for two terms to the London County Council School of Art in Southampton Row. But she was disillusioned. At fourteen, she had been considered very good—but she had never got, nor would now get, any better. She gave up, but she regretted the lost gift, and transferred its qualities to writing: "It seems to me that often when I write I am trying to make words do the work of line and colour. I have the painter's sensitivity to light. Much (and perhaps the best) of my writing is verbal painting".[4]

Even before the art school experiment, she was writing. At nineteen—some time before the garrison dances and John Anderson—she was cagily writing poetry. At her father's wedding to Mary Gwynn, she had met her first author, Mary's brother Stephen Gwynn: talking to him confirmed her idea that "generally, authors lived in London".[5] After the art school, she took a course in journalism.

There was never any question of her just being a girl at home. She had a horror of unlived lives, of, in her phrase, "a life to let". She sometimes said that if she had not been a writer she would have been an architect. She wrote that she saw the writer as a "free-lance maker" (in *Why Do I Write?*), and went on to say cheerfully that if she had not written "I should probably have struck out in designing and making belts, jewellery, handbags, lampshades or something of that sort— my aim being that these should catch people's fancy, create a little fashion of their own". To see the writer as comparable to the maker and seller of a product was characteristic of the practical, unpretentious side of her that got genuinely fed up with readers' and critics' constant references to her "sensitivity"; she hated being thought of as a sensitive plant. This has to be meshed with her remarks about extensions of childhood fantasy, uncertainties about adult status, and the compulsion of an insecure girl, "dislocated" by "race" and circumstances, to try to make sense of the half-understood situations around her. These threads meet in a simple way in another remark from *Why Do I Write?*: "I am sure that in nine out of ten cases the original wish to write is the wish to make oneself felt . . . the non-essential writer never gets past that wish".

She began writing stories when she was twenty, when her career as an art student was in the process of evaporating. The first story she ever completed—"Breakfast" (it begins, " 'Behold, I die daily', thought Mr. Rossiter, entering the breakfast-room")—was to be the opening story in her first published book. She wrote it, unromantically, in Aunt Laura's Harpenden house, in a high-windowed attic. There was a patch of damp on the wallpaper under the window, at eye-level when she sat at the table. Outside, the Midland Railway broke the silence. "Breakfast" finished, she wrote more. She had not read the stories of Hardy, Henry James, Maupassant, or Katherine Mansfield. She was not following any genre theoretically familiar to her—the short stories she did know, from Downe days, were Richard Middleton's collection *The Ghost Ship* and E. M. Forster's *The Celestial Omnibus*. She was very much on her own.

She herself, years later, characterized these early stories as "a mixture of precocity and naïveté".[6] It was in these stories that she recognised that desire both to level up with and to "demolish" her elders and betters. In several, a quietish younger person observes the emotional bangings-about of older women, the younger one feeling, as Lydia in "The Return", "suddenly hard and priggish and immature". The older people are easy enough to score off: they are muddled, self-deceiving, vain, messy in their emotions. They form conspiracies: two against two, the dead against the living. In "The Lover" and "The Shadowy Third", there are glimpses of an ideal love-relationship, concealed almost from its own realisation by the author's merciless eye: it is not quite safe, one feels, to trust the vision. In "Mrs. Windermere", Elizabeth hit the note of deadpan comic caricature that was struck again in her first novel.

The story from this period that carries the most emotion is one that is avowedly autobiographical—"Coming Home". The child Rosalind returns from school aglow with the success of an essay only to find that her mother, "Darlingest", is out. Disappointment, resentment overcome the child. And fear that something has happened to her mother leads—classically —to the fear that it is Rosalind's own fault:

> How could she ever have left Darlingest? . . . A person might be part of you, almost part of your body, and yet once you went away from them they might utterly cease to be. . . . There was no security. Safety and happiness were a game that grown-up people played with children to keep them from understanding. . . .

And later the child thinks:

> What have I done? I did love her. I did so awfully love her.
> Perhaps she was all right when I came in: coming home smiling. Then I stopped loving her, I hated her and was angry. And it happened. She was crossing a road and something happened to her. I was angry and she died and I killed her. . . . Life's nothing but waiting for awfulness to happen and trying to think about something else.

The saddest part about "Coming Home" is that when Darlingest is safely home, the child sulks and rejects her; and later, in anguish imagining Darlingest's loneliness and distress, she goes to her mother's room—but Darlingest has forgotten all about it. She is "standing in the middle of the room with her face turned towards the window, looking at something a long way away, smiling and singing to herself and rolling up her veil". Her emotional world is not so concentrated on Rosalind as Rosalind's is on her.

"Coming Home" is as near as one gets, and as one has the right to get, to the young Elizabeth in her feelings for and loss of her mother—to the Elizabeth who was away in another house while her mother died, to the Elizabeth who wrote, when she was over forty, that her mother, when away from her, had "thought of me constantly and planned ways in which we could meet and be alone". As she makes the writer St. Quentin Miller say in *The Death of the Heart*:

> "Memory is quite unbearable enough, but even so it leaves out quite a lot. It wouldn't let one down as gently, even, as that if it weren't more than half a fake —we remember to suit ourselves. . . . if one didn't let oneself swallow some few lies, I don't know how one would ever carry the past. Thank God, except at its one moment there's never any such thing as a bare fact. Ten minutes later, half an hour later, one's begun to gloze the fact over with a deposit of some sort. The hours I spent with thee dear love are like a string of pearls to me."

Elizabeth sent her stories round to the editors of periodicals. They were, without exception, rejected.

She moved her London base from Lillie Road to grander quarters with her great-aunt Edith at 32 Queen Anne's Gate. Aunt Edith was Lady Allendale, the widow of Sir George Colley, who had been killed at Majuba Hill in 1881 in the Transvaal revolt. Afterwards she married a Beaumont, who became Lord Allendale, and thenceforth worked almost continuously on her first husband's memoirs, out of remorse. Aunt

Edith liked to have a Colley girl around the place, and fancied herself as a matchmaker. Her blind spots in this line are evident from the fact that the kind of person she would have preferred for Elizabeth was someone like Eddie Marsh, a man of letters who was not noted for his interest in women.

Aspiring authors need luck or patronage as well as talent. Elizabeth haunted the fringes of literary London. Like the older married lady in her early story "The Evil That Men Do—", she went to poetry readings: at the Poetry Bookshop "upstairs, after dark, in a barn-like room, I listened to Ezra Pound reading aloud what was hypnotically unintelligible to me by the light of one candle".[7] The turning point came through her old headmistress Olive Willis. Miss Willis had been at Oxford with Rose Macaulay, and Rose Macaulay asked Elizabeth to tea at the University Women's Club. Rose was by then in her middle thirties, well established as a critic and novelist, and happily in love with Gerald O'Donovan (though Olive Willis thought she ought to give him up).

Elizabeth showed Rose her stories; and Rose, she said, "lit up a confidence I never had". Rose showed that "kindness with a touch of imaginative genius" which every young person needs. Her influence was not restricted to intangibles. Through Rose, Elizabeth met Naomi Royde-Smith, then editing the *Saturday Westminster*, in the pages of which a story of Elizabeth's appeared in print for the first time. Elizabeth started going to the regular Thursday parties for fifty or sixty people given by Rose and Naomi at 44 Prince's Gardens in Kensington: "Inconceivably, I found myself in the same room as Edith Sitwell, Walter de la Mare, Aldous Huxley. . . ."[8]

A friend—the "M.J." of the dedication—paid for having the stories typed, and they were sent to Sidgwick & Jackson with a letter of recommendation from Rose. Frank Sidgwick accepted them, and it was he who thought up the title— described as an "alluring" one by L. P. Hartley, reviewing the book in *The Spectator*. *Encounters* was published in the summer of 1923.

And in that same *annus mirabilis*, Elizabeth got married.

Audrey Fiennes's mother, recently widowed, was living at Bloxham, in Oxfordshire. Audrey spent some time there with her. The new incumbent at Bloxham church was one Fothergill Robinson, fortyish, a bachelor, artistic, temperamental, and sociable. Living with him was a younger man whom he had met when at Oxford and included, rather incongruously, in his aesthetic and literary circle. The young man was Alan Charles Cameron.

Since leaving the Army at the end of the war, Alan had been recuperating—he had been wounded and had had gas poisoning—and was looking around for something to do; he was thinking of teaching. Meanwhile Alan's mother joined the two men in Bloxham to keep house, and in 1919 the three were living together somewhat inconclusively: for the relationship between Alan Cameron and Fothergill Robinson, which had had its charm in Oxford days, had lost lustre now that Alan was a twenty-five-year-old war veteran.

It was Alan and Audrey who, under the circumstances, paired off. The village had them as good as married. But she gave him little real encouragement: "He was an inexpert handler of young women, and I was as green as most of us were in those days". They went for walks, and she tried to teach him to dance. Audrey was not all the time in Bloxham; and over the next couple of years Elizabeth came often alone to see her Aunt Gertrude, of whom she was very fond. Before long, news reached Audrey in Ireland of Elizabeth's literary discussions and long walks with Alan Cameron. She was not enormously surprised when Elizabeth wrote to say that they were engaged. Then and always, she loved both Elizabeth and Alan.

They were married quietly on August 4, 1923, in Uncle

Wingfield's church at Blisworth, Northamptonshire. Elizabeth was twenty-four, and Alan thirty. Elizabeth wore for her wedding an amber crêpe-de-Chine dress made by herself. She didn't even get the hem straight, said the committee of aunts. Since 1921, Alan had been working as Assistant Secretary for Education for Northamptonshire (much of the later phase of their courtship took place at Blisworth Rectory), and this determined their place of residence: 73 Knights Lane, Kingsthorpe, Northampton. "Elizabeth has made the best of a horrid little house", said Aunt Edie.

Alan Cameron, like Elizabeth, was an only child. Theirs was a very Celtic union: she was Welsh/Irish, and he was a Scottish Highlander on his father's side and Cornish on his mother's. Alan's maternal grandfather, who married a Miss Owen, was Sir Charles Lanyon, M.P. for Belfast. Elizabeth Helen, Alan's mother, was the second child of six; the sons all went into the services. One of Alan's uncles was Colonel Sir Owen Lanyon, the first military governor of the Transvaal. Elizabeth Helen Lanyon married Henry James Cameron (born 1844), H.M. Inspector of Factories, and Alan was born in 1893 to rather old parents. His father retired to Donington, near Exmouth, where he died in 1909. The only paternal instruction to young Alan that has survived the years is that "the men must not use the upstairs lavatory during the day—that is for the ladies".

Alan was brought up in Exmouth by two rightful tenants of the upstairs lavatory—his mother, a detached person much given to following cults, and an elderly nanny. Mrs. Cameron, by the time Elizabeth met Alan, was a tall, slight, white-haired lady, at that time a devotee of British Israelism, to her son's expressed disgust. Elizabeth got quite fond of her; and she lived until 1936, when she was run over by a car.

Alan had, even as a boy, a mannered voice and way of expressing himself that caused him some trouble at Radley, where he was sent to school; as a junior boy, he was laughed at. But once at the top of the school he made an impressive Senior Prefect; and he was a good cricketer. As a personality, he rather fell between categories: he was intelligent, well-read, and sensitive without being an intellectual; he was extremely conscientious; and, as the *Times* obituary said when the time came (in the inimitable *Times*-obituary antithetical style), while "hearty in manner, he was never 'a hearty' ". All the qualities, in fact, that make a first-class administrator: which he became.

The Radleian of 1912 includes a terrifically bad and heartfelt poem by Alan, entitled by him "A Mood", which owing to a printer's error appeared, confusingly, as "A Wood". In the same year, he won an exhibition to Hertford College, Oxford, where he failed to distinguish himself greatly, achieving a third class in Mods.* The war came within two years of his going up to Oxford; he enlisted in the Devon Regiment. He was in the opening battles of the Somme in 1916, and later saw service in Italy; here he distinguished himself as he had not at Oxford. He came out of the war as Captain Cameron, M.C., but in poor shape. The gas had affected his eyes, which were to give him trouble all his life. His qualities of courage, straightforwardness, and conviviality made him a natural as a soldier; he had a good war. Later, feeling himself to have become a bore to Elizabeth's literary friends, it was to anecdotes of the war that he eternally returned.

Elizabeth's great-aunt Edith, she of Queen Anne's Gate and the designs on Eddie Marsh, was not pleased about Alan. When Elizabeth first brought him to see her, she said: "My dear, I do not like your young schoolmaster. His buttons are too tight". And when Elizabeth made some excuses: "My dear, he's the kind of man whose buttons will always be too tight".

But in 1923, when Elizabeth's success was still a small

* Honour Moderations—the first classics examination.

56

and uncertain phenomenon, and she was still a rather gauche, insecure young woman, it was Alan who was the dominant partner. This was even true on an intellectual level: he had been to Oxford, he had been through the war, he had read a lot, he could talk about what he had read. To the unbookish Colleys, it was a case of "Bitha's marrying an intellectual". (Elizabeth remained Bitha to many of those who had known her from childhood, even after announcing that from now on she was Elizabeth. One's near and dear like to keep one from moving too far out of their orbit—which the assumption of her full name and her writing-self perhaps threatened. But no one ever had a stronger sense of family than Elizabeth.)

Alan "made" her in other, more worldly ways. Her clothes sense was very astray and, in spite of his own tight buttons, he took her in hand. She was not conventionally pretty as a young woman—she had the sort of strong, long face that is grown into in maturity. "Isn't it funny", says a character in *The Hotel*, "that for everybody there seems to be just one age at which they are *really* themselves?" Elizabeth was probably at her handsomest in her thirties and forties, when she had enormous charm and distinction; and it is in later years still that her face, softened, prompts the word "beautiful". As a girl, her taste and her means led her into wearing rather dotty, flamboyant, often home-made clothes. Her short sight contributed to her lack of judgement. She was always striking: large-boned, with white skin and pink cheeks, good features. Alan put her into clothes with style; she was always thereafter "smart", and her things were, when she could afford it, expensively tailored. She retained, in her *farouche* inner self, a penchant for overdressing on occasion. She used a lot of make-up, and the earrings—large clip-on ones—became a *sine qua non*. She wore them so incessantly that sometimes an infection was set up on the lobes of her ears, but she would not leave the clips off even then, because the sore places were unsightly.

She had very long feet, and Alan put her into sensible, expensive shoes bought at Fortnum's; in these and her tweeds he took her for long country walks. Alan liked to walk, totally shod, through any stream they might encounter. He said it was nice and cool, and did the shoes good. He was very keen on shoes. Just after World War II, Blanche Knopf sent Elizabeth three pairs of American shoes from Saks. Not only Elizabeth was delighted with them but Alan was, too, and Elizabeth wrote to Blanche: "You know how he loves shoes! (Short, I trust, of being a fêtichist.)" (The unwarranted circumflex she gave to "fetichist" gives that word an uncommonly festive air.) In *Joining Charles*, her 1929 collection of stories, there is one called "Shoes", about a young English couple abroad. The wife's large brogues are accidentally replaced by the hotel staff with a pair of dainty sandals far too small. The husband is attracted by the pretty little shoes and by the pretty little woman who turns out to be their owner, while loyally protesting scorn of such women. The servant returning the brogues adds insult to injury by referring to them as *"les chaussures de Monsieur"*. Thus Elizabeth put to ironic and profitable use Alan's enthusiasm and her own elegant, outsize feet. Her hands, too, were big, with long, spatulate fingers: "Strong, masculine hands", said an ex-lover who was familiar with them at a later date, and "an androgynous waist".

Alan and Elizabeth entered into marriage with great enthusiasm. Elizabeth was not domestically inclined (she rarely cooked, but general servants were customary and inexpensive), though they both loved good food and drink. She was not very interested in entertaining his colleagues, and produced horrid teas with no "little cakes" when he brought them home after work. She was not a fastidious housekeeper, and was by nature very untidy. But she and Alan understood one another. And she had the gift of "making" a house. There were always flowers in abundance, arranged *au naturel*, and their combined collections of books, treasured objects, and records. They were children of their time, and this was the 1920s: by their elders' standards, they lived informally; and they had single beds because that was the modern thing to do, and they took marriage cheerfully rather than soulfully.

On the principle that there is always one who loves and one who is loved, it would be Alan who did more loving; he adored her, looked after her, while she accepted, loved, and sometimes teased or scolded. "Darling" was a much-bandied word between them, often in tones of loud expostulation. Even later, when she was a famous author and he was—as he put it—Albert the Good, she always depended on him more than her newer friends knew. He was the safe harbour, the "location" for her dislocated life. To say that she could not buy a pair of shoes without him was true both literally and metaphorically.

Whether she was passionately in love with him when they married is doubtful. A voice from the past says: She married him because he proposed to her. Writing about her Downe House days, she said:

> I and my friends all intended to marry early, partly because this appeared an achievement or way of making one's mark, also from a feeling it would be difficult to settle to anything else until this was done. (Like passing School Certificate.) Few of my friends anticipated maternity with either interest or pleasure, and though some have since become mothers it still seems inappropriate.[9]

Alan had the romance of the soldier about him. He was intelligent. He was, then, very good-looking. He talked with her about the things that passionately interested her. Her first engagement had recently ended in failure. More than anything, she needed an emotional base and a simple, dependable kind of loving. The beginnings of success only accentuated this need; she wrote in *The House in Paris*: "All your youth, you want to have your greatness taken for granted; when you find it taken for granted, you are unnerved". And if she was never in love with Alan, she always loved him.

Their marriage, which as the years passed sometimes seemed incomprehensible to the outside world, lasted. She moved into a milieu where some of her closest friends were married two or three times, where liaisons, heterosexual and homosexual, were everlastingly, if painfully, formed and dissolved. Elizabeth greeted each new partnership with perfect politeness. She wrote in her essay "The Big House", "Well why not *be* polite—are not humane manners the crown of being human at all? Politeness is not constriction; it is a grace: it is really no worse than an exercise of the imagination on other people's behalf". She was not a disapprover; she disapproved only of disapproval, and thought that people should have what they needed. Her approach to life was a vigorous one. She had no patience with moral attitudes, or the sort of rigidity that passes as "goodness". Matchett, the marvellous maid in *The Death of the Heart*, tells sixteen-year-old Portia about old Mrs. Quayne, who so nobly "gave" her husband to his mistress, thereby banishing him from the home he loved and had never thought to leave:

> "Sacrificers," said Matchett, "are not the ones to
> pity. The ones to pity are those that they sacrifice. Oh,
> the sacrificers, they get it both ways. . . ."
> "But Matchett, she meant to do good."
> "No, she meant to do right."

Elizabeth believed in goodness, which did not always in her eyes coincide with rectitude. She believed in behaving properly—even if to behave properly meant, on occasion, to behave very badly.

But there was never any question, whatever the intricacies of her own private life, of her leaving Alan. "He is not a person that one could leave", she said. Nor was she a person to do the leaving. She believed in institutions and in sacraments, and she needed him. "She played the game according to the rules", William Buchan said of her, "and still made it exciting". She played the game according to her own as well as society's rules and was firm on some points, flexible on others; and besides (*The House in Paris* again) "no one speaks the truth when there's something they must have". Elizabeth certainly did leave Alan in the sense that in later years she absented herself from him quite often; but she always came home to roost.

The image of them as a pair of homing birds—something larger and more substantial than love-birds, however—is apposite. They were great trippers as young marrieds, travelling to un-obvious places abroad in a way that people then did not much do; and at home, they took endless days out in the car. Once, in an argument as to which was the way home, Alan, at the wheel, insisted on having his way. "Great grey pigeon", Elizabeth called him then, with great affection, "flapping its way home".

Alan and Elizabeth only lived at 73 Knights Lane for two years, but in that time she wrote two more books: another collection of stories, *Ann Lee's*, and her first novel, *The Hotel*. Neither was published until they had left Northamptonshire for Oxford; *The Hotel* was in fact written between the completion and the publication of *Ann Lee's*—and some of the stories in the latter were written while *Encounters* was still in the press. All this writing activity was fitted in between spring visits to Italy, journeys to Ireland to see her father and Bowen's Court, and frequent train trips to London.

Mostly, though, she worked, and in very different psychological circumstances from before: "I was now located, the mistress of a house; and the sensation of *living* anywhere, as apart from paying a succession of visits, was new to me".[10] She was working with an uninterruptedness that later she was

61

to look back on enviously, her writing-table now in a bow-window from where "a flat but reposing view of vegetable gardens stretched away . . . the nearest high point in *that* direction being, I was told, the Ural mountains".[11] The landscape of the English Midlands is not dramatic.

As she wrote the new stories, she sent them to magazines, as before; with a little better luck, but not much. John Strachey, running the literary side of *The Spectator*, published an abridged version of the title story of *Ann Lee's* (the first story *The Spectator* ever carried); he also advised her to go to the cinema, from which much, he said, was to be learnt. The *Queen*, the *London Mercury*, and *Eve* took three more. Elizabeth was now using an agent—Curtis Brown, Rose Macaulay's agent—and they sold two of the best stories, "The Parrot" and "Making Arrangements", to *Everybody's* in America.

The reason so many of her stories, however, still attracted only rejection slips was, Elizabeth thought later, that they fell halfway between the "first bright stage of experimentation and the required next degree of command . . . the disarming naïveté of *Encounters* is missing".[12] Also, perhaps, her suggestive, "atmospheric" style was not always dramatic in the sense that fiction editors understand it; read in isolation, before her name and her appeal were widely recognised, her quality was too easily passed over.

It is hard to remember, reading *Ann Lee's* now, that these stories were written by a young and energetic and newly married woman. Two of them—the two inspired directly by her environment—have a sense of moments of vividness snatched from a life in abeyance. In "The Parrot" (the idea came from imagining an escaped parrot in the branches of a chestnut tree on the corner of their road), a paid companion, Eleanor, in pursuit of her employer's parrot, has a glimpse of life next door, dramatic and irregular; when the bird is caught and she can take it home, her stolen hour will be "a nothing, an irrelevancy; a lost hour that had slipped through a crack in her life and vanished". In "Human Habitation" (inspired by a canal-side walk), two students, on an over-long walk along the towpath, call at a house and become briefly involved in the emotional drama going on within. As they left, "they felt like candles wavering, soon to be extinguished". One of the young men dives past his hostess "into the cave of darkness beyond the threshold". Out of the emotional whirlpool it is drearier, but perhaps safer?

This image of people leaving or having left, disappearing, ceasing to exist for each other, recurs again in almost the same form in this collection in "The Contessina", when the title-girl rejects the blundering Barlow: "The Contessina could no longer see him; it was as though he had slipped out of her vision down a crack, and the crack had closed above him for ever". Other words besides the "crack" recur and reinforce the sense of obsession with connections and disconnections. "Enisled" is one such word. In "The Visitor", the child is "alone, enisled with tragedy". In "Making Arrangements", the deserted husband remembers his wife's farewell letter "enisled . . . lonely, gleaming and defiant" on the silver salver where she used to throw down her gloves.

In "The Contessina" there is a great dwelling on the sheer minxish prettiness of the young girl—her clothes, her hair, her affected, enchanting little ways. There is much celebration of prettiness in *Ann Lee's*: Elizabeth said of herself that "the younger sister of beauty at that time delighted me". It is rather like the way in which George Eliot dwelt upon the soft skin, the tendrils of hair, the graceful ways of women such as Rosamond Lydgate in *Middlemarch*. Physically, Elizabeth was not unlike George Eliot. At a pageant in Oxford in the 1930s got up by the Buchans (John Buchan was Newman), she appeared as George Eliot and achieved, in costume and wig, a startlingly effective likeness.

Whatever Elizabeth herself said about the *Ann Lee's* stories' lacking the "required next degree of command", one in particular shows the ability to use and be objective about her own past. There is in "The Visitor", as there was in the earlier "Coming Home", her own childhood; but it is transformed, *used*. The child in "The Visitor" is a boy, Roger, staying with two maiden ladies, suspecting his mother is dying. The boy's father is not Henry Bowen, and certainly not the Henry Bowen of Elizabeth's mother's last days; but there are echoes here of the little that Elizabeth knew of her father in earlier, sicker days:

> Up and down the room he'd go, up and down the room, then dart sideways as though at a sudden loophole and disappear through the door in the garden. But he always came back to where Roger was; he couldn't let one alone . . . and the hands always reaching out to Roger to grab him with "Come on, old man, let's talk. Let's talk for a bit."

And Roger's self-consciousness, knowing the adults are discussing him:

> He walked past them, through the trees, consciously visible, oh, every line of him conscious—this was how a little boy walked while his mother was dying. . . . Then he hated himself: he did not like being looked at.

Elizabeth knew this feeling; when her mother died, "sometimes I wanted nonentity, sometimes celebrity". One was a person set apart. And there is one memory that Roger will not torture himself with: "He wouldn't remember *coming in to tea*—not that". But Roger is not Elizabeth, as Rosalind in "Coming Home" was Elizabeth; he is externalised; he is himself, a new person.

Ann Lee's, like *The Hotel*, uses very largely material from the past, from girlhood; the imagination naturally turns that way, and works its transformation on things that are already partly absorbed, or completes thus the process of absorption. So it is silly to deduce too much of Elizabeth's state of mind at the time of writing from these books. But she does, in her later foreword to a reissue of *Ann Lee's*, acknowledge the tenseness that is in them and that was in her:

> I do not know whether the mood of aesthetic restlessness in which I wrote them has left any mark on the *Ann Lee's* stories. It possibly made for tenseness, for over-anxiety to justify my medium. I was beating myself against human unknowableness; in fact, I made that my subject—how many times? The stories are questions asked: many end with a shrug, a query, or, to the reader, a sort of over-to-you.[13]

Things, she says, are left unexplained: "I cannot consider these to be trick endings; they were the admission of my predicament".

She puts the restlessness, the tenseness, the anxiety about human unknowableness down to literary, aesthetic preoccupations. This is no doubt so; to the reader, it also comes across as personal anxiety, tenseness, restlessness, "unknowableness". This is borne out by *The Hotel*, which, whatever other and quite different things it is, is a study in immature sexuality. There is one other thing to remember before going any further with this: and that is that every highly imaginative person— every natural novelist—not only notes everything that is actually going on within a relationship, but also follows up the thread of everything that *could* happen; he makes structures, writes scripts, that take off from the actuality. Love-relationships with and for persons of this kind can be fraught with ambiguity for this reason, though very often the partner in the relationship, firmly planted in reality, is unaware and untouched. Elizabeth knew all about this. In *The Hotel* the girl Sydney imagines the vapid, hypochondriacal female relation she is in Italy with to be suddenly dead, and wonders what she

.will do now; the lady is not dead, Sydney does not wish her dead: "But imagination often divorces itself from feeling".

Imagination often divorces itself from feeling: but there is one story in *Ann Lee's* that is so sexually violent in an unassertive way—Elizabeth never wrote anything like it again—that it draws the attention like a magnet. This is "Making Arrangements". Hewson's wife, in this story, has left him; and the essence of the story is a sort of rape of his lost wife through the medium of her evening dresses. His wife was the amusing one of the ménage, and at her dinner parties

> all the way down the table the shirt-fronts and pink quarter-faces veered intently towards Margery would veer round, guffawing, towards Hewson . . . their mirth drawn out into a sigh. "You must forgive us," they implied, "but your wife is really *so* amusing!" And Hewson sat on solidly and kept the wine going.

This particular scene is prophetic. It may have happened, a little, at the parties Alan and Elizabeth gave in Northampton; it was to happen over and over again in subtler, crueller company in Oxford and London. It is like something Rosamond Lehmann, in *The Swan in the Evening*, described: a situation in one of her novels that had parallels with something actually going on of which she was ignorant at the time of writing: "Did I invent the fictional 'plot'?—or subconsciously sneak up on what was going on unknown to me, and reveal the gist of it under the guise of fiction?" In Elizabeth's case, she was perhaps with the Hewsons' dinner parties imaginatively "following through" an actual situation; in any case, it is, with hindsight, painfully on target for what was to come.

Hewson, his wife departed, goes upstairs to pack up the dresses she has sent for. The dresses are described in detail—the black, the flame-colour, and "a creamy slithery thing with a metallic brilliance that slipped down into his hands with a horrible wanton willingness", and a red one that tore between his hands. He piles them all on the bed:

> It seemed to him, as he softly, inexorably approached them, that the swirls, rivers and luxuriance of silk and silver, fur and lace and velvet, shuddered as he came. His shadow drained the colour from them as he bent over the bed.
>
> Half an hour later, Hewson once more crossed the landing and went up to the box-room to look for Margery's trunk. He was intent and flushed, and paused for a moment under the light to brush some shreds of silver from his sleeve.

Whatever Elizabeth's "predicament" was, she understood or intuited frustration and the blacker side of love. In her novel *Friends and Relations*, Janet, explaining why she married (partly, unlike Elizabeth, in spite of and to spite another man), said: "You see, I had no experience, nothing outside myself. . . . But all I thought (then at first) was 'Here is a place for me.' . . . When Rodney came it was like being given directions". And whatever their difficulties, Alan's affection was always a place—the place—for Elizabeth.

E B

CHAPTER IV

The Oxford Connection

I N 1925, Alan Cameron was appointed Secretary for Education for the city of Oxford. They found a house in Old
Headington, the original village from which new Headington
has grown and was then growing; over Magdalen Bridge and
up Headington Hill, it is about a mile and a half from the
town. Their house, Waldencote, was a stone-built cottage
converted from the coach-house of Old Headington House. It
faced on to the Croft, a path that runs along the outside of the
high garden wall of the big house (into which Waldencote was
built) and opens on to the old High Street. Waldencote is still
there, though extended and modernised; and the Croft still
has a perfectly rural air. In this little house, which was blue-
washed inside, with a curly iron staircase, they lived for ten
years. In Oxford, Elizabeth came into her own professionally,
socially, and emotionally. She would have built a life had
they stayed in Northampton; but Oxford was heaven-sent.

John Buchan (later Lord Tweedsmuir) lived at Elsfield
Manor, a couple of miles from Headington. With him and all
his family Elizabeth and Alan became close friends. (Elsfield
was as great a centre of hospitality as Lady Ottoline Morrell's
Garsington, but, given the very different temperaments of the
two families, the clientele only partially overlapped.) It was
John Buchan's wife, Susan, and Alan who met first. They were
both members of the Oxford Committee formed to help the
massive unemployment in the South Wales coalfields in the

late twenties. Mrs. Buchan was impressed by the forcible way Alan spoke at one of the meetings:

> I had no idea who he was, and I asked someone, who told me that he was Mr. Alan Cameron. . . . The person whom I questioned said vaguely that he thought his wife wrote novels.[1]

At about the same time, the president of the Headington Women's Institute joined the committee of the Oxfordshire Federation of W.I.s, of which Susan Buchan was a member. The president of the Headington W.I. was none other than Elizabeth. "She came looking quiet and well dressed. I eyed her from the other side of our large table", said Susan Buchan, "and wished I could talk to her. She was a silent Committee member, and hardly ever made a remark". Elizabeth, however, loved the W.I., and was particularly involved with the drama group; the Headington contingent put on a play in a large barn in Islip called *The Wedding Morning*, in which she refused to act because of her stammer, but which she directed to great effect. The W.I. was one aspect of country life that she regretted when they came to leave Headington. She told Virginia Woolf in 1941, "I do very much miss W.I.s: since I came to live in London I feel I don't live in England at all".

Susan Buchan and Elizabeth finally coincided in a third-class carriage from Oxford to London, talked all the way, and were thenceforth close friends. The Camerons dined at Elsfield very often—the first time to meet the writer Anne Douglas Sedgwick, the American wife of Basil de Selincourt. There were many Elsfield evenings, and many visits to Waldencote and Elizabeth's "little tobacco-scented and dusty drawing-room"; but one evening in particular at Elsfield stands out, in the early thirties, when Elizabeth, Virginia Woolf, and Rosamond Lehmann were all there together, and all dressed (or so it seemed to Alice Buchan, then a very young girl) in misty-silvery dresses.

Elizabeth became Susan Buchan's friend; they used to go to each other's houses to write, to get away from the distractions of home. Elizabeth's rather grim story "Reduced" (included in the collection *Look at All Those Roses*, dedicated to Susan Buchan) was written at Elsfield, in John Buchan's upstairs library. But, falling as she did in her late twenties between the two generations of Buchans, Elizabeth was also the friend of all the Buchan young. She was specially fond of young William—blond, enchanting, and an aspiring writer. All her life Elizabeth was good, endlessly supportive, and helpful to certain chosen young people. Billy Buchan was the first in a long line of protégés. He and his brothers and sister, Alice, used to go to the Waldencote parties, where huge amounts of food were eaten off plates balanced on the knees. And William used to go over in the afternoons and literally sit at the feet of Elizabeth and her growing number of Oxford friends. Alan was particularly fond of Alice Buchan (who later married Brian Fairfax-Lucy) and used to say delightedly—but not to her—that there was something about her that made him want to beat her.

There were also old friends regained. In 1926, Eric Gillett, who was at Radley with Alan, was married in Lincoln College chapel; at the wedding he met Elizabeth for the first time. Eric had literary contacts through having worked with Harold Monro at the Poetry Bookshop, and he introduced Elizabeth to Cecil Day Lewis. Both *Encounters* and *Ann Lee's* had been praised by the reviewers, and L. P. Hartley, reviewing for *The Spectator*, was one of her earliest and most vocal champions. Hartley told Lord David Cecil, then in his first year as a young don at Wadham College, that he had found a really good new author, and asked him to lunch at the Ivy to meet her. Finding that they both lived in Oxford, and liking each other very much, within a fortnight Elizabeth and David Cecil had become friends.

In Oxford, from then on, Elizabeth and David Cecil met

about twice a week. She was the closest friend David ever had. It was an extremely intense, intimate, literary friendship; they were not lovers. She attended his very first lectures, on the Victorian novel; he lunched and dined regularly at Headington, and met there her close woman friends such as her cousin Noreen and Beatrice ("B") Curtis Brown. Alan was generally absent. But Alan and David got on—perhaps because David was the first of the "clever friends", he did not become categorised.

However intense the friendship, Elizabeth was not one for false sentimentality. She was very direct. David Cecil thought of her as an eighteenth-century woman and as a modern one—but not as a nineteenth-century woman. He found that she did not like refinement (though she approved of tradition and ceremony) or too much "sweetness". If anything was wrong between them, she believed in having it out, even in having a row, and clearing the air. Relationships, she said, should be "like a pearl in an oyster—a little friction producing the pearl". David did not agree with this.

Personal and social life, a necessity to Elizabeth, blossomed after meeting David, who introduced her to Oxford. She said, after reading his biography *The Young Melbourne*, "If I had been able to live like those women I'd never have written a line". By "those women" she meant Lady Melbourne and the Spencer sisters, especially the enchanting Lady Bessborough (whose portrait she resembled). She had a belief in the value and significance of "private life" as opposed to "public life": "taking 'private life' both in its broader, social, entertainment aspect and in its more intimate aspects—individual personal relationships, all the different varieties and degrees of friendship and of love", according to David Cecil. She was no feminist in the usual sense; she didn't like the "professional woman" image. This seemed to her to diminish the importance of non-professional women who ran the private and social side of life—if you underrate them, you rate personal relations pretty low. She did not think women ought to be rated highly only because they did things that men traditionally did.

So, even though from this time on she began to lunch and dine and weekend with her own friends, without Alan, it was because they were her friends, her world; she would not, for example, dine on Wadham high table on "women's evenings". She would often refuse invitations from people who were not her personal friends—lion-hunters as she became a lion—that did not include Alan. She always asked to be introduced as "Mrs. Cameron" and not as "Elizabeth Bowen"; there was extreme diffidence (which she never lost) in this, as well as self-defence and principle. It could sometimes cause retrospective embarrassment. During the war, at a party, Angus Wilson introduced Francis King to her:

> He must, I suppose, have mumbled "Elizabeth Bowen" first but all I heard in the cocktail-party noise was "Mrs. Cameron". I therefore had no idea who this handsome, big-boned, shy woman with a stammer could be. When she asked me what I did, I said that I was a novelist. (I had published two novels but I was, in fact, still an undergraduate.) I then lectured her for a considerable time on the modern novel with all the conceit and arrogance of the young. She listened sweetly and deferentially.[2]

As he left, Angus Wilson said, "I'm glad you and Elizabeth Bowen got on so well". The poor young writer was appalled. And at a party during the Spoleto Festival once, Harold Acton spent a whole evening trying to extract from "Mrs. Cameron" who she was—for it was clear to him that this remarkable woman was "someone". He did not succeed. Elizabeth was capable, too, of completely freezing strangers who approached her in hotels and restaurants simply because they recognised her. As St. Quentin Miller, the writer-character in *The Death of the Heart*, says, "writers find themselves constantly face to face with persons who expect to make free with them". Elizabeth did not suffer fools of the pretentious kind gladly, if at all; but it was not only "interesting people" in whom she was interested. Nice bores, and the oddest and most unlikely people, received her sympathetic and undivided attention. Nevertheless, in Oxford she did begin to meet "interesting people" in large numbers for the first time. And the Oxford generation with which her arrival coincided was by any standards an extraordinary one. Through David Cecil, she met Maurice Bowra, who, then in his mid-twenties—he was a year older than Elizabeth—was fellow and lecturer in classics at Wadham. (He became Warden in 1938.) Bowra was already a celebrated talent-spotter and host; among those who were just finishing their undergraduate careers in the mid-1920s, and who came and went within his circle, were Rex Warner, Cecil Day Lewis, Brian Howard, Cyril Connolly, Kenneth Clark, Henry Yorke (Henry Green), John Betjeman, Evelyn Waugh, Anthony Powell, John Sparrow, Isaiah Berlin, A. J. Ayer. . . . There were giants in the earth in those days, but if in those days they were giants it was still within the context of their own circle: just a very talented group of young men. Many of these became Elizabeth's friends; those she did not meet in the early years at Oxford later caught up with her in London or elsewhere. The publication of *The Hotel* two years after the move to Headington reinforced her reputation, and it was from then on that she began to play, as Bowra put it in his *Memories*, "a vivid part in our lives".

Both the books of stories had been published by Sidgwick & Jackson; with her first novel she changed her publisher. In July, 1926, Rose Macaulay wrote to Michael Sadleir at Constable, "I believe Curtis Brown is sending you *The Hotel*, a novel by Elizabeth Bowen, who wrote two very clever books of short stories. . . . This is only to say that I've just read *The Hotel*, and thought it extraordinarily clever and good—I wonder if you will?" She apologised for any possible officiousness and told him to read it for himself. He did, and Constable published it the following year.

Frank Sidgwick had urged Elizabeth to write a novel. But she had felt she had "a flitting mind", and could not extend her vision outside the range of an hour; until one afternoon "in a flash" the idea of hotel life on the Italian Riviera, where she had spent the winter of 1921 with Aunt Edie and her children, came to her.

The Hotel is full of women. "You know, women's lives are sensational", says the most sensation-mongering of them. The men are bulls in their china shop, to be "managed" or headed off. The women are vacuous, like Veronica who gets herself engaged "because everyone's the same and I must have some-body"; or sentimental, like Miss Pym and Miss Fitzgerald, whose tender friendship is rocked by a quarrel; or stiff, gypsy-ish, detached, like Sydney, the heroine, afraid of her own emotions. In *The Hotel* that ubiquitous early Bowen char-acter, the powerful older woman, blooms most wickedly: Mrs. Kerr, on whom Sydney has what is commonly—and not by Elizabeth—called a crush. Her charming, manipulative ways dominate the novel; it is she who breaks up Sydney's precipitate engagement to Mr. Milton, almost indetectably, trickling doubt into his mind. Mr. Milton sees through her: " 'Yes, you are charming,' he doubtfully thought, 'you injurious woman.' " But he is no match for her—"he sees spikes everywhere and rushes to impale himself".

Mr. Milton's sexual self is more than Sydney is ready for. Elizabeth knew exactly what she was doing (there is a kiss): already, she has the art of saying, about these matters, every-thing and nothing. The frightening impersonalness of passion is here: "Eye to eye they looked at each other questioningly, as though trying to learn from one another if they had been together; then each looked away, as though afraid to read they had been forgotten". Milton tries to reassure Sydney by reminding her of Curdie, "who opened a door straight on to the sky and was told to walk through it". Sydney does not want this. "I'd have gone back through the door", she said.

John Anderson had had a primitive appeal for Elizabeth that both frightened and attracted her, though John Milton, the clergyman, is not John Anderson; and Elizabeth all her life had been dominated by various well-meaning older women— Aunt Edie had greeted the news of her engagement in Bordighera with less than enthusiasm. But Aunt Edie was not a beautiful witch. Mrs. Kerr, with eyelids that "delicately and sadly fluttered", was "a lovely thing"—an inspired figment, the good/bad fairy godmother.

The important thing about *The Hotel* is that it is very, very funny. The picnic organised by the terrible, pathetic Lee-Mittisons is high-level farce; as is the scene in the hotel drawing-room where the bored, silly matrons sew and gossip —the atmosphere is so stiflingly feminine that poor Colonel Duperrier needs all his courage to go in and get a pen. They gossip, crabwise, about Mrs. Kerr and Sydney. " 'I have known *other* cases,' said someone else, looking about vaguely for her scissors, 'of these very violent friendships. One didn't feel *those others* were quite healthy.' "

And in Colonel Duperrier himself there is someone who is to reappear with variations in *The Last September*: the kind good man who married an enchanting girl only to find years later that she has become a neurotic and demanding invalid. He loves pretty girls still; he could be blissfully happy again with one, but there *she* lies upstairs, fretful, alone, waiting for him to come up. Colonel Duperrier is nice, far too nice, to look his predicament in the eye. Others see it for him. The young Elizabeth did. She had watched the middle-aged. Aunt-figures and uncle-figures were and remained her mythology.

Elizabeth's descriptive style, so inimitable in spite of imitations, flowers already in her first novel, as in her picture of an Italian cemetery:

> A wreath of black tin pansies swung from the arms of a cross with a clatter of petals, trailing colourless ribbons; a beaded garland had slipped down slantwise over the foot of a grave. Candles for the peculiar glory of the lately dead had been stuck in the unhealed earth: here and there a flame in a glass shade writhed, opaque in the sunshine. Above all this uneasy rustle of remembrance, white angels poised forward to admonish. The superlatives crowding each epitaph hissed out their "*issimi*" and "*issime*" from under the millinery of death. Everywhere, in ribbons, marbles, porcelains was a suggestion of the *salon*, and nowhere could the significance of death have been brought forward more startlingly.

A more experienced writer might have omitted what comes after that last comma, and trusted the rest to make the point. Elizabeth in *The Hotel* found it hard to pass up an insight; she "puts everything in". Later, she practised—and wrote about—the art of exclusion. But *The Hotel* is on every level a very good novel. And for a first novel it is extraordinary.

Elizabeth had great personal success in Oxford. The academic world does not always take kindly to creative artists, as Bowra said, "since its purposes are of a different kind", but she got taken up enormously. Her conversation was original, amusing, trenchant, punctuated by her stammer; shy in a large or largely unfamiliar group, she blossomed among sympathetic friends. It was still the golden Oxford, now much documented by Elizabeth's contemporaries, of cherished college wine-cellars, pleasure, privilege, and private dinner parties in college rooms for those who could afford it. After a dinner at Wadham in 1931 for W. B. Yeats, at which Elizabeth was present—with John Sparrow, Nancy Mitford, and the Kenneth Clarks—the poet told Bowra that "no emperor does himself so well as an Oxford don".[3] Oxford is a community of gossips, and Elizabeth thrived on gossip; she did not have that tight-lipped brand of loyalty which forbids talking about friends to other friends. Maurice Bowra has left a portrait of how she appeared to the Oxford of the 1920s and early 1930s:

> She was tall and well built and had the manner of someone who has lived in the country and knows its habits. She was handsome in an unusual way, with a face that indicated both mind and character. Unlike some Irish, she did not talk for effect but kept the conversation at a high level and gave her full attention to it. . . . She had the fine style of a great lady, who on rare occasions was not shy of slapping down impertinence . . . with all her sensibility and imagination, she had a masculine intelligence which was fully at home in large subjects and general ideas. . . .[4]

Elizabeth's presence always imposed a sense of fitness and propriety—people did not tell dirty stories in her presence. Even a person who was sometimes difficult in other ways, like Cyril Connolly, behaved when with her—lots of jokes, but no sulks. This faculty of hers strengthened as she grew older. Cyril Connolly was rather ruthless about getting his hands on books that he wanted; and once, years later, at dinner at his house, he told Elizabeth that he didn't have first editions of her first two or three books, and could she give them to him? Elizabeth firmly said that she had only one copy of each. He continued to wheedle and plead but she had no intention of giving in. Then he poured out a claret of which he was very proud and asked Francis King, who was also present, to try it. Francis thought it tasted odd but was too polite to say so. Elizabeth sipped hers and said firmly, "Cyril, this is awful. It must be corked". With unusual docility he fetched another bottle.

Elizabeth could be tough with Cyril (and not only with Cyril); but they were enormously fond of each other. Cyril admired her writing greatly—in a rather abstract sort of way: "Marvellous writer, Elizabeth . . . never could finish one of her books". (He must, however, have finished at least one—her first novel, *The Hotel*, was the subject of his first-ever novel review for *The New Statesman*.) He admired her style, the way she looked: Sean O'Faolain once questioned her handsomeness, and Cyril replied indignantly that she was "a most beautiful woman".

What Elizabeth did was to stimulate, charm, stir up, excite the company and the conversation, while keeping things —on the surface—within bounds. Very different from Bloomsbury, as Raymond Mortimer remarked; Bloomsbury would say anything, and the more *outré* the better.

She fitted into Oxford, Bowra thought, because she believed in it, its past and its traditions. Not that she was much of a historian; indeed, she was no historian at all. (She never got round to reading Lecky, the classic chronicler from her own country.) Yet she had, according to Bowra, "a historical insight lacking in many historians", springing from her sensitivity to place and to the past. She took him, on a visit to Ireland, to the ruins of Kilcolman, a few miles from Bowen's Court, where Edmund Spenser wrote part of *The Faerie Queene*, and to a big house burnt out in the Troubles; and he noticed how she combined "a historian's impartiality with a novelist's commitment". She had, too, the gift of making everywhere visited in her company seem magical and mythical, and everyone she was with feel nicer and better than they really were, and everyone one encountered with her more interesting than they really were; quite dull people, first met in her company, retained afterwards a spurious fascination.

Twice a year at least, Alan and Elizabeth travelled from Oxford by car and boat to Ireland and Bowen's Court; the new friends sometimes came, too, and often Audrey Fiennes. Elizabeth and Alan had a bull-nosed Morris, and for these trips it would be packed to the roof, "the poor little car clawing the air"—Elizabeth, like Rose Macaulay, anthropomorphised her cars. With Audrey, who adored them both, Elizabeth and Alan were at their best and happiest. The two young women never stopped talking. "You *are* two VITAL great women", said Alan, "the noise is rather like the Small Cat House at the Zoo". But then Alan was extremely fond of cats. So they always had cats, and Elizabeth tolerated them for his sake. She gave a self-sufficient little cat called Benito, "a dear little bore", a small part to play in *To the North*. And she herself had much that was catlike in her personality and even appearance, as Alan was the first to appreciate.

Henry Bowen liked Alan and got on well with him—on these holidays they walked up and down together in the Bowen's Court grounds, each with his hands behind his back. It was to the world of her girlhood at Bowen's Court that Elizabeth returned in her second novel, *The Last September*.

She said that *The Last September* had "a deep, clouded, spontaneous source".[5] Danielstown, the house in the story, is Bowen's Court. Lois, the girl in the story, the niece of the house, "derives from", but is not, Elizabeth at nineteen. Lois is still capable of displays of "unfathomable silliness" and still feels "a distant pride at having grown up at all, which seemed an achievement like marriage or fame". If she is at the crossroads between childhood and adulthood, her country is at a grimmer crossroads. The story is set in 1920, in the Troubles. In Danielstown and the houses around, the vapid fatuities, the traditional cosinesses, the Anglo-Irish dinner parties, tennis parties, dances continue. There is threat in the air, in the very landscape, in the sunsets; beyond the demesne, "behind the trees, pressing in from the open and empty country like an invasion, the orange bright sky crept and smouldered". The young men with whom Lois and her friend Livvy dance and flirt do not always return from their patrols. The young man Laurence, made desperate by the unreality of the social round and longing for a "crude intrusion of the actual", says, "I should like to be here when this house burns".

In *The Last September* there is that juxtaposition of two dissimilar women that was to become a pattern in Elizabeth's novels; both are drawn from polarised aspects of her own personality, her self and her sub-self, as she expressed it. There is Lois; and there is Marda, a visitor to Danielstown, ten years older, whom Lois admires and longs to please. Marda, with her big hands and elegant clothes, worldly, assured, adequate, detached, will marry coolly, in order to be married. She is loved briefly and hopelessly by Mr. Montmorency, who has a wife with a weak heart, and who never, now, will achieve or become anything: a bloodless, sadder version of Colonel Duperrier in *The Hotel*. Marda is something like the person Elizabeth in Oxford was becoming—or, rather, how Elizabeth's Oxford self might be perceived by someone like Lois, her own inner, younger self.

The Last September is the classic Bowen novel of arrivals and departures, felt vividly and painfully by Lois, for whom they changed the quality of the outer air and her own inner weather. Sir Richard Naylor, the vague master of Danielstown, perceives them in his own way:

> Visitors took form gradually in his household, coming out of a haze of rumour, and seemed but lightly, pleasantly superimposed on the vital pattern till a departure tore great shreds from the season's texture.

In this novel, too, as in *The Hotel*, the young girl's engagement is broken by the interference of an older woman—this time by Lois's high-minded, high-handed aunt, who convinces Lois, with sadly little effort, that she does not "really love" her young soldier. "You have no conception of love", she says:

> "Go to a school of art."
> "But I don't think I really draw well."
> "That is no reason why you should marry."

The Last September, while centered on the doomed world of Danielstown and on Lois, has everything to say about the English-Irish relationship in the Troubles (and not only in the Troubles). It is done through social comedy, through "manners", but is none the less sharp for that. The land-owning Irish, like Sir Richard and Lady Naylor, are bound by interest and tradition to the union with England. They hope for a "favourable" end to the Troubles; they entertain the British officers and their wives. And yet they find the English among them vulgar and insensitive; they comment on this among themselves. Some of the Naylors' own tenants, familes known to them from their fathers' time, are probably among the rebels. The arrests on suspicion, the harassment of these families, cause pain to people like the Naylors—as it did to the Bowens. They are caught between loyalties. So there are tensions at the tea-parties, and talk between the women becomes a little spiteful. The English officers' wives, delighting in the hospitality, "so Irish", have little inkling of the emotional minefields on which they walk. The instinctive hostilities are absorbed almost subliminally by the reader of *The Last September*, for no character is so ill-bred as to fail in courtesy. *The Last September* is the perfect illustration of Elizabeth's tenet that life with the lid on is both more frightening and more exciting than life with the lid off. She expressed this in print when writing about Jane Austen (in *English Novelists*, 1942): "The constraints of polite behaviour only serve to store up her characters' energies; she dispels, except for the very stupid, the fallacy that life with the lid off—in thieves' kitchens, prisons, taverns and brothels—is necessarily more interesting than life with the lid on." (She is, in the same book, markedly lukewarm in comparison about George Eliot, of whom, curiously, she seems to have had only a moderate appreciation, feeling her to be over-intellectual for a novelist.)

"Life with the lid on" is the essence of Elizabeth's early fiction, as it is of her upbringing and her temperament. Passion and terror lie beneath, partly controlled, partly controlling. Meanwhile there are the flowers to be arranged; and after dinner the family will sit out on the front steps of Danielstown, of Bowen's Court, in the twilight of the day and of the old order.

And it is in *The Last September* that Elizabeth, writing about the country and the county that she knew best, gives her best and most characteristic description of it. The house itself is described here in its setting in a passage about nightfall that is written with the sharpened vision of apprehensive love:

> Square cattle moved in the fields like saints, with a mindless certainty. Single trees, on a rath, at the turn of a road, drew up light at their roots. Only the massed trees—spread like a rug to dull some keenness, break some contact between self and senses perilous to the routine of living—only the trees of the demesne were dark and exhaled darkness. Down among them, dusk would stream up the paths ahead, lie stagnant on lawns, would mount in the dank of garden, heightening the walls, dulling the borders as by a rain of ashes. Dusk would lie where one looked as though it were in one's eyes, as though the fountain of darkness were in one's own perception. Seen from above, the house in its pit of trees seemed a very reservoir of obscurity; from the doors one must come out stained with it. And the kitchen smoke, lying over the vague trees doubtfully, seemed the very fumes of living.

Danielstown burns, as Bowen's Court never did. In *The Last September*, Elizabeth described what her father had told her to steel herself to expect, when she was in Italy. But Elizabeth has mercy on her fictionalized younger self, and Lois is abroad and does not see what the Naylors see, their front door standing "open hospitably upon a furnace". "Bowen's Court survived", wrote Elizabeth (in her preface to the 1952 Knopf edition of this novel). "Nevertheless, so often in my mind's eye did I see it burning that the terrible last event in *The Last September* is more real than anything I have lived through".

Elizabeth's response to the stimulus of Oxford was to produce two books in one year—*The Last September* and the short stories *Joining Charles* in 1929—and a book every year except one until she and Alan left Oxford in 1935.

Joining Charles is a very mixed bunch; three or four of the stories, if she had not already been established as a writer, would never have passed a publisher's muster. The best ones are imaginative extrapolations of her "young married" situation. In the title-story, a young wife, staying with her in-laws, wrapt in their accepting affection, suddenly is afraid she does not love her husband. "The Working-Party" is about tea in the young farmer's wife's sitting-room while a dead man slumps on the kitchen stairs—cakes, daintiness, and doilies inside, nameless horror outside. There are two returns to earlier days: In "The Dancing-Mistress" we attend, from the teacher's point of view, a dancing-class like the one where seven-year-old Elizabeth learnt to waltz; and "The Jungle" is about the excitement and misery of a school friendship, which ends in a moment of intense closeness between the two girls, a flash of emotions they know nothing about.

Joining Charles is full of domestic interiors, of a sense of "house" not always benign. (The collection includes a ghost story.) In the descriptions of houses there are long sentences that become as labyrinthine as the corridors, where the construction is as dislocated as the people within: this one, for example, from "The Cassowary", like a sequence from a film:

> The uneasy house grew familiar to Margery, the loud shutting of the heavily-moulded doors, the cold limey breath from the passages, the sheen along empty rooms where one wandered of paint and marble in the immoderate glare of the windows, and, most of all in the rooms they inhabited, a suggestion about the general arrangements of being provisional;

The camera—the sentence—continues on after the semicolon, to come to rest beautifully, provisionally, on three women sitting in a room.

Henry Bowen was ill again. He had completed, after sixteen years, a book on statutory land purchase in Ireland—which ironically turned out to be of historic interest only, since changes in Irish land-law after the Treaty put the system out of effect. He and Mary planned to live all the time now at Bowen's Court, the first time the house had been a full-time home for nearly twenty-five years. He loved the place, but he did not thrive there. His physical health deteriorated, and his mental illness returned; the doctors said the end would not be long. Elizabeth went over to be with him. He lay in the room in which his mother had nursed him through smallpox so long ago. He died in May, 1930, a beautiful sunny May. Bowen's Court now was Elizabeth's: "I went upstairs to the Long Room, where I walked up and down."

Hundreds of the country people came to the funeral, to accompany the coffin from the house to Farahy church:

> The crowd would just part, to let my husband and me keep our places close to my father, then it came round

us, with friendly closeness, again. The people, now naturally talking, because in Ireland death makes no false or inhuman hush, swept over the grass alongside the avenue, pressing down almost to the verge of the woods. When we came to the churchyard, the service was read there, so that the friends who were Catholics should not be left waiting outside the doors. . . .[6]

Elizabeth's father was buried against the wall facing north towards the house, which backed then on to trees planted in his own time; they are felled now, and nothing blocks the view towards the house; only there is, now, no house.

The Bowen's Court that Elizabeth inherited was much as it was when the third Henry Bowen moved in in 1776. For a house so loved and so lovable, it had a very austere façade, unrelieved and bare. The main rooms were not so very many, but they were large and high. The drawing-room with its old grey paper had three great windows looking south and two to the west; the windowless walls held Robert Cole Bowen's vast mirrors. The drawing-room opened off the hall to the left, and the library—the most comfortable, lived-in room— to the right. The dining-room was behind the drawing-room, and, from the back hall, stairs went down to the working parts of the house and to the kitchen, where Sarah Barry and Molly O'Brien worked. The wide front hall was a room in itself— Elizabeth used it as her dining-room—and in it the Bowen family portraits hung. In good weather, the front door stood always open, and the wide, shallow front steps, which got the sun, formed a sociable extension to the house.

The staircase, lighted by a Venetian window, had oak banisters and opened on to a gallery on the second floor; from here the stairs were to have been extended upwards, but no Bowen had ever had the money to do it; as it was, the Long

Room could only be reached by humble back stairs. On the second floor there were two large corner bedrooms over the library and the drawing-room, with dressing-rooms behind them, and one other large bedroom and dressing-room at the head of the stairs, over the dining-room.

There was no bathroom at all in 1930. The maids brought up tin baths to the bedrooms, and hot water in wickerwork containers whose crimson padding was stuffed with hay. The lavatories, those installed by Robert Cole Bowen, were ancient but adequate. Idyllic in summer and always drenched in light from the great windows, Bowen's Court was hard to heat; guests were on occasion issued with their own personal electric fire to carry from room to room. The bedrooms and the beds were sometimes damp. One visitor tested the sheets by putting her hand-mirror down the bed; finding it misted up, she prudently slept in a mackintosh.

In compensation there was the beautiful setting, the walled garden to which Mary Bowen had brought new order, the grace of the house itself, and Elizabeth's lavish, loving hospitality. Food and drink were of the very best and came in huge and unmeasured quantities. Elizabeth gave, and never counted the cost. Or only once a year, when she went down to settle her grocery bill with Mrs. Annie Cleary, who kept the little shop at the bridge at Farahy: a ceremonious occasion, with a sit-down chat and a drink.

The Long Room right at the top (with six small rooms opening off it) was startling in its length, running from front to back of the house, and empty of furniture. It was meant as a ballroom—but the floor would never have stood it. It always seemed to Elizabeth the heart of the house—on coming back to Bowen's Court "one never feels one has really come home again until one has been up to the Long Room". Used for pacing in times of stress, as a wet-weather playroom for generations of Bowen children, it came into its own again as a grown-ups' playroom for Elizabeth, Alan, and their visitors.

Elizabeth, who played as intensively as she worked, liked to *do* things. Writing from Oxford to Cyril Connolly's first wife, Jean, in 1931, describing the summer spent at Bowen's Court, she said they had

> played deck-tennis and a mock Basque game . . . very stretching and nice, with wicker shovels, on the lawn or in the Long Room at the top on wet days. Vingt-et-un in the evenings. The Cork Aero club had its head-quarters at Fermoy and I looped the loop and did spinning nose-dives which I am very glad to have done as I was so terrified of them. The loop is not so very exciting, is it, more like a Victorian bedroom mirror coming loose on its hinges and swinging forward at one when one looks at it.

She was a great person for games, and this was a great period for games—paper games, card games, parlour games. Rummy and vingt-et-un were her card games, and Scrabble her last love. Consequences was a perennial; and after the summer spate of visitors to Bowen's Court in 1937 she wrote to William Plomer:

> The Cecils imported some rather nice new paper games —one called Things Left Behind—do you know it? You have to give a list of 4 characteristic objects found in a spare room, and the others have to guess who the person is. And I invented one called Bad Parties—you have to invent a list of the most excruciating eight people (though they may be nice individually) possible to combine. Also to make out a menu of the most re-pulsive (though it must be credible) dinner you can imagine. With drinks. And, if possible, the games played afterwards.

Such games require a delicate malice and a large acquaintance in common, both of which conditions were satisfied. Another game was played with Norah Preece and her children. (Mrs. Preece—née Hely Hutchinson, and formerly Mrs. Oliver— first knew Elizabeth when she lived at Byblox, not far from Bowen's Court, and later Elizabeth was a frequent visitor at Kells House, Kerry, where the Preeces lived.) The procedure in the Byblox game was for everyone to declare what physical attribute they hadn't got but had always longed for.

> The players included Elizabeth, Honor Tracy, Eddy [Sackville-West], and assorted young daughters and nieces: these mostly banged on about their legs; Honor wanted Big Brown Velvet Pansy Eyes, instead of Little Green Piggies, Eddy rather strangely wished to reinforce his neat features with Great Big Nigger Lips, and Elizabeth said that Golden Curls would have made ALL the difference.[7]

Acute commentators have remarked that in this game people are very rarely perfectly sincere, for fear of drawing attention to what they secretly imagine to be their one major imperfection, which, by some miracle, may still have escaped the world's notice. Elizabeth's wish, in any case, was nostalgic rather than fantastic: she once had been the possessor of golden curls—or, at any rate, of golden waves.

Alan took over a lot of the practical running of Bowen's Court, though he could not, because of his job, spend so much time there as Elizabeth did. He kept the estate accounts, as well as putting in a fair amount of physical work in the garden and woods. Both of them loved Bowen's Court, though the upkeep of it was a perpetual anxiety. There was never enough money. Once, when Elizabeth was living in London, she opened the door of the Clarence Terrace house and, going in, picked up some letters from Ireland from the hall table. She said to the writer Elizabeth Jenkins, who was with her: "I sometimes wonder what I should feel if I had a letter saying Bowen's Court had been burnt to the ground. It might almost be a relief". When times were hard, Bowen's Court, her inheritance, was a responsibility in the same way that a beloved but subnormal child is a responsibility. But there was never, never any question of their not keeping the house on, or of not being there as much as possible; it was, simply, home.

E B

CHAPTER V

The Grand Chain

"WRITERS OF MEMOIRS", wrote William Plomer in the first volume of his autobiography, "often say nothing about the most usual process by which acquaintanceship is extended. It is like the movement in the Lancers which used to be enjoyed by children of my generation at their dancing-classes and was known as 'The Grand Chain'." Elizabeth and William Plomer became part of the Grand Chain at about the same time and touched hands with many of the same dancers, and with each other.

Before the Second World War one could still speak of "society", which centred on London and spread to country houses at the weekend. There were servants, so dinner parties and weekend guests, however racking emotionally, were not unduly taxing physically for hostesses. The big difference between then and now was that the upper-middle-class world of society and the world of the arts very largely coincided. A talented person from a less privileged background—the Irish writer James Stephens, for example—was absorbed into literary society and generally conformed: conformed, that is, to the accepted modes of social or sexual non-conformism. There were exceptions—Bloomsbury could not absorb D. H. Lawrence. Charm, wit, and cleverness were at a premium, and good manners and "civilised" behaviour were not yet discredited among people whose values dominated even the depression years.

There were, of course, in the smartest drawing-rooms rebels and social consciences and Socialists. It is a cliché to remark that the 1930s was a period of mainly left-wing political awakening among English intellectuals. The tides of Communism and Fascism in Europe were recognised to concern Britain and her remaining empire and the future of mankind. Rose Macaulay wrote of this decade in *Life Among the English* that "the slump blew like a cold draught at its birth, war stormed like a forest fire at its close; between these two catastrophes Communists and Fascists battled and preached". If there was one thing that excited writers in the thirties, John Gross has written, it was the idea of themselves as "men of action".[1] Since it is possible to see the end product of both Fascism and Communism, from the private individual's point of view, as much the same point on a circle approached from different directions, it is hardly surprising that the ideologies and aspirations of some literary radicals seem, now, confused. Commitment and involvement were important to them; but involvement in what precisely does not always bear analysis. Nevertheless, many people then and now would agree with Stephen Spender that the inner life should not be the only life: "Sensibility is not enough".[2]

Sectarianism—whether political, religious, or aesthetic— gives opportunity to settle old scores and personal prejudices. The leftish magazine *New Verse*, for example, shaped by Auden and by its editor, Geoffrey Grigson, was "against", among heterogeneous others, "Edith Sitwell, but also Bloomsbury, the Book Society, Laura Riding, Michael Roberts . . . a long procession of Georgians, academics, *New Statesman* reviewers, middlebrow pundits, neo-romantics".[3] Elizabeth (leaving aside her Anglo-Irish heritage) was heir, in literary and aesthetic terms, to Bloomsbury. She was no part of the new left. She was never involved in party politics, and her politics, such as they were, were Conservative as far as Britain was concerned. Otherwise she was eclectic. She was, as Bloomsbury was, appalled by Fascism; after a visit to Italy in the early thirties she wrote to Virginia Woolf that she had been given a seat in a grandstand "to watch, a few feet way, Mussolini on a white horse reviewing police—dogs, bands, tanks—that was awful".

She certainly fitted into several of the categories disapproved of by *New Verse*. Not that she would have approved of everyone on that arbitrary list herself: she warned William Plomer against "Miss Riding; how disconcerting that she liked you—be careful, she's most tenacious". Aspects of the left-wing world might have attracted her; John Gross's phrase about the politicised writers seeing themselves as men of action echoes one of her own: "I'm tired of queers and intellectuals, I want a man of action". But, in the nature of things, the action of left writers, before the war, with the exception of those who went to the Spanish Civil War, remained mostly cerebral. And Elizabeth's real-life men of action tended to be not connected with literature.

Elizabeth in her early thirties—her own and the century's—was interested in her work and in her friends. She was not peculiar in this. There was in England a profound refusal to contemplate disaster. Europe, for as long as possible, still meant the Salzburg Music Festival and French Impressionism and the Italian lakes. With her, it was not a refusal to envisage disaster, but an unwillingness to do anything so pointless as to talk about it. Even after the war, she held firmly to her belief that art and politics do not, in any case, mix. In *Why Do I Write?*, in 1948, she said that writers should keep out of pulpits and off platforms and should not sign petitions about things they didn't know much about. Certainly, from art's point of view, political or moral axe-grinding of however high an order can only damage the art.

In short, you have to choose. Elizabeth's position was that of Virginia Woolf, who deprecated the preoccupation of writers such as Auden, John Lehmann, and Stephen Spender with outside events in the thirties—though Stephen Spender did invite Elizabeth to contribute to *Left Review*. Elizabeth thought that the most that should be asked of a writer publicly was demeanour: "He should try not to be too far, personally, below the level of his work".[4] And the demeanour of those who, like Elizabeth, fiddled while Europe smouldered was, after war came in 1939, by no means unworthy or uncourageous. Elizabeth was very alive to all social change, but from the individual's point of view; it was a "happening", a challenge. Karen, the heroine of *The House in Paris* (1935), the character with whom one identifies says this:

> "I wish the Revolution would come soon; I should like to start fresh while I am still young, with everything that I had to depend on gone. I sometimes think it is people like us, Aunt Violet, people of consequence, who are unfortunate: we have nothing ahead. I feel it's time something happened."
>
> "Surely so much has happened," said Aunt Violet. "And mightn't a revolution be rather unfair?"
>
> "I shall always work against it," said Karen grandly. "But I should like it to happen in spite of me."
>
> "But what would become of your Uncle Bill? He has always been so good, and no one would think of him."
>
> Karen saw this was too true. . . .

Elizabeth is ironic at the expense of both Karen and Aunt Violet here. In fact, revolutions, and violent ones, overtake them both, but not of the sort that they are discussing. Personal life, for Elizabeth, held most of the drama life could offer.

Elizabeth never shared the feeling of some creative artists who, depressed by the state of the world, find it futile or pointless to go on with their work. Talking (in a B.B.C. broadcast in 1959) about the war years, which affected her strongly, she added:

> But on the whole I'm much more egocentric—I'm less morally, psychologically sensitive—than quite a number of the novelists I know. I've got a sort of imperviousness. Just as, apart from the work I did in the war, I went on writing and writing away—not, I think, altogether wrongly, but feeling, "Well, this is the one thing I can do and what's the point of stopping it? . . ."

In 1930, Virginia Woolf was forty-eight and at her zenith. (*The Waves* was published in 1931.) When Elizabeth was beginning to write in the twenties, she had been conscious of an "establishment", "the great elder group . . . the people in Bloomsbury".[5] Virginia Woolf was the acknowledged head of her profession, certainly as far as Elizabeth was concerned; but there were also the new names, writers in their twenties and thirties, children like Elizabeth of the twentieth century: Rosamond Lehmann, Stephen Spender, Evelyn Waugh, L. P. Hartley, the whole list of young Oxford lions—with Raymond Mortimer and other established critics and writers filling the gap. But London society and the literary world were still small enough for anyone who received good notices to be very quickly known to other writers. Social life could be intense, if that was what you wanted: as Stephen Spender wrote to Elizabeth, "I am having tea with Rosamond this afternoon, lunch with Eliot, dinner with A. P. Herbert, coffee with Virginia! A very literary day".

Elizabeth said in the 1959 broadcast that she had never belonged to any group and that "so far as we worked our way along, Graham Greene, or Evelyn [Waugh] or Henry Reed or Rosamond Lehmann has a certain prestige and influence; but I wouldn't say that the establishment consisted of the novelists who were at work so much as the critics and the circle they create". Her generation was far less cliquey than Bloomsbury had been. "Like a large loosely knit family", Stephen Spender said, "most of them under the rather remote guardianship of their parent of Bloomsbury".[6] Elizabeth perhaps took this further than most people—she tended, especially as she grew older, to keep her friends in separate compartments, and everyone had his own Elizabeth. Looking back on those days from the 1950s, she wrote to William Plomer:

> What an agreeable life we all had, seeing each other without being "a group". Perhaps ours was, is, the only non-grouping generation; the younger ones now sound as though they'd started doing that again—or haven't they, really?

Publishers' lists were small, fewer titles were published, it was a more personal business. Authors were not yet so numerous or so heterogeneous that a critic receiving a letter of thanks for a sensitive review would not be perfectly prepared to embark on a correspondence, or a friendship, and to introduce the new author into his circle.

If reviewers were one way of entering the Grand Chain, hostesses were another. Rose Macaulay and Naomi Royde-Smith had given Elizabeth her first experience of literary society; now, by 1931, she knew Lady Ottoline Morrell—an aging, unwell (she died in 1938), but still flamboyant Ottoline, still the tireless hostess and patron. Garsington was given up now, but she was At Home at 10 Gower Street on Thursdays. Sometimes she would invite one specifically, but it was quite all right to send a note—as Elizabeth frequently did—and propose oneself. "It is *delightful* to have you on Thursdays", wrote Ottoline to Elizabeth, "but I should also like you to myself some time!" Frequently she pressed Elizabeth to a "nice long tête-à-tête". She gossipped confidentially with Elizabeth as Virginia Woolf did not: she wrote to Elizabeth how "terribly moved" she was, reading the published letters of

D. H. Lawrence (one of the people she had most loved): "I see more than ever how Frieda broke him as *a man*—not as a writer perhaps". Elizabeth was greatly intrigued by Lady Ottoline, asked for and was granted a photograph of her, and wrote to her assiduously and—"How happy you make us all!" —flatteringly.

Elizabeth and Alan had a share with Audrey Fiennes in a London flat, which Elizabeth naturally enough used more than Alan did, because of his work. Also his health, even now, was not always good. There was the trouble with his eyes; when they were bad, Elizabeth would keep him company in Headington and do little "except go for walks with him and read out, and see a few friends here". Oxford had lost its gloss a little. Elizabeth wrote to A. E. Coppard in December, 1932: "I do want to travel a great deal, *not* vicariously and *soon*. . . . Are you ever in London? . . . I spend most of my time there as I don't like Oxford very much these days". There was, however, a new friend at Wadham, Humphry House, and always Maurice Bowra—she attributed a greater animation in Oxford to the return of "the dynamic Maurice Bowra" from his visit to Europe with Adrian Bishop in 1932: "I like vitality, don't you? it seems to get rarer and rarer", she wrote to Lady Ottoline.

In that year David Cecil, the beloved friend, married. Elizabeth, maternally, approved:

> She is charming, attractive and *good*, and I feel sure, does thoroughly understand him. I had been getting so worried about him last winter: he seemed to be eating himself up nervously, never relaxing. . . .[7]

"She" was Rachel, daughter of Desmond MacCarthy, lead reviewer of *The Sunday Times*. The wedding, Elizabeth told Lady Ottoline, was just as it should be:

> . . . graceful, formal, romantic, utterly un-sentimental. Cynthia Asquith said: "Like the marriage of a pair of

royal children"—and it was like a little Valois marrying a still younger Velázquez princess. And both looked transparent and serious, like a pair of children.

"What a delicious couple they are", she wrote after her first visit to the newly-weds. She never lost David, and he and Rachel went every summer for years to stay at Bowen's Court. But one particular chapter was over. Another one began. She was godmother to their son Jonathan—to whom she gave the vast and vastly heavy bust of the Duke of Wellington that he found in the attic in Bowen's Court when he was a little boy, the one that in Elizabeth's father's youth had stood in the hall. David Cecil dedicated his book *Hardy the Novelist* to Elizabeth in 1942; not that she was particularly a "Hardy woman", but because he wanted a book of his to be dedicated to her.

There were so many strands to Elizabeth's life in the early thirties—her work, her life with Alan, social life in Oxford and London, visits to Rome and Italy, her first visit to New York—that Ireland and Bowen's Court were, briefly, seen by her with an outsider's eye:

> *Here* feels a long way from everyone, though at a distance one can think over one's friends, can't one, and it is very spacious and restful and nice. . . . The thought of London and friends in the autumn makes the contrast of this solitude (which month after month and year after year would be frightening, I can see how people round here go either all vague and sloppy or else take to drink) rather funny and nice.

The child of Bowen's Court is, temporarily, writing like a stranger in her own land. But then, she was writing to Lady Ottoline. She wrote about Ireland differently, lyrically, to Virginia Woolf—but, to both of them, self-consciously.

The Grand Chain also brought Elizabeth to the T. S.

Eliots—whose marriage was approaching the rocks. "Do keep up with the Eliots", Lady Ottoline urged Elizabeth. "I feel it is such a pleasure and joy to Tom . . . it will give him life". In April, 1932, Elizabeth, after dining with them, wrote that she found their flat very sinister and depressing. Not that there was anything wrong with the flat itself; it was the atmosphere of "two highly nervous people shut up together in grinding proximity". But as for Eliot himself, "he is so very funny and charming and domestic and nice to be with, besides being so great. I love knowing him". Among other things, Eliot told her the ignoble but not unencouraging fact that without alcohol he would never have got into the mood for his poems.

What with knowing the great, and loving knowing the great, it might be supposed that Elizabeth was not working so intensively as before. The reverse is true. Magazines were now asking for her stories. She began to review for *The New Statesman*—under the literary editorship of Raymond Mortimer—and for *The Tatler*. She published a novel in 1931—*Friends and Relations*—and another, *To the North*, the following year. All Elizabeth's books found publishers in America, but with *To the North* she moved to the firm of Alfred A. Knopf, who remained her American publishers for the rest of her life. With *To the North* she was also persuaded to change her English publisher from Constable to Gollancz. Victor Gollancz did not particularly enjoy Elizabeth's writing, but wanted her on his list as a prestige point—for she was now a prestige commodity. They had lunch together *à deux*; and when his wife asked him when he got home what Elizabeth Bowen was like, he replied: "A brilliant baby".

Friends and Relations, with its misleadingly Compton-Burnettesque title, is the Elizabeth Bowen novel that even Elizabeth Bowen enthusiasts tend to forget about. This may be because the characters—the central pair of sisters and their respective husbands, the older generation pressing on them from above and the younger from below—are tonally on the same plane; there are no stark outlines, no spotlit figure. It is about the strength of family both for good and ill, about the clash between obligation and freedom and "the fatal distinction between kinship and affinity". Two members of the older generation are found "difficult" by the family because they flouted convention (have lived life with the lid off) and, worst of all, survived whole and smiling. The novel is divided between those who can, with time, encompass and tolerate such deviation, and those who cannot. It is the younger generation who have to work this out. The first step is recognition (of unheard-of goings-on), the second outrage, the third, with luck, acceptance. But the show—the family show—must go on.

Friends and Relations and *To the North* are in many ways a pair. Both centre on two young women, and both feature the by now familiar influential aunt-figure: Lady Elfrida in *Friends and Relations* is a stirrer-upper, a deviant, a lady with a past (Theodora, another deviant, but hostile to deviancy in her elders, calls Elfrida "the most tiresome kind of *cathédrale engloutie*, full of backwashes and large drowned bells"); while Lady Waters in *To the North* is a self-satisfied interferer, a self-appointed and destructive mother confessor, an elaboration of the "Mrs. Windermere" of *Encounters*. (What has happened to aunts since the war? In Elizabeth's generation they had enormous stature. They are still with us; in the nature of things, people still have them. But they have lost caste horribly.) Both novels, too, have intolerable, calculating, self-conscious schoolgirls in them, and glimpses of school life— Elizabeth found girls at boarding-school irresistible copy.

But there is one crucial reason why *To the North* is a better novel than *Friends and Relations*. In *Friends and Relations*, Elizabeth, involved in the conflict between personal desire and family duty, between following one's anti-social nature and "keeping the lid on", sits on the fence abominably.

(Virginia Woolf used another image to describe to Elizabeth the mixed feelings provoked by *Friends and Relations*: "I feel you're like somebody trying to throw a lasso with a knotted rope".) Problems of personal versus public good are never resolved. But authorial caution does not make for strong fiction; and the writing is too nervous, too questioning, too highly tuned for one to compare the story to Chekhov's manner, or even to the *Brief Encounter* manner. There are too many knots in the rope. And over all the other characters hover Lady Elfrida and her ex-lover Considine, old now, like Cheshire cats, having behaved shockingly, and having survived.

The questions posed by *Friends and Relations* are eternal ones, and the disturbance Elizabeth experienced in thinking about them makes it a disturbing novel—that and the comedy in it are the strongest things about it. And some of the writing is Bowen at its very best (for example, the shocked atmosphere in Lady Elfrida's drawing-room in Trevor Square after a tense interview between unacknowledged lovers. The man leaves, and: "The long low little room, left alone with Janet, was mortally disconcerted; the lamps staring. A room does not easily re-compose itself, laugh, remark some inconsequence, remember a tune".) Yet, in spite of such things, *To the North* is a better book. Not that *To the North*, the first of Elizabeth's books to be published by Gollancz, was much of a commercial success. This was as much due to the depressed economic situation as to anything else. Victor Gollancz told Elizabeth that sales of the novel were "not frightfully impressive"; but then, "We have had the misfortune to bring out *To the North* in the worst publishing season since the war".

Elizabeth nevertheless felt she had done something new with this novel—as she wrote to A. E. Coppard after its publication:

> I never did think, really, that I ought to write novels—
> most of my others would have contracted into short

stories and I've had the vaguest possible feeling of guilt about them. But I couldn't have written what happened to Markie and Emmeline in a short story. So I feel "To the North" justified.

In *To the North*, too, Elizabeth makes London her own for the first time. There is London—a tentative London—in *Friends and Relations*: Edward and Laurel's house in Royal Avenue, Chelsea, and Lady Elfrida's in Trevor Square. Elizabeth could absorb and apprehend interiors always. But as she spent more and more time in London she learnt the street-feel of London, its larger atmosphere, and the special nature of each district. In *To the North* there is a delicious account of the route of the number 11 bus, considered by housekeeper Mrs. Patrick to be "an entirely moral bus":

> Springing from Shepherd's Bush, against which one has seldom heard anything, it enjoys some innocent bohemianism in Chelsea, picks up the shoppers at Peter Jones, swerves down the Pimlico Road—too busy to be lascivious—passes not far from the royal stables, nods to Victoria Station, Westminster Abbey, the Houses of Parliament, whirrs reverently up Whitehall, and from its only brush with vice, in the Strand, plunges to Liverpool Street through the noble and serious architecture of the City.

Regent's Park will always be the essential Elizabeth Bowen London, because she had a house there for seventeen years, and because of *The Death of the Heart* and *The Heat of the Day*. When Cyril Connolly moved to Sussex Place, they jokingly agreed, for the purpose of writing, to carve up the Park between them; the Rose Garden, and the bridge over the lake by Bedford College, was and is Bowen territory. (Anthony Powell and his wife also lived in Regent's Park; but on the other side, in Chester Gate.) Places Elizabeth had known first in books were to her "more than themselves" for that reason: so some parts of London, to Bowen readers, are known in a heightened way. St. John's Wood is one of them. Emmeline and Cecilia in *To the North* share a house in Oudenarde Road, which is off Abbey Road in St. John's Wood,

> that airy uphill neighbourhood where the white and buff-coloured houses, pilastered or gothic, seem to have been built in a grove. A fragrant, faint impropriety, orris-dust of a century, still hangs over part of this neighbourhood; glass passages lead in from high green gates, garden walls are mysterious, laburnums falling between the windows and walls have their own secrets. Acacias whisper at nights round airy, ornate little houses in which pretty women lived singly but not always alone. . . . Nowadays things are much tamer: Lady Waters could put up no reasoned objection to St. John's Wood.

This is more like Colette than like anything written in English. And like Colette, Elizabeth, though no gardener, filled her books and her houses with flowers—especially roses:

> Cecilia . . . looked at the roses battered apart by rain. Rainy petals littered the earth; more white roses, loose globes of colourless shadow, were still to fall; the La France were blanching. But glowing in early dusk the dark crimson roses, still close and perfect, drank in the sweetening rain; on their spined stems and dark leaves the crimson were like a painting—that drop so bright, so *real* on a petal's lip—but these were live roses, living through to the heart. Hoping that crimson roses might be her affinity, Cecilia resolved to go quite soon to America.

Both these bits from *To the North*—the description of St. John's Wood, and of the roses—are characteristic in that the suggestive lyricism is earthed in the final sentence each time by a peculiarly prosaic human observation. (Lady Waters cannot object to St. John's Wood; Cecilia may go to America.) The veil between the imaginative world, "a world elsewhere", and the everyday world is for Elizabeth very thin; she moves between the two without jarring; every story is in some sense a ghost story, or ghost stories are everyday. There is also a simple technical point—these terse earthings bring us back to the story. Enough is enough.

To the North—dedicated to D. C.—is the first of Elizabeth's novels in which the men really count; in the earlier three, the women are perceived with a disproportionate intensity. Julian in *To the North* is low-sexed, repressed, good at intimacy but bastioned against passion, "estranged from all women by a rather morbid sense of fraternity". But Markie is frankly, and in the terminology of the times, a cad; he is a new, but from now on recurring, figure in the Bowen gallery—possessing, like the young girl doomed to lose innocence, a special place in Elizabeth's imagination: "the kid and the cad", as Sean O'Faolain has expressed it. It ties in with the sense of delinquency that O'Faolain found in her writing, and with the untamedness that remained part of Elizabeth's complex personality; Elizabeth herself summed up the significance of the juxtaposition once and for all in *The House in Paris*:

> . . . young girls like the excess of any quality. Without knowing, they want to suffer, to suffer they must exaggerate; they like to have loud chords struck on them. Loving art better than life they need men to be actors; only an actor moves them, with his telling smile, undomestic, out of touch with the everyday that they dread. They love to enjoy love as a system of doubts and shocks. They are right: not seeking husbands yet, they have no reason to see love socially. This natural fleshly protest against good taste is broken down soon enough;

their natural love of the cad is outwitted by their mothers. Vulgarity, inborn like original sin, unfolds with the woman nature, unfolds ahead of it quickly and has a flamboyant flowering in the young girl. Wise mothers do not nip it immediately; that makes for trouble later, they watch it out.

Elizabeth, though she flowered as a girl, flowered "flamboyantly" as a woman. The cad-figure interested her: the non-intellectual, worldly, self-regarding, masculine sort of man. Markie in *To the North* is rational, social, and witty, and emotionally shallow. His appearance is Maurice Bowra's, as was immediately apparent to their friends. Bowra used to refer cheerfully to his "celebrated caddishness". H. G. Wells identified with Markie for less superficial reasons. He read *To the North* in France, on the train south to join Odette Keun at their villa Lou Pidou, from where he wrote to Elizabeth:

> The car smash at the end came, so far as I was concerned, in the Wagon-Lit between Lyons and Avignon. Then I lay awake for a time thinking how like I was to Markie, how like all men are to Markie, and how much better women are than men, as [in] the novel. Either you have an imagination beyond compare or all the people in your book, the weekend in the cottage and everything really happened—and you know all about it. Emmeline is charming.

He ended on a technical note: "In your next book you may have pelmets in one room but you must not notice them in more than one room. Pelmet is a rare and therefore an arresting word. Q.E.D."

The two young women in the story both have aspects of Elizabeth. Cecilia, the young widow, is her unworthier side: she is overbearing, restless, brittle, unable really to fall in love. "Poor Cecilia's horrid, isn't she", Elizabeth wrote to A. E. Coppard. "But I have quite a feeling for her". But the novel belongs to the gentle young woman, to Emmeline—short-sighted, simple, serious, innocent, vulnerable. Emmeline's love affair with sophisticated Markie is played by each of them according to different rules. "I'm not dependable", says Markie, and indeed he is not. He can't be blamed. Emmeline in love has no sense of moderation—she enters "the region of the immoderate". Elizabeth makes in her creation of Emmeline the point about innocence expressed by Graham Greene in *The Quiet American*:

> Innocence always calls mutely for protection, when we would be much wiser to guard ourselves against it; innocence is like a dumb leper who has lost his bell, wandering the world meaning no harm.

Innocence, so single-minded, so immoderate, "walks with violence" in *To the North*. "There is no doubt", wrote Elizabeth in this novel, "that angels rush in before fools". That innocence can so little be accommodated in the world is no doubt a judgement on the world, but that does not lessen the havoc it causes.

The violent ending of *To the North* seems, on first reading, contrived and gratuitous (for the lid is kept closed on the impending disaster until the last moment—and then, St. John's Wood is so leafy, so civilised). This is a novel that must be read twice; reading it again, knowing the outcome, one sees pointers all the way—how could one not have seen them before, and been prepared? Not long before her death, Elizabeth was approached by an admirer who told her how particularly she liked *To the North*. "I have just been rereading that", Elizabeth said. "Poor Emmeline! It was inevitable".

In *To the North* Elizabeth allowed Emmeline to fall in love, act on her instincts, suffer the consequences, and cause others to suffer with her.

In early 1933, the year after the publication of *To the North*, Elizabeth herself fell in love. However great the strength and nature of the bond that united Elizabeth and Alan, it was not primarily a physical one. The man she fell in love with was brilliant, highly sexed, introspective, susceptible—much too introspective and susceptible to be classed as a cad—and eight years younger than herself. She first met him at lunch with Bowra, and afterwards used to go by bus to visit him at his lodgings outside Oxford. By the time the friendship developed into something more, he was already engaged to be married to someone else.

Elizabeth, in the grip for the first time in her life of a *grande passion*, was pretty ruthless about this, and knew it; she told him that when she had described in *To the North* "that prehensile quality Markie detested in women", she made him express, as in other parts of the book, "a good deal of dislike I feel for the less good woman in me". She saw and wrote to him continually even after he married at the end of 1933; the woman he married was well aware of the situation. Early on she asked him, "Do you want a divorce so that you can marry Elizabeth?" "Good heavens, no", he replied.

Yet this man, who except where women were concerned was capable of taking the most drastic moral stands, was torn between the two of them. Elizabeth wanted him to keep his two loves in separate compartments; he needed her, she assured him; without her, if his marriage failed, he would fall back on "muddles and lust". Love—hers and his, that is—was "the gates of the spirit". She deplored what she saw as his descent into domesticity. (Once, after staying with them, Elizabeth sent his wife a present of a tea-service; the wife took this as an insult, since Elizabeth had seemed always so scornful of the domestic virtues. She did nothing for two weeks, then sent her thanks by telegram.)

Elizabeth wrote to him with the lofty erotic lyricism which the articulate woman overtaken by sexual love tends to adopt: she wanted, she told him, "perfection in intimacy", and for "the word to be made flesh". A platonic relationship was not what she had in mind for the future: "If our sensuous feeling were to be cut away there'd be nothing left."

He tried to compromise, tried to make Elizabeth a family friend. But that wasn't really what Elizabeth wanted. The two women got on perfectly well, curiously enough, when he wasn't there; and once the wife, with her small baby, even went to stay alone with the Camerons at Headington. But in a threesome of Elizabeth and the husband and wife there was uneasiness, which is hardly surprising. Yet the disquiet in the situation was something Elizabeth disliked; she would have preferred clarity, honesty. This was impossible for him, since he was at that time uncertain about absolutely everything, at a crossroads in his career and in his intellectual orientation. Elizabeth wrote to him: "Until the torturing uneasiness of your relationship with [your wife] resolves itself, your relations with anyone else, friend or lover, will be poisoned, distorted and uncertain". Since she herself was the cause of at least some of the "torturing uneasiness" she diagnosed, she was on dangerous ground.

Uncertain and inexperienced as the man was, he allowed himself to be subjected to what amounted to emotional bullying. Yet this wasn't what Elizabeth wanted either. She longed for him to be the traditional dominant male. She wrote to him about the subjection latent in every woman; she told him that she wanted to be "towered over". But he was not really the man for this. (Nor, when in her right mind, was Elizabeth really the woman for it.) He was, as most people were, charmed and fascinated by Elizabeth. He was flattered by her concentration on him; he admired her; he was enormously involved emotionally with her. But he was ill-equipped, and in no position, to live at the pitch she wanted. He tried to put this into words to her, to modify the intensity of her communications. She replied that her "flood of nervous talk" was defensive;

when it came to matters of feeling, there were many disadvantages, she said, in being considered "a clever woman". She described one of his letters as being a blow not at her head, but at her breast.

Sorry though one may feel for his wife—who held on—and even for the man himself, caught in a complicated situation he could not live with, there is something gallant about a woman in her thirties, a reticent, over-controlled woman, and a highly successful author, giving herself so entirely into the hands of this inexperienced and very young man. There was good reason for it. The wife herself saw that Elizabeth was "avid for experience"—that she needed this affair for her own fulfilment, for her development, for her writing. Certainly in the worldly sense she can be seen as ready for some big emotional experience. Her success and life in Oxford had stimulated her, given her confidence, and opened her eyes to a wider world. Her close friendship with David Cecil was intense and emotional, but not sexual. And her need was not merely emotional; there were aspects of Elizabeth's nature that had never been released or resolved in ten years of marriage with Alan. Her lover believed—as he told his wife—that he had taken Elizabeth's virginity. Little wonder that it was a case of *"Vénus toute entière à sa proie attachée"*.

Alan was protected from the whole thing. The affair had absolutely no bearing on her marriage as far as Elizabeth was concerned. However much she deprecated domestic ties, she would never have wanted to jeopardise her life with Alan. Nor would she have inflicted pain and embarrassment on Alan by "telling him everything". Equally, she would not have considered renouncing her lover's company for Alan's sake, and she did not inflict upon herself the added agony of guilt over this: "Guilt is squalid" was one of her tenets. This was not callous so much as practical: masculine rather than feminine, if you like.

Most women as deeply involved as Elizabeth was do not

find it at all easy to keep their feelings in such politic compartments; how much of the love from her side was, as it were, contrived, self-induced? She knew all about herself, and wrote to him:

> What you say about my overwhelming love for you makes me feel dishonest. You must not mistake an artist's impulse and wish for everyone to live at full height for an ordinary or better woman's craving for love. I am dishonest and play-act more than you know.

Not at the beginning; but by this time self-knowledge, self-defence have the upper hand. Nor was she above hitting back in less subtle ways: she told him that he had "distorted and vulgar ideas about love".

The important thing is that after the first intoxication of love was over, she became self-conscious, she saw through herself, she knew that what she was doing was "living at full height"—which she had not before, and which she believed everyone should—and that she was gaining experience, tapping sources within herself crucial for her as a writer.

Compulsive writers labour under two disadvantages when it comes to their private life. One of them is that they dramatise and fictionalise their own activities, rather like an obsessional diary-keeper who ends up experiencing nothing directly but only in terms of how he will record it when he gets home. Many writers, like other neurotics, find it hard to fuse the watcher and the watched within themselves. The other disadvantage is expressed in a letter that Elizabeth wrote to her lover in the summer of 1934, a year after the affair began. It is a statement of both victory and defeat; it is written in both arrogance and humility.

> I do blame myself for being high-handed and, where behaviour was concerned, exacting. Being impatient, in fact, because you wouldn't play my way.

Remember that you had Elizabeth Bowen to contend with—I mean, a confirmed writer. Someone accustomed to getting herself, or himself, across without outside opposition. (The whole struggle, where work goes, for clear thought and absolute feeling is inside oneself—the writer.) One spends one's time objectifying one's inner life, and projecting one's thought and emotion into a form—a book. Which, once one's inside difficulties are overcome, is the exercise of an unchecked power.

This isn't as irrelevant as it sounds.

Because it is hard for me (being a writer before I am a woman) to realize that anything—friendship or love especially—in which I participate imaginatively isn't a book too. Isn't, I mean, something *I* make what it is by my will that it shall be like that.

One may—I may—easily forget that a relationship with a person isn't a book, created out of, projected by, one's own imagination and will. That it is not, in fact, a one-man show. And that the exacerbations, perils and snags of joint authorship all lie in wait. That is where I went wrong with you.

Not that it was over, even then; nor was it until he took a job abroad in 1936. When he returned, they were friends.

To the outside world Elizabeth always spoke of him in kind, if rather elder-sister terms. Writing to a friend about a visit to Bowen's Court that had terminated earlier than planned, she said: "His wife's state of health and mind crystallised into telegrams which made him have to go, and made us send him off. A bit of a barren muddle, and deteriorating in the long run, I feel". In fact, the roof had blown off the house back in England where his wife was expecting her second child. Whatever sort of a muddle awaited him at home, it was hardly "barren". Elizabeth sent a note back with him for his wife saying how sorry she was that he had to go; and that she was feeling particularly saddened because she herself would have so much liked to have a child. But the roofless and pregnant wife was in no condition to be moved by this candour.

Just before he went abroad—where his wife, after the birth of this child, joined him—Elizabeth wrote to the same friend that she and he "had an awful row which is so sad: I am not a quarreller but really I don't think it was my fault. . . . I don't like him going off under a blight. Who would be young again?"

When he came back to England after a couple of years, Elizabeth continued to take a dim view of his ménage, and as for his wife, "poor little creature, I always feel at once sorry for and depressed by her". (She was a very able person with, later, a professional life of her own.) Elizabeth wrote about the man himself now in terms entirely appropriate for an older, married, more worldly friend:

> . . . really very sweet, now he's back, but I agree with you that I *don't* think he's more than half digested anything he found there. When he went out there, he was a person of so little experience (except of the most hectic and bemusing kinds) that I feel he had too few terms of reference—really no means of sorting anything out. . . . It will be very interesting to see how he shakes down in England now. I do hope well—he's so nice.

Elizabeth did revise history, did make something what it was —when she could—"by my will that it shall be like that". Very much on the credit side of this, she presented always a charitable face to the world. Her revisions were never revengeful, however self-protective.

It was well over. By now Elizabeth had moved on, in all senses. She spent a day in Brighton with him at the beginning of the war, when they went to "an entertainment called

'1001 laughs for 2d' which included siren screeches in a dark room, and being biffed on the head by a sudden skeleton arm"—and this, but not he, gave Elizabeth palpitations. Intensity was over. He was anything but broken by the experience; it had been an important episode in his life, and taught him a lot. He remained brilliant, introspective, and highly susceptible. His marriage continued.

The most significant thing in this episode—other than the fact that it enabled Elizabeth to break, as it were, her sexual silence—is the primacy of her writing life, which it revealed and reinforced. It is in the aftermath of losing yourself that you most surely find yourself. When Elizabeth was having a conversation with Elizabeth Jenkins about emotional crises, she said that even in the worst of them she always found herself thinking: "What effect is this having on me *as a writer*?" Elizabeth Jenkins mentioned this to Victor Gollancz, who found it unsympathetic. But Elizabeth felt, on occasion at least, that she was a writer before she was a woman.

CHAPTER VI

The House in London

BOTH ALAN'S PROFESSIONAL MOVES came just at the right time for Elizabeth. Ten years earlier, his work had taken her to Oxford; now, in 1935, they were coming to London. His new appointment was as Secretary to the Central Council of School Broadcasting at the B.B.C. Elizabeth wrote to Lady Ottoline that "we have found a very nice (I think) house in Clarence Terrace, Regent's Park: it is not nearly so large as most of the Regent's Park houses: I had always wanted to live there but their size oppressed me". It had taken her only five days' house-hunting to find 2 Clarence Terrace—"I fell in love with the house at first sight". She described it in greater detail to Virginia Woolf:

> It is about 3½ minutes from Baker St. Station and over-looks the park lake with those coloured-sailed boats and a great many trees. It is a corner house, which I think is nice, don't you, as the windows look different ways. It has high windows and ceilings, and pale-coloured modern parquet floors. The excuse for taking it, and taking it so soon, is that it is a bargain, only just in the market and not very expensive, in fact cheap, because of there being only an eight years' lease. The reason to take it is that it is, in a bare plain way, very lovely with green reflections inside from the trees such as I have only seen otherwise in a country house.

The Regency terraces—completed by the end of the first quarter of the nineteenth century—which bound the Outer Circle of Regent's Park, are, arguably, the most beautiful houses in London: cream stucco, with columns, porticoes, and pediments, and set back in curves from the curving road. Clarence Terrace in spring faces on to flowering chestnut and pink may, with tulips and grass and the lake beyond. Elizabeth Bowen could not have found a finer setting. These houses—and their occupants—took a lot of punishment from German bombs during the war; some of them are no more. But Clarence Terrace still stands, greatly "restored" and altered, and arranged in flats, but still among the most beautiful houses in London.

In the year the Camerons moved, the Buchans went to Canada, where John Buchan was to be Governor-General; their son William, now nineteen, who was working at Elstree "under Mr. Hitchcock learning to make films", had for a short time a big bed-sitter at the top of the Camerons' new house. "I had always said I would not have anyone else in the house on any account", Elizabeth told Virginia, but "tentatively Alan and I talked it over and thought it would be a pity not. . . ." So the little household of three, with a housekeeper from Ireland and some more of the furniture from Bowen's Court —including the fine Empire sofa—established themselves.

Shortly before the move, Elizabeth had published another novel, *The House in Paris*. There had been another book of stories between this and *To the North*, called *The Cat Jumps*. (The first edition, of 1,500, sold out almost at once.) Sending a copy to A. E. Coppard, she said that she knew that they were "*very* uneven, not only in execution but intention"; some had been written for magazines over the past three to five years, "commanded", as she put it, "which always makes work metallic". She told Victor Gollancz that she considered the stories in *The Cat Jumps* all had an "escape from life" theme, and had suggested to him the title "Hard Fantasy";

"One hears much of 'hard fact'. Fantasy can, to my mind, be more of a tyrant".

The hard fantasy that she herself liked best in this collection, "The Disinherited", is one of the key half-dozen or so Bowen stories. However unpolitical she was in the understood sense, she had a keen ear for the shaking of the foundations, an eagle eye for class and social climate. It is a story that encapsulates the confusion of social change. The two young women—one from the old house on the village green ("gentry") and one from the raw new housing estate—go to a party in a rotting, uncared-for country house. The lordly host is absent. The guests are a rag-bag of types halfway up or halfway down, temporary kings or permanent failures, drunk, promiscuous, floating. Of one guest Elizabeth wrote: "The old order left him stranded, the new offered him no place". So it is for all of them. "We have everything to fear", she wrote in *Bowen's Court*, "from the dispossessed". Davina, the aimless girl from the old-order background, delinquent and desperate, accepts this orderless world as the only group to which she can relate; and she makes love with her aunt's vicious chauffeur, Prothero, whose own scandalous history is incorporated, in a piece of flagrant self-indulgence on Elizabeth's part. The whole Prothero bit is a sub-Lawrentian fantasy that dilutes the story's subtlety, but Elizabeth's imagination wants him in; and perhaps this breaking of all the rules of shape and structure suits the anarchy in the air. Prothero is more than a cad, he is a criminal; and Davina had, "in some strange fashion, fed her own pride by the hasty sale of her kisses, feeling set free of herself each time those anonymous lips without pleasure had claimed her own".

It's vulgar but it's vivid; and most of the girls in *The Cat Jumps* are cut off beyond redemption by childhood, circumstances, or temperament from any hope of being "free of themselves" or anyone else—though some of them, especially two parked-out, displaced little girls (in "Maria" and "The

Little Girl's Room") fight back like the trapped little monsters they are.

Whatever one thought about the end of the old order, Elizabeth, at Clarence Terrace and at Bowen's Court in the few remaining years before the war, was able to give that old order, in its positive aspect of grace and hospitality and congenial intimacies, a late and lavish flowering.

In the year she moved to London, she was chiefly anxious about the reception of *The House in Paris*. She had sent two copies to Virginia Woolf: had she read it? "But I did read *The House in Paris*", wrote Virginia, and added that she liked it best of all Elizabeth's books. Virginia was suspicious of the "cleverness" in Elizabeth's writing, and found that in this novel "the cleverness pulls its weight instead of lying to dazzle on the top". Yet did it? For after adding some more and positive comment, Virginia returns to the same point:

> . . . my old grumble, that we are afraid of the human heart (and with reason); and until we can write with all our faculties in action (even the big toe) but under water, submerged, then we must be clever, like the rest of the modern sticklebacks.

The House in Paris draws on her love-affair. The sandwiching of past and present, the complexities of the plot belong to imagination. But the central triangle of Karen, Naomi, and Max (the latter two being engaged to be married) contains the essence of Elizabeth's real-life triangle. Karen, in her illicit love, comes up against her new self: herself as deceiver (of her parents and of Naomi), and by this is isolated, as never before; because "never to lie is to have no lock to your door, you are never wholly alone". Now she must lie. The politics of passion are explored through Karen—it was in this book that Elizabeth wrote, "Nobody speaks the truth when there's something they must have". Also explored are feelings about having a child. Karen, during the night of love in Hythe (they are in the Swan—called in the book the Ram's Head—though Elizabeth in life favoured the nearby White Hart), longs for Max's child, to perpetuate and make sense of the experience. And yet, "The child would be a disaster". Karen, in the novel, bears Max's son, and virtually abandons him.

Max is not a physical portrait of Elizabeth's lover. Elizabeth did seem to model Naomi on the wife, or on her own version of her, however. Karen's mother in the novel says how the nervous, emotional Naomi's eyes "start out of her head", and Elizabeth in a letter referred to the wife as "pop-eyed with anxiety the whole time". Elizabeth found it hard to make her characters live until she had found a physical shape in which to crystallise them. Portia in *The Death of the Heart* looked like a girl Elizabeth had seen serving in a shop; the physical model for Eva in *Eva Trout* was glimpsed at an airport. "Nothing physical can be *invented*", she wrote in her "Notes on Writing a Novel".[1] In a letter to A. E. Coppard about how she visualised her *House in Paris* characters, she said: "I can see . . . Karen's figure, movements and ways but I don't know what kind of nose she had". (In the book, she says of Karen that "the nose was her mother's nose".) "Max is a portrait of someone I knew quite passingly and superficially once, so of course I *do* see him. . . . Naomi Fisher I see the whole time, even her clothes".

The most dominant figure in *The House in Paris* is, however, neither Karen, Max, nor Naomi, but Mme Fisher, Naomi's dying mother, who has herself loved Max. The account Max gives of his entanglement with this much older woman is interesting. For the first but not the last time, the omnipresent "older woman" figure in a Bowen novel incorporates bits of Elizabeth herself. Max is speaking to Karen here, about Mme Fisher:

". . . Her sex is all in her head, but she is not a woman
for nothing. In my youth, she made me shoot up like a

plant in enclosed air. She was completely agreeable.
Our ages were complementary. I had never had the
excitement of intimacy. Our brains became like senses,
touching and drawing back."

"Then you acted on her, too?"

"To an extent only. She was ready for me when I
was not ready for her. She had waited for years for
what I had not had time to miss. We met in her house,
in all senses. Women I knew were as she made me see
them: they were not much. Any loves I enjoyed stayed
inside her scope: she knew of them all. . . ."

One must beware of glib assertions about who "is" who in a
novel. Some novelists deny hotly that they used any models for
their characters, or any autobiographical material; they copied
nothing from life. This is arrant nonsense, but it is a perfectly
legitimate piece of self-defence—or in some cases an un-
awareness of their sources, and an instinct not to enquire into
them. Elizabeth preferred not to have this area probed, partly
out of natural reticence, partly for fear of damaging the intuitive process of writing. Francis King asked her in 1971
whether she would be prepared to be the subject of an "Ex-
ploration" such as he had conducted with L. P. Hartley. This
was part of her reply:

> I should not be a good subject for this purpose. As a
> "kind" of writer, I am the exact opposite of Leslie
> Hartley—one of my oldest friends, and one of the living
> novelists whose work I enjoy most and like best. You
> would find me neither frank nor informative. I do not
> find the idea of an "Exploration" intimidating; I find it
> (better to say this point-blank) repugnant. It would be
> against the grain with me—and, more, I should find it
> injurious to such powers as I have.
>
> This does not mean that I should not enjoy talking

to *you*: I could wish that we met more often. But even to friends, I don't find I talk much, often or easily about "my writing". As for outside people, I never can see why I should. Why can't they just read my books—if they care to—and leave it at that?

The same, she said to him, applied to her life. There was nothing particularly mysterious about it, but it was her own affair. "It is a non-literary life":

As a succession of experiences, and my reaction to them, it clearly must have some connection with the stories I write, but that is a connection *I* should find it damaging publicly to explore, or to have explored, in my presence, by others.

Yet it is very often writers themselves who say, "A put B into that book", "C is the original of D in such-and-such a novel", especially to each other; but then they know exactly what they mean by it—and also writers tend to be such dedicated gossips. But we are back to Elizabeth's statement that "imagination divorces itself from feeling"; imagination also divorces itself from what actually happened and in what order and with what consequences; it shares out attitudes and experiences between several characters that in life are embodied in one, and vice versa. Imagination gives the original idea a life of its own, and invention transforms it in the cause of personal myth, poetic truth, fantasy, structure, or—sometimes—revenge. Pure transcribed autobiography usually makes dreary fiction. Elizabeth wrote in the preface to a selection of her stories made by herself, published in 1959, that:

I find myself rejecting stories which reek to me of myself, by exhibiting sentiments—or betraying them. In some, I do not seem to have been enough on guard. Such stories seem overwritten or, still worse, yoked to my personality. I am dead against art's being self-expression. I see an inherent failure in any story which does not detach itself from the author.[2]

This preface expresses the delicate balance between art and life, for she goes on to say that one cannot eliminate oneself wholly for a second: "any fiction . . . is bound to be transposed autobiography. (True, it may be this at so many removes as to defeat ordinary recognition.)"

But to abstract, for the purposes of biography, certain elements from a novel tells you less than nothing about the quality or the total effect of that novel. To read *The House in Paris* is a very intense experience. Victor Gollancz, not given to gushing to Elizabeth, told her he thought it was "one of not more than half a dozen contemporary novels that I have really enjoyed during the past ten years. . . . I wonder if you realise how *un-English* it is? It will be appreciated most by Maxes, Frenchmen and Jews". H. G. Wells on the other hand disliked it for, as he said, "primarily a non-literary reason." His sympathetic identification with the "cad" Markie in *To the North* was not extended to Max. "This Max of yours is incomprehensible and detestable. What in him *got* Karen?" *The House in Paris* provokes strong emotional reactions.

Elizabeth, who in life was tolerant, empirical, and an enjoyer, sometimes behaved like the God of Genesis in her novels. Once "the crack across the crust of life" appears, the process of fragmentation cannot be stopped. There is no remaining in Eden, but little hope outside it. There is no virtue in remaining within stifling conventions, but only trouble awaits the delinquent. Her women are so often stultified or trapped, but when they take steps to free themselves they open Pandora's box. It's a can't-win situation. Everything in *The House in Paris*, so ambiguous at the beginning, collects itself together into a shape that is the shape of disaster. The children in their different ways have hope, have potential—Leopold will "see the illuminations"; but the past limits their potential, and human nature is their legacy as it was their parents'.

Elizabeth said that in writing "shape is possibly *the* important thing".[3] She is a writer whose atmospheric descriptions of place, other-worldly perceptions, hyperaesthetic responses to shifts of mood, light, pace, mass make one characterise her as an impressionist. And yet there is this inexorability with which she brings her characters toward their fate; and her endings are seldom ambiguous—in the novels, as opposed to the stories, they are often unequivocally violent. It is this perhaps that Virginia Woolf was trying to pin down when she wrote that one should write with all one's faculties "but under water, submerged"—for every real question only leads to another set of questions, and not to a final judgement or a smart answer, which are nursery solutions. But Virginia Woolf took steps into the dark in her writing, as in her mind. As Elizabeth wrote in *English Novelists*, Virginia "has put behind her, having no need of, devices that make all other stories work". Elizabeth found it hard at this stage to sidestep her own "cleverness", and "shape" can be a strait-jacket as well as a strength.

The House in Paris is a very strong novel. None of Elizabeth's novels is without comedy, this one included. But for a quite uncanny and un-comic rendering of family atmospheres, of childhood fortitude, of being in love, it is remarkable. The fierce logic of *The House in Paris* gives it, too, the strength of myth. It certainly felt that way to Elizabeth: twenty-one years after it was published, she said that it "never does seem to me to be a book *I* wrote":

It really did impose itself in the most extraordinary way, like a sort of deep gripping dream. When I wrote it, it was much more like hunting for language and images which would most strongly transcribe something which had happened or which I already knew, and yet

I myself had not been any one of the characters in the dream. In fact, to put the matter more shortly, I don't feel I in any way invented or, as it were, devised "The House in Paris", which I suppose really is the ideal feeling to have about a book.[4]

Virginia Woolf paid Elizabeth the tribute of taking her seriously. The Elsfield dinner was not their first meeting; they first met at tea in the garden of Lady Ottoline's house in Gower Street. Virginia was wearing a lavender muslin dress and a hat worn forward over the face. With Elizabeth she was kind and formal; they talked about ice-cream. When Elizabeth went home to Clarence Terrace, she told Alan it was rather like meeting the wife of a very distinguished soldier.

They became friends, but not intimate friends. Elizabeth revered Virginia not only for her genius but for her beauty. She discussed with Elizabeth Jenkins what it must be like to be so beautiful that you never looked in a glass. Her genius Elizabeth described as "some extra dimension that can't ever be quite accounted for in terms of intelligence or emotion. Something almost out of control, only it isn't".[5]

Virginia exercised on Elizabeth her customary eager curiosity, fantasising lightly about Elizabeth's life as she imagined it ("Oh, you, when are you going back to your ancient Irish castle?"), but perhaps because Elizabeth did not belong to the inner circle of gossip and intimacy, she did not probe deeply. Elizabeth at times saw Virginia's uncontrollable manic teasing in action ("Oh, she was awfully naughty. She was fiendish", said Elizabeth), but not directed on to herself. Virginia was capable of charming the birds off the trees; and of a terrifying bleakness. She was capable of saying to Desmond MacCarthy's wife, "Molly, you are dull. DULL, Molly, you are DULL, aren't you?" Elizabeth was aware, too, of Virginia's professional sensitivity and jealousy about work: "that was a side of her that one had to watch". As far as work was concerned, apart from the repeated "Don't be too clever", Virginia warned Elizabeth of the influence of Henry James. "She foresaw him as a danger to me". This was sound enough.

Hugh Walpole recorded in his diary in late 1938 a tea-party at Virginia's, where Elizabeth was also, "dressed very smartly with a hat like an inverted coal-skuttle. She and Virginia sat together like two goddesses from a frightfully intellectual Olympus. Thank God I'm no longer frightened of them".[6] Thus, by 1938, was it possible for Elizabeth to be seen by outsiders. But when she was alone with Virginia, she used herself to have at first a feeling of "awe and alarm. As a rule, that wore off. But sometimes she seemed tired, or extra remote". Elizabeth, who had the stamina of a horse, would not have realised the extent of Virginia's vulnerability. Virginia wrote in her diary in October, 1935:

> I am again held up in *The Years* by my accursed love of talk. That is to say, if I talk to Rose Macaulay from 4–6.30: to Elizabeth Bowen from 8–12 I have a dull heavy hot mop inside my brain next day. . . .[7]

The friendship with Virginia was not one that included Alan, and Elizabeth cultivated it. Virginia at her best was, to use one of the phrases of the period, a life-enhancer. In her preface to a 1960 edition of *Orlando*, Elizabeth wrote that friendship with Virginia was "entering, in her company, into the rapture caused her by the unexpected, the spectacular, the inordinate, the improbable, and the preposterous". But she did not altogether sacrifice Alan on the altar of Bloomsbury. The first time that she was invited to stay with the Woolfs at Rodmell, she had to decline; she had arranged to be at an educational conference in Oxford with Alan:

> I do wish I could have come to Rodmell: I did so fear-fully want to. But I am so seldom a useful wife to Alan, and in the course of that conference week it began to appear that it really would be rather mean of me to go

away leaving him over-run with people that he must be genial to.

Being genial included Elizabeth and Alan taking "twelve foreign educationalists for a drive in a file of taxis across the Cotswolds".

Virginia Woolf came to Bowen's Court once, with the Connollys. Elizabeth told Sarah Barry, her cook, that their guest was the most famous living English novelist. Sarah, unimpressed by this, conceded "I can see she's a *lady*". And Elizabeth stayed twice at Rodmell, the first time in the summer of 1940, and wrote in thanks that "I don't think I'd ever imagined a place and people in which and with whom one felt so perfectly happy that one felt suspended the whole time, and at the same time wanting to smile, *and* smiling, continuously, like a dog". They had picked currants and raspberries, and Elizabeth had come away with a cactus in bloom, and some garlic. "If I began to write about affection for you, Virginia, I should degenerate into sheer gush".

The second visit was only a few weeks before Virginia's suicide. Elizabeth spent two nights in early February, 1941, at Rodmell. In her thank-you letter she wrote:

> I was miserable coming away on Saturday. . . . I do hope happiness doesn't make me too bouncing: I felt so awfully happy. I still can't see much but your upstairs room with the cyclamens on the window-sill . . . and those two arum lilies, and your embroidery. I mean, even apart from you and Leonard. All I have got to look at are the scratches from the beautiful apache cat. The moss is now in the middle of my dinner table, in a sort of white Wedgwood basket dish.

She had left behind a green-backed hand-mirror and two jars of cold cream. "May I make them an excuse to come back to you before I go back to Ireland?"

But on March 28th Virginia Woolf, mortally afraid of the return of her mental illness, drowned herself. Elizabeth, by then at Bowen's Court, heard the news from someone who had heard it on the wireless; English papers, because of the war, were arriving a week late.

Elizabeth's memory of Virginia remained that of the enchanted, enchanting companion:

> The last day I saw her . . . I remember her kneeling on the floor—we were tacking away, mending a torn Spanish curtain in the house—and she sat back on her heels and put her head back in a patch of early spring sun. Then she laughed in this consuming, choking, delightful, hooting way. And *that* is what has remained with me.[8]

Elizabeth disliked the tragic, martyred image of Virginia Woolf that grew up after her death. When she read the first volume of William Plomer's autobiography, *At Home*, in 1958, she told him that "only you seem to bring back Virginia's laughter—I get so *bored* and irked by the tragic fiction which has been manufactured about her since 1941". His book reminded her of things she had forgotten; in it he described watching George V's funeral, and then:

> In the afternoon I went to the Woolves, where I found Elizabeth Bowen and Iris Origo and Ethel Smyth. . . . I went on to Elizabeth's dinner and Eliot was there. His gravity seemed decidedly male in comparison with those exceptionally quick-witted women with their shining eyes and brilliant, rapid utterance (in Iris Origo's case extremely rapid) outpaced by the quickness of their brains and senses.

"I *can't* believe", wrote Elizabeth to William, "though I'd believe it if you say so, that I went to tea at Virginia's, and met you there, on the afternoon of George V's funeral". All she remembered was that she, her young cousin Noreen Colley, and Billy Buchan had got up at 4 a.m. to watch the procession in the Edgware Road, and later, exhausted, had looked for food for that night's dinner party with all the shops shut. "I remember finally coaxing a large veal-and-ham pie, at black market price, out of a little restaurant in the understructure of Baker Street Station. . . ."

Elizabeth's feeling for Virginia was always tinged with respect. Virginia was someone set apart. Elizabeth found the title of Edward Albee's play *Who's Afraid of Virginia Woolf?* rather offensive. Virginia was, she told William Plomer, one of "the only two of the dead whom I *truly* miss". Virginia's personality seemed a guarantee of some continuity, some afterlife: "She ended, as far as we know, in darkness, but—where is she now? Nobody with that capacity for joy, I think, can be nowhere".[9]

But a few months before her own death, and thirty years after Virginia Woolf's, Elizabeth, thinking again about Bloomsbury, wrote to Rosamond Lehmann: "Noble though they all were, they were *smug*. And their godlessness gives me—always did give me—a feeling of depression, and what else—claustrophobia?"[10]

Existence at Clarence Terrace took shape gradually. The house for a long time had a provisional, undefinitive look. The Billy Buchan experiment worked out; Elizabeth told Rosamond Lehmann the first winter they were there that Billy was being "so good. He disappears like a ghost in the mornings, before I'm even awake, to the studio". In Clarence Terrace the Oxford and London worlds fused. Maurice Bowra came to stay for a party, and immediately fell ill: "I was rather rattled as he was full of the gloomiest apprehensions". She was writing this letter just before going out to dinner with the

Cyril Connollys—"I wonder what it will be like". So much was new:

> No rhythm of any kind seems to have established itself in this house yet. I mean no everyday feeling—that is partly, I suppose, because of Maurice's illness, I don't like a house till it's ordinary. But I think it will be very soon, and it does meanwhile seem to me beautiful.[11]

The rhythm, when it established itself, was very social indeed. Elizabeth became a compulsive and inspired hostess. "I feel I am casting my mantle on you", Lady Ottoline wrote to her. "Do you mind? I hope not". A growing circle of writers and critics, often leavened by visiting Colley cousins, came to Clarence Terrace for tea, for drinks, for dinner. The few remaining years before the war were the halcyon years, but it did not all stop with the war; and Elizabeth Jenkins called Elizabeth Bowen "the last *salonnière*". Her energy was prodigious. Stephen Spender said that all the hostesses he had ever known (which included Elizabeth) "have something about them of the athletic champion—the Channel swimmer or the Olympic runner".[12]

People came because Elizabeth was enchanting, amusing, stimulating; her company had the same heightened quality that Virginia Woolf's had, but without the unpredictability and fiendishness; she had the Irish warmth, fostering and welcoming. The parties did not always work for all of the guests, who tended to be mixed indiscriminately; sometimes one could find no one to talk to. Those who enjoyed themselves least were the very young wives or girl-friends who were brought along as mere attributes of their partners; to some of these young women Elizabeth could seem affected, or formidable, or bizarre. It did not help matters to see their husbands or lovers so devotedly and animatedly in their element at Elizabeth's table. They were grateful, often, to talk to kind, avuncular Alan.

Elizabeth, as she grew older, had considerable *tendresse* for *jeunes filles en fleur*, especially those whom she could identify with her own younger, uncertain self. But for those whose presence was purely circumstantial she had a fine disregard. A pretty daughter of Robert Lynd, visiting Bowen's Court in 1935 in company with Isaiah Berlin, regretted that "alas", they could not stay longer. "I can't bear girls who say 'alas'," announced Elizabeth; not, one hopes, within hearing. Two undergraduates, admirers of her work, came one day to Bowen's Court when Veronica Wedgwood was staying there. The blonde the young men brought with them was anything but dumb, and knew and cared nothing about Elizabeth Bowen or about her distinguished friend. Her father had been in Cairo. So Veronica Wedgwood asked her about Cairo. "Cairo's hell", said the blonde, "not a decent night-club in the place". Elizabeth, afterwards, said, "Some people really ought to be left in the car with the dogs". (Alan found the whole thing hugely funny.)

That story is echoed by what happened at a party Elizabeth Jenkins gave in her Hampstead house. One of the guests brought a very beautiful Rumanian girl, who spoke no English, and sat in silence most of the evening. Elizabeth Jenkins, after the party, was worried that the girl might not have enjoyed herself. Elizabeth briskly reassured her: "Girls like that are brought along at owner's risk". All in all, it's hardly surprising that some young women found Elizabeth formidable.

The young women whom Elizabeth did accept she accepted totally—for a while. May Sarton, the American novelist and poet, was one of these. She was introduced into the Cameron household by John Summerson, in early summer, 1936. At her first dinner party at Clarence Terrace, John Summerson and May—who was in her early twenties, eager, shy, and ready to adore—had Isaiah Berlin and David Cecil as fellow guests. She described her reactions in her autobiography (to which she gave the startlingly Bowenesque title *A*

World of Light: Portraits and Celebrations): "It was a good example of culture shock as I floundered, paralyzed, in the abyss between American and Oxford English, and wondered whether I would ever even catch one word". Alan took care of her. May was surprised that this man should be Elizabeth Bowen's husband: "He was quite stout, had a rather blimpish look, a red face and walrus mustache, and spoke in a high voice, near falsetto". But she found him kind and sensitive, and it was he who went out of his way to put her at ease. When she knew them better, she and Alan would sometimes walk together across the Park to the Zoo when Elizabeth was out. "There before the abstracted gaze of a tiger or panther Alan inevitably exclaimed, 'Elizabeth!' "

May Sarton came to feel like an adopted daughter at Clarence Terrace. Her most precious moments were when she had Elizabeth to herself, and Elizabeth would sometimes abandon her customary reticence: "On those late nights when I stayed at Clarence Terrace . . . and, after the guests had gone, she fetched a pillow from the bedroom and stretched out on the sofa to smoke a last cigarette, she did tell me a great deal about herself. . . ." And this is what May saw, when she gazed at Elizabeth in her mid-thirties, in 1936:

> Hers was a handsome face, handsome rather than beautiful, with its bold nose, high cheekbones, and tall forehead; but the coloring was as delicate as the structure was strong—fine red-gold hair pulled straight back into a loose knot at her neck, faint eyebrows over pale-blue eyes. I was struck by her hands, which she used a great deal, often holding one in the air before her with a cigarette in it. They were awkwardly large; the heavy bracelets she wore became them.

The guests at Clarence Terrace were almost all Elizabeth's friends before they were Alan's; it was for Elizabeth that they came, not for Alan. The young Oxford dons, the

London critics, the writers had little to say to him. There were exceptions. But some of them were very wayward, very rude. They talked across him, they ignored him, while accepting his hospitality. Among themselves, they discussed the Cameron ménage. Why had she married him? What did Elizabeth *say* to Alan? Clearly, he must either be much cleverer or much stupider than he seemed. Which?

But, however close and intense the friendship enjoyed with Elizabeth, one was not allowed to criticise or discuss Alan with her. One was cut off short. She was, in this, totally loyal. She spoke of him with affection and respect. She gave one to understand that one did not appreciate his qualities. She was grateful to friends who were patient when he bored them, who "did not notice". Francis Wyndham, calling one day to see Elizabeth—alone, as he supposed—arrived early and found Alan and Elizabeth sitting talking on the sofa in the drawing-room. He felt as if he had arrived at a theatre before it was time for the curtain to go up. In a little while, Alan withdrew. But they had been talking. They talked, always.

Apocryphal stories grew up about Alan and the clever friends, perhaps the most graphic being that about a party at Bowen's Court where a guest, blundering off to look for a lavatory, opened a door to find Alan alone in a small room eating his supper off a tray. Apocryphal stories have a poetic, if not a historical truth; they express what a sufficient number of people feel to have been the truth. And the truth is that to an outside observer Alan seemed to be having rather a thin time.

Alan's job at the B.B.C. was rewarding and time-consuming; a lot of Elizabeth's friends visited her when he was not there. He referred to them as the Black Hats, on account of the rows of them hanging in the hall when he got back from the office. (The same term was also used to describe the admirers of another lady at much the same time—

coined, seemingly, independently.) He would rarely join them in the drawing-room, but went into his study. He talked loudly and bitterly about the Black Hats; but when one day Audrey Fiennes sympathised with him, he said to her, "Don't you see —all these things minister to something in Elizabeth". And as far as his feelings for Elizabeth were concerned, it did not matter how many Black Hats there were.

May Sarton indeed gave a different and much happier picture of Alan's homecomings; there were not Black Hats on the premises every day:

> When Alan came home at half past five, the tensions subsided and everything came cozy and relaxed. He embraced Elizabeth, asked at once where the devil the cat was—a large fluffy orange cat—and when he had found her, settled down for a cocktail and an exchange about "the day". As in many successful marriages, they played various games. Alan in his squeaky* voice complained bitterly about some practical matter Elizabeth should have attended to, and she looked flustered, laughed, and pretended to be helpless. Alan's tenderness for her took the form of teasing and she obviously enjoyed it. I never saw real strain or needling between them, never for a second. Love affairs were a counterpoint.[13]

He did suffer; but he kept his end up the best way he knew, and was, at the parties, a good host. He got his own back—wittingly or unwittingly—by telling long and repetitious stories at the dinner-table. He got his own back once, accidentally, in a more dramatic way. The critic and editor John Hayward was a cripple; Alan elected to carry him down to the

---

* May Sarton is mistaken in her choice of words to describe Alan's voice: it was penetrating, rasping, often booming—but not "falsetto" or "squeaky."

car. Outside the house he dropped Hayward, squealing, into the gutter.

Also he took refuge in whiskey. He drank a great deal, and increasingly so as he grew older and his eyes gave more trouble. He was sometimes short-tempered, and shouted at people. He lived, in these pre-war years, under something of a strain.

The answer to the Black Hats' question as to whether Alan was stupider or cleverer than he seemed is, of course, that he was cleverer. He was a very shrewd man and a very good man. He did not pander to Elizabeth, in private not at all; in private her dependence on him for all things practical and administrative, but not only for these things, came to the fore. He was extremely protective of her; and when she was learning to drive a car in Ireland, he stood on the steps of Bowen's Court in a frenzy, listening for the sound of the returning motor, dreading disaster. (Elizabeth was, in fact, one of the most alarming drivers of all time—an honour she shared with her friend Rose Macaulay.) He was not above a gentle dig, generally directed at the more reverent of her admirers, but sometimes at her as well. Watching appreciatively from his chair as she struggled myopically with the (then new) dialling system, he said: "Just watch the *whole great mind* concentrating itself on a mere telephone!" She was cross. Naturally.

Alan was not isolated. He loved his work. He was a very good administrator. His colleagues were fond of him. Mary Somerville, who worked with him, said that no one who attended his committees would ever forget his way of "twisting his wiry locks into a row of perpendicular rats' tails, which on receipt of a note from his secretary, or so we believed, he would furtively unwind and smooth into place again in the act of expounding some intricate piece of council business".[14] This twisting of his "cockatoo crest" was a characteristic mannerism, not only at meetings. Another colleague said that in the 1930s, in his prime, there was something "exceptional and reassuring" about Alan—and this was at the height of the Black Hats period. The same colleague, Eric Gillett, said that "there was no malice or pettiness in his make-up";[15] Eric found him the perfect intimate friend. Elizabeth's family were devoted to him, especially Noreen and Audrey. Audrey and Alan went on country outings together when Elizabeth was away. "I must have lambs", she said to him once in spring. "Well, Audrey, I think I can manage *lambs* for you". Which he did. "Do ring him", Elizabeth wrote to John Hayward from Bowen's Court in 1936, "and make him go for a drive. He'd love it, but is as you know sluggish, or rather despondent, about making plans".

The trips into the country, always so much part of the Camerons' life, continued whether there were visitors or not. May Sarton shared their Sunday ritual of a drive out of London, a walk, a picnic—and then a long nap lying on the grass. On one occasion, wrote May Sarton, "they looked, fast asleep, so much like figures on a tomb that I tried, to no avail, to wake Elizabeth by throwing small twigs at her".[16] In this final piece of Sunday ritual Elizabeth and Alan eluded, side by side, all outsiders.

Alan loved Elizabeth. He knew that he wasn't enough for her. He was pleased that she was given by the world everything that he thought she deserved. He thought he was married to the most interesting woman in England. For that there was a price to be paid, and he paid it. He was repaid by her dependence, her need of him, and by the fact that she stayed with him and that, as time passed, they grew closer and cosier. If he knew of her infidelities, it made no difference; and would in any case never have been discussed between them. And as for Elizabeth—she wrote in *The Death of the Heart*: "One's sentiments—call them that—one's fidelities are so instinctive that one hardly knows they exist: only when they are betrayed or, worse still, when one betrays them does one realise their power".

Perhaps it was gratitude, perhaps it was repressed resentment, or martyrdom, or alcohol, or simply love, that made Alan say, "Elizabeth is a saint". It was at dinner at Clarence Terrace; Stephen and Natasha Spender were there. There was a conversation about character. "Elizabeth is a saint", said Alan. She, embarrassed, demurred. Emphatically, without irony, he repeated it. Elizabeth got up and left the room.

As Henry James said (at the beginning of the story "Louisa Tallant"), "Never say you know the last word about any human heart".

CHAPTER VII

"People in Their Thirties"

S O MUCH OF WHAT IS CHARACTERISTIC of Elizabeth's writing hinges on journeys, arrivals, departures; and she was not only a hostess, she was an enthusiastic guest. She dined out, with or without Alan, and went to stay with friends, generally without him. She went to stay often with the "Crichel boys"— Edward Sackville-West had a house at Long Crichel, in Dorset, which he shared with Raymond Mortimer and Desmond Shawe-Taylor. Raymond, the nicest of the Bloomsberries in the opinion of many, had been one of her earliest literary supporters; Eddy she was to become very close to rather later; Desmond, Anglo-Irish like herself and best known as a music critic, was, in the mid-thirties, writing film criticism for *The New Statesman* under the pseudonym "Peter Galway" —sometimes Elizabeth went with him to the morning screenings for critics. This had for her an element of truancy, as she habitually worked in the mornings; she enjoyed the sense of minor delinquency, as she enjoyed the champagne that was sometimes provided on these occasions.

She used to stay with L. P. Hartley at his house near Bath. This friendship, which had begun with his review of *Encounters*, remained always. Once, arriving together at a Royal Society of Literature function, they were mistakenly introduced as husband and wife. "If I had married anyone", said Leslie Hartley (it was most unlikely), "it would have been Elizabeth".

On their frequent visits to Ireland, Elizabeth and Alan went to Corkagh, to see Aunt Edie and the Colley cousins; at Bowen's Court they were sometimes alone, or with family. Often, in the 1930s, the London and Oxford friends turned up there as well, and had to adapt themselves to what they found. It was always great fun; Elizabeth, happy to have her friends round her, made her friends happy. They found the hospitality warm and loving, and the amenities spartan; and most of them met a staple of the life at Bowen's Court, Jim Gates, whom Elizabeth had known all her life. The visitors' first meeting with Jim was often on his own doorstep with soap and towels in their hands; for the Gateses' small modernised house in Kildorrery had a bathroom, which Bowen's Court before the war did not. As an alternative to the hip-baths and hot cans in the bedrooms, Elizabeth would dispatch her guests in an open farm vehicle into the village to ring Jim Gates's doorbell.

Jim Gates was the manager of the creamery in Kildorrery, an enterprise that was to become part of the empire of Cow & Gate. He organised things for Elizabeth, was always at hand whether for a party, a game of cards, or an excursion; and it was he who taught her to drive a car. Jim Gates was completely non-intellectual, genial, a life-and-souller, and he got on fine with Alan. Elizabeth loved him. Not that there was anything remotely like an affair between them; the relationship was subtly feudal.

Elizabeth needed men like Jim Gates: extrovert, practical, a little coarse. It wasn't *nostalgie de la boue*—that would be grotesquely unfair to Jim. Rather, it was *nostalgie* for the basic demotic male principle. In the same way, she liked sometimes to be taken to rough pubs and seedy night-spots. The novelist's hunger for copy, perhaps, although she did not put these things into her books. Men like Jim met the gypsy side of her own temperament, and were a relief and a liberation from preciosity, from too much literary sensibility. With Jim she had, simply, a good time, with lots of drinks and lots of cigarettes and lots of easy laughter and shared memories. His company was a liberation not only from the excessive sensibility of others but from her own—that sensibility which was at the centre of her talent and also, some have thought, its limitation. Sean O'Faolain, who rated her writing very highly indeed, nevertheless said that "one longs occasionally for a good, warm, passionate howl, like an Italian mother baying over her dead child". Too much elegance, he thought, over elemental things, "too much *dressage*".[1] It is precisely this tension in her—the fact that she could not howl—that gives her writing its peculiar pent-up intensity. One cannot write baldly of despair and loneliness, but one can instead describe the falling of the petals of a rose on to an escritoire. This is not symbolism: it is a sort of displacement activity. The "life with the lid on" thing is part of this. In pursuing a policy of "not noticing" (as she learnt in her childhood), one notices instead, in sharpest detail, something just to one side.

Her friendship with Jim Gates was not always unclouded. Writing to Virginia Woolf from Bowen's Court during a very bad patch in the war—January, 1941—she said:

> This letter was interrupted by a telephone call: I got up and was cruel to a neighbour called Mr. Gates. I said, "How can you be so absolutely stupid when you have got an Austrian grandfather?" which is really an unforgivable thing to say to a country neighbour: if one is even a degree more imaginative than anyone else, one ought to be nice to them, but how hard it is. And this is certainly no time to be querulous. In principle I feel very humble indeed. I have been cruel to Mr. Gates because I made the mistake I so often make, of idealising at the outset a stupid person.

It passed. Jim Gates was her friend, was part of the Bowen's Court set-up. In the letter just quoted, Elizabeth also asked Virginia most particularly for her opinion on the story "Summer Night", which had just been published in a new collection, *Look at All Those Roses*. "Summer Night" belongs, with "The Disinherited", among Elizabeth's very best stories. (It was written rather fast, as a makeweight, because Victor Gollancz said the collection was too short.) "Summer Night" is perhaps *the* best: the resonances and implications it leaves behind it go so far beyond its relatively restrained narrative. As in "The Disinherited", there is a liaison between a woman of the officer class and an other-ranks man; but in "Summer Night" the class difference is not so extreme, nor is it the point; the contrast is one of temperament. Elizabeth told Reginald Ross-Williamson, a friend in the British Embassy in Dublin, that Jim Gates was the starting point for Robinson in "Summer Night".

In the story, the major's wife leaves her gentle, baggy husband and drives through the dark, tense and keyed-up, to an assignation with Robinson. Robinson, a factory manager in a small Irish town, with an "imperturbable male personality", is meanwhile entertaining two acquaintances, brother and sister. The brother, Justin, is a nervous, susceptible, literary creature. Robinson attracts and baffles him: "[Justin's] talk became excessively cerebral, and he became prone, like a perverse person in love, to expose all his own piques, crotchets and weaknesses". Justin asks Robinson suddenly: "What's love like?" Robinson just laughs. The Justins of this world cannot accommodate themselves to the Robinsons. They end up hysterically beating their fists against such unimaginative self-sufficiency. "Incapable of being haunted, you are incapable of being added to", Justin tells Robinson. Justin's sister is stone-deaf: to her, Robinson seems delightful. "She does not hear with her ears, he does not hear with his mind. No wonder they can communicate".

The guests leave, the woman in the car arrives for her night of love: "Farouche, with her tentative little swagger and childish, pleading air of delinquency, Emma came to a halt in Robinson's living-room". Her heightened romantic mood is quenched by Robinson's matter-of-factness: "Here she was, being settled down to as calmly as he might settle down for a meal".

> She was becoming frightened of Robinson's stern, experienced delicacy on the subject of love. Her adventure became the quiet practice with him. The adventure (even, the pilgrimage) died at its root, in the childish part of her mind. When he had headed her off the cytherean terrain—the leaf-drowned castle ruin, the lake—she thought for a minute he had broken her heart, but she knew now he had broken her fairy-tale. He seemed content—having lit a new cigarette—to wait about in his garden for a few minutes longer: not poetry but a sort of tactile wisdom came from the firmness, lawn, under their feet.

Robinson's feet are on the ground. He is unself-consciously having a pleasant affair with a married woman; while she was attempting a picnic in Eden. Only the deaf woman seems the winner in this story. She dreams blissfully of Robinson that night, fusing him in her mind with a boy she had known long ago. Her Eden is an illusory one; but perhaps that's the only sort going, and she is happy. All this in the context of the war, of battles elsewhere, of changing values and new questions creeping in on neutral Ireland. "Who shall stem the black tide coming in?" There is more to "Summer Night"—it is nearly fifty pages long—even than this; and yet virtually nothing "happens".

It was not only the Black Hats who, in Alan's phrase, "ministered to Elizabeth", both to her sociability and to her private creative self. It was Jim Gates and men and women

like him, "incapable of being haunted", as well. If she sometimes reacted against them like Justin in the story, as is shown
by the letter to Virginia, she still relied, in a world where
Eden—the fairy-tale—was mostly disallowed, on the "sort of
tactile wisdom" that they offered her instead. "Not that there
is, really, one neat unhaunted man", says St. Quentin Miller,
the worldly-wise writer in *The Death of the Heart*. "I swear
that each of us keeps, battened down inside himself, a sort
of lunatic giant—impossible socially, but full-scale—and that
it's the knockings and batterings we sometimes hear in each
other that keeps our intercourse from utter banality".

Also from *The Death of the Heart*: "Unwritten poetry twists
the hearts of people in their thirties". And—"Frantic smiles
at parties, overtures that have desperation behind them,
miasmic reaches of talk with the lost bore, short cuts to
approach through staring, squeezing, or kissing—all indicate
that one cannot live alone". There was sometimes something
rather febrile in Elizabeth's social behaviour in her thirties.
The first affair had started something that was not finally laid
to rest until ten years after. In the 1930s, she was still finding
out. The house-party at Bowen's Court—the house-party for
which the extra blankets, the four new teapots were bought
in September, 1936, the year her lover went abroad—tells
its own story. Elizabeth was emotionally exhausted when she
arrived at Bowen's Court that summer; she went to bed for
twenty-four hours and "drank bromide", and kept on losing
her voice. And she had a lot of work on hand; but felt happy
"in a strange, steamy, half-awake way".

David Cecil and Rachel had been and gone. Noreen
Colley was there; the next arrivals were Roger Senhouse and
Rosamond Lehmann. Elizabeth had known Rosamond since
early Oxford days. They had friends in common, including
the Buchans, the Connollys, and William Plomer; Rosamond,

married and with two young children, lived at Ipsden, not far from Oxford. She was a few years younger than Elizabeth. Her first novel, *Dusty Answer* (1927), had made her name; the year of her visit to Bowen's Court saw the publication of her fourth, *The Weather in the Streets*. (Elizabeth reviewed it in *The New Statesman*.) She was famous not only for her talent but for her looks. She was unequivocally beautiful—dark-haired, creamy. There was a splendid appropriateness in the rapturous reaction of an American in County Cork to whom Elizabeth introduced her on this visit: "Not Miss Rosamond Lehmann—in the *flesh*?" Alan was very fond of Rosamond; and Rosamond on this occasion thought she was partly invited for his sake, since Elizabeth's preoccupations were elsewhere.

Roger and Rosamond arrived one morning; the same evening came Isaiah Berlin with two of his undergraduates, Stuart Hampshire and Con O'Neill. Isaiah had been at Bowen's Court the year before; this was the first time that Elizabeth met Stuart Hampshire, who was to become, as a result, a Black Hat and a friend. Then came John Summerson, whose book on Nash—the architect of Regent's Park, Elizabeth's London—had recently been published, and Michael Gilmour, a young solicitor. The guests who came by sea (Isaiah and his friends arrived from Killarney) were met in Cork by the Bowen's Court car.

The first couple of days were taken quietly. Elizabeth worked in the mornings; Alan and Rosamond went for walks. People sat about reading books. Another guest was expected and, pending his arrival, Elizabeth was tense, over-excited, smoking even more than usual.

The expected guest was Goronwy Rees, with whom Elizabeth had formed an attachment that was to be, in the event, short-lived. Goronwy was ten years younger than Elizabeth; she had first known him in Oxford, when in 1931 he got a fellowship at All Souls. Now, five years and a stint

on *The Manchester Guardian* later, he had just become assistant editor of *The Spectator*. He was a Black Hat, and his
new relation to Elizabeth was of recent date. Goronwy was
very clever, very unpredictable, and very attractive to women.

Goronwy arrived, in Isaiah Berlin's phrase, "like a
toreador". Immediately the quiet party was no longer quiet.
There were expeditions, lively games of deck quoits in the
Long Room, paper games in the evening. They played archi-
tectural Consequences—all except Goronwy, who would not
or could not draw. Goronwy sat on the arm of Rosamond's
chair. Alan no longer had the pleasure of Rosamond's company
on walks. She was taken over by Goronwy and Stuart. Then,
entirely by Goronwy. And Goronwy neglected Elizabeth. For
the *coup de foudre* had struck both him and Rosamond—
they fell in love there and then. It was a matter of now or
never, since Rosamond was due shortly to go back to her
family.

Noreen Colley was very pretty, very innocent, and still
in her teens. Because of the disposition of the bedrooms, she
could not avoid knowing much too much about the consequences of the *coup de foudre*. She got up and sat on the
stairs in acute misery. Her distress was not directly on
Elizabeth's account—she had no idea of her cousin's attachment—but because she thought it was such a terrible thing
to be going on under Elizabeth's roof, a betrayal of hospitality.
She was devoted to Rosamond, too; it all seemed incomprehensible. In the morning she poured the whole thing out to
Isaiah, whom she had always found sympathetic. Should she
tell Elizabeth what was going on? No, said Isaiah, firmly and
without hesitation. (And indeed Elizabeth didn't know the
whole of it until Noreen told her weeks later, when she was
staying at Clarence Terrace. Elizabeth said she had friends
coming for drinks, and she did hope Noreen would be in;
Noreen said that if the friends were Goronwy and Rosamond

—and they were—she would rather not see them—and then all the rest came out.)

But Elizabeth had the evidence of her own day-time eyes. Rosamond left as arranged, with no word of reproach from Elizabeth, who was, however, wretched. The atmosphere in the house was uncomfortable, though soothed by another, un-involved visitor, Myles Dillon from Dublin. Probably the only person totally unaffected by the undercurrents was young Michael Gilmour; he was living his own drama. He had pro-posed to a young poet named Elise Cumming, and while at Bowen's Court he received her letter saying yes. How much Alan noticed or knew is unfathomable. In the remaining day of Goronwy's visit, letters for him in Rosamond's handwriting were on the breakfast-table. He stayed on with Elizabeth and Noreen after everyone else, including Alan, had gone back to England. Elizabeth suffered, and she made Goronwy suffer. "My father went mad here", she said to him. "Wouldn't it be nice if you and I stayed here and went mad too?" Goronwy, to escape the intensity and the pain, went for long solitary bicycle rides. In the end, Elizabeth was not sorry to see him go.

It was the end of the story as far as Elizabeth and Goronwy were concerned, and the beginning of a story for Goronwy and Rosamond. Rosamond later wrote to Elizabeth to apologise for their behaviour; Elizabeth wrote back per-fectly kindly, adding, "I have another love". There was a slight awkwardness between the two women for some time, but later again they were close, closer than they had ever been.

If the reader will now look back to the letter to John Hayward, quoted in the first chapter of this book, in which Elizabeth describes this house-party ("Rosamond looked quite lovely, was sweet and I think enjoyed herself"), it will be apparent that her dignity, charity, control, and sense of self-preservation were of a very high order indeed.

There are only two end-pieces to add to this particular episode. The first is that when, in 1940, Goronwy announced that he was going to marry Margaret Morris, a very young and pretty girl, both Rosamond and Elizabeth—before they had met her—wrote him long and severe letters asking him whether he was quite sure it was such a good idea. He found this upsetting; his bride, on the other hand, was not excessively disturbed. She was in the position of Cinderella who has won her prince: and for her the other two were, if anything but the Ugly Sisters, hardly a threat, being twenty years older than herself. She went with Goronwy to parties at Clarence Terrace. She—not surprisingly, under the circumstances—was one of the girls who were happy to talk to Alan. The second end-piece to Elizabeth's episode with Goronwy Rees has to do with the novel she published two years after the house-party, *The Death of the Heart*.

Elizabeth was not one for banging her head against a brick wall. She was a romantic, but a picaresque, unself-destructive romantic. She did not mourn long for Goronwy. While perhaps over-anxious in these years to test her attractiveness to the opposite sex, she was, as she had said, a writer before she was a woman and chalked these things up to experience. She said of another friend of whom she was briefly enamoured that he was "one of those people who do not understand that affairs have their natural termination". "One wants to say", she remarked on another occasion, "break my heart if you must, but don't waste my time".

The years between *Encounters* in 1923 and *The Death of the Heart* in 1938 were the most intensely productive of Elizabeth's life. After *The Death of the Heart* came the war and its dislocations, and a new orientation; her next novel was not published until 1949, though she did publish all through the war, both non-fiction and short fiction. During these productive years, in between writing and reviewing intensively and living intensively, she had also been constantly reading, often in the fallow periods at Bowen's Court. In the early thirties she had read a lot of French, starting with Stendhal: and a chunk of his *De l'amour*, in the French, found its way into *To the North*. In 1932 she was reading for the first time Flaubert's *L'Éducation sentimentale*, and told Lady Ottoline:

> What perfect writing, and what a clear powerful mind, and what a perfect picture of an enchantment he can produce. And what compass he has: this picture of colour and movement compared with the sad immobility of poor Bovary.

A few months later she began translating it, "because it seems to me one of the best books in the world". She wrote to A. E. Coppard that she imagined the translation had no future: "Probably it's been done (tho' not as well as I meant to do it). But there's an excitement about examining and transposing someone else's style". The French interest persisted. In 1937 she was having "a heavenly time" reading Montherlant, and writing a piece on him for *The New Statesman*.

Maupassant never meant as much to her as Flaubert, or as Proust. She was reading collections of Maupassant's stories in mid-winter at Bowen's Court when she wrote to Virginia Woolf:

> I suppose he had sharp sense but really rather a boring mind. You soon get to know his formula, but there is always the fascination: it's like watching someone do the same card trick over and over again. I did feel the fascination so strongly that I wondered if I were getting brutalised myself. There is a particularly preposterous story called *Yvette*. . . .

In print, she called Maupassant "that rare thing—the first-rate *un-literary* writer".[2] She said in 1942 (with some exaggeration, since she was speaking in Ireland and a little defensive about her apparent Englishness): "The English novelists simply don't influence one. But the French *do*. They both excite *and* influence".[3]

As to reviewing, which she always did a great deal of, she was ambivalent. She was a notoriously kind reviewer of novels; she preferred not to write about a book she could not praise, and was known in the business as a very soft touch. But "it is a perfectly awful business", she wrote to Virginia Woolf about *The New Statesman* fiction-reviewing stint she was doing in 1935, alternating weekly with Peter Quennell. Once when Henry Reed was staying at Bowen's Court and she was very involved with her own work, "Henry even did some of my *Tatler* reviews for me, which left me more time for the novel: a friendly act". It was indeed. Like most novelists, Elizabeth felt that it did her no good to write reviews; and like most novelists, she reviewed endlessly—on and off for *The Listener*, *Vogue*, and *Harper's Bazaar*, as well as for *The New Statesman* and *The Tatler*. During the six months' life of the weekly *Night and Day* (1937–38), which Graham Greene edited, she wrote its theatre criticism, which she enjoyed doing. (*Night and Day* was ruined by a libel action brought against Graham Greene on account of an article about Shirley Temple. Writing from Mexico, Graham Greene told Elizabeth that "I found a cable waiting for me in Mexico City asking me to agree to apologise to that little bitch Shirley Temple—so I suppose the case has now been settled with maximum publicity. How I shall miss your theatre criticisms".)

Elizabeth was also involved in the thirties with literary projects peripheral to her own work. Faber & Faber, in the person of Tom Eliot, asked her to select and edit a collection of modern short stories, which was published in 1937. It turned out to be rather a chore, even though she was able to include work that she admired by people she was fond of (including A. E. Coppard, Frank O'Connor, William Plomer,

Peter Quennell, Edward Sackville-West, and Stephen Spender; she included her own "The Disinherited" and wrote an introduction). She wrote to William Plomer from Bowen's Court just before the 1936 house-party:

> Yes indeed I am doing those abominable short stories (the collection I mean). As far as I ever do read here, I read nothing else. ⅘ of what I try out shows a level of absolute mediocrity; arty, they are, and mawkishly tender-hearted. Quite a large number of short stories are told, do you notice, by hikers. "As I crossed the horizon" they so often begin, and the heroine is generally just called "the woman". Really they are the hell. . . . I long more and more to make a collection of *Great Middlebrow Prose*. Would this be actionable? Would you collaborate? I suppose it would ruin one.

The only stories she came across that seemed to her remarkable were Sean O'Faolain's collection *Midsummer Night Madness* (she included one in the Faber book), which had come out in 1932 and "which I do think *grand*". "Have you met him?" Elizabeth asked William. "Is he nice? He might possibly be quite dim".

Although Elizabeth had never met Sean O'Faolain (who was anything but dim), they had already collaborated from afar. In 1932 A. E. Coppard and the Golden Cockerel Press had commissioned nine writers to each write one section of a story based on the paper game Consequences. It was a very pretty little book, in a limited edition of 1,000 unsigned copies and 200 numbered copies on handmade paper signed by all the authors; there was a woodcut by Eric Ravilious as a frontispiece. Elizabeth was allotted the episode "She Gave Him". Deep in completing *To the North*, she had found it hard to come to grips with the assignment: "To tell you the truth", she had told Coppard, "I liked the scene (yours) but disliked the characters so made heavy weather of it: there's something

147

about exposing the poseur I find very unrewarding; I could wish that He and She had been more straightforward and picaresque. I very much wish that my part were better". Her brain, she said, felt like scorched porridge. As to her contribution: what She gave Him, after circling for several pages, was "the cold shivers". (The idea of collaborations, however, interested Elizabeth—she suggested to Coppard another project on the Seven Deadly Sins.) In *Consequences* the other contributors, apart from herself and A. E. Coppard, were John Van Druten, G. B. Stern, Norah Hoult, Hamish Maclaren, Ronald Fraser, Malachi Whitaker, and—"He Said to Her"— Sean O'Faolain.

Sean, too, was from County Cork; he had been teaching in London in the very early thirties, but Elizabeth did not meet him then. Not that she was cut off from other Irish writers. She was made a member of the Irish Academy of Letters in 1937, and when she spent a few days in Dublin, as she did in early summer, 1938, she visited "Some of the grand old boys"—

> like Yeats, with whom I spent an evening, who was an angel, in his own house, less showy and more mellow: he has a superb white cat. I spent a day with Frank O'Connor, who's at present living in Wicklow; he's a very nice creature: the most contemporary (I mean the least up-in-the-air) of the younger Irish, at least to talk to, I think.[4]

Sean's Irish background was very different from Elizabeth's. This in the early years of their friendship was not unimportant. Before they met, in the spring of 1937 (but having arranged to meet), he wrote to her from the Thackeray Hotel, opposite the British Museum. He had been reading her books, and was moved by them: "I find so much trembling loveliness in your books that they have given me quite a bad time . . . lonely folk shouldn't read lovely books. *Friends and Relations* specially hurts", and he continued:

> I am looking out at the mourning-card of the B.M. opposite the window and I know that if you wrote about it the great pillars would Blake-ify and it would all become charged with that tender melancholy feeling that you seem to find in things. . . .

Do for God's sake, he told her, write a book about Ireland. He had not then read *The Last September*. She lent it to him, and the letter he wrote about it from Ireland expresses painfully the problems of the new Ireland, of Irish writers, and the tensions that underwrote their own friendship. "It's so entirely Irish", he said of *The Last September*, "if that matter a damn. (We're so sick of hearing our Nazionalists ask for Irish literature—so thirsty for just literature.)" Now that the Troubles were in the past

> each side has to make up its losses. Do you feel any of that? Or is the wall between Danielstown and Peter Connor's farm as high as ever? I fear to think it is. Last summer I was walking near Foynes and called at a Big House. . . . I had met the people in the train from Dublin. It was now a kind of guest-house. They "allowed" me to stay. Nice people. . . . The boy was studying in London for the Foreign Office. There was an Austrian baroness there, and two Anglo-Irish ladies. We sat on the steps, like your house, and looked at the trees below the meadow and the far line of hills. My folk came from those hills—I had put them into A Nest of Simple Folk; my father left the little farm to become a constable in the R.I.C. As we sat on the steps a man came up sidling with his hat in his hand, an old man with drooping moustaches. He might have been my

father. The butler came out to fend him off from the
lady of the house. The butler was possibly the old man's
second-cousin, and he might have been mine. I felt
something turn over in my bowels to see the two men
talk to one another in that way, and to have to keep
silent, and not say, "Hello, Tom," or Jerry, or whatever
his name was. It seemed that wall was just as high as
ever. It made me feel like a spy inside it.

Elizabeth, he said, should write about a Danielstown House
"that was at least aware of the Ireland outside . . . that,
perhaps, regretted the division enough to admit it was there".
He would love, he said, a book revealing the life of the
Ascendency *"now"*:

> I am writing like a fool. You will look up at the cars
> swishing quietly along the road in the park, and at the
> graceful movements of boats or people or the little trees.
> And this Ireland will seem a ragged, untidy thing, like
> a man in a poorhouse trying to pretend he is free and
> rich. You will say, These people are in a mess, and I
> cannot be bothered; this is work for a social reformer
> not a novelist. Still, *Dead Souls* did, for Gogol, link
> up divided worlds, and Tchekov [*sic*] has many stories
> (about doctors) that climb walls. All our Irish stories
> have been in water-tight compartments.

Sean stayed at Bowen's Court; but her commitment to the
"absurd ridiculous house", which was not even comfortable,
he found in the end excessive.

That first summer—1937—that they knew each other,
Elizabeth went to Salzburg with Sean, Isaiah Berlin, Stuart
Hampshire, and Sally Graves[5] for the Festival. They all went
round together, and to all the concerts, and enjoyed themselves hugely:

Salzburg was great fun, and had some funny moments. The Connollys turned up, looking well in mountaineer get-ups. Our party didn't go into those, as we were all either too fat or too small. The weather was heavenly and we drove about in fiacres. There was a great deal of conversation and eating, and the music, which I really did enjoy.[6]

Elizabeth, while strictly unmusical, was on occasion greatly affected by opera; *Don Giovanni* once moved her to tears. (She identified strongly with Don Juan; it was for him she wept. She had no time for Donna Anna.) Of *Tosca* she said (this was years later):

It certainly does hit one with a bang. *I* enjoyed it: I underline the "I" because Isaiah said it was to him the most horrible opera, stuff and essence of Fascism. But I am so very naïve about opera at all, I think I like one to be about the passions: so many seem to be about long, tedious impersonations and practical jokes.[7]

In 1937, on her return, she wrote a lively piece about Salzburg and the Festival for *Night and Day*, which contrived to refer only once and obliquely to the Festival's object: "Almost everyone admits to hunger during the Opera. . . . Hunger is so exalting that during a last act you practically levitate".[8]

Goronwy Rees read *The Death of the Heart* when it came out in 1938 and recognised himself in the character called Eddie. At first this delighted him, and he told Rosamond the novel was brilliant. Then he changed his mind; he wrote Elizabeth a very bitter, upset letter and planned to sue her for libel. In this he was dissuaded by his friends, notably E. M. Forster.

The novel is set in a house in Regent's Park, in

"Windsor Terrace". The house is Elizabeth's own, with its house-telephone, its upstairs drawing-room occupied by charming Anna Quayne, its downstairs study where her husband, Thomas, waits alone for her visitors to take their leave or, "home from the office, [sits] at his study table, drawing cats on a blotter, waiting for Anna to come back from a lunch". Eddie, a frequent visitor, is young and irresponsible; and he made the mistake of trying to kiss Anna because "he wanted to repay some of her niceness in a way he thought she could but like. It had been his experience that everyone did". He tries to get off with people because he cannot get on with them.

Life in Windsor Terrace is controlled, edited, passionless. Anna suffers from "the shut-in room, the closed-in heart". Her emotions are half-frozen, like the lake in wintry Regent's Park in which she walks on the first page of the book. Portia, Thomas's orphaned half-sister, is parked on the Quaynes. She watches, she judges, she keeps a diary that Anna reads: Anna is threatened by Portia's presence, her "perfectly open face", her candour—"is she a snake or a rabbit?"

Portia—Elizabeth's sub-self—is more innocent even than Emmeline in *To the North*, and she loves Eddie with the same blind whole-heartedness with which Emmeline loved Markie. Eddie, who is fond of the sixteen-year-old girl, and flattered by her devotion, tells her she is "innocent to the point of deformity". And the authorial voice-over—particularly strong throughout this novel—spells out again the predicament of the innocent:

> The system of our affections is too corrupt for them.
> They are bound to blunder, then to be told they cheat.
> In love, the sweetness and violence they have to offer
> involves a thousand betrayals for the less innocent. . . .
> Their singleness, their ruthlessness, their one continuous
> wish makes them bound to be cruel, and to suffer

cruelty. The innocent are so few that two of them seldom meet—when they do meet, their victims lie strewn around.

For Eddie, too, is a kind of innocent; he constantly makes false moves. He tells Portia that girls like her "have a lunatic instinct for picking on another person who doesn't know where he is". It is not at all an unsympathetic portrait; even as regards his treatment of Portia, he is *genuinely* ungenuine:

> "How can I keep on feeling something I once felt when there are so many things one can feel? People who always say they feel as they did simply fake themselves up. I may be a crook but I'm not a fake—that's an entirely different thing."

What, really, was there for Goronwy to take such violent exception to? (If indeed Eddie was entirely based on Goronwy—the charming, handsome, unsettled boy who haunted "Windsor Terrace" also has a look in his eye of Elizabeth's sometimes lodger in Clarence Terrace, William Buchan, though the family background ascribed to Eddie must have sounded rather familiar to Goronwy, and not at all to William.) Goronwy felt that it was a betrayal. But the aspect of Eddie that reflects least well on anyone presuming himself to be the model also reflects ironically on Anna Quayne/Elizabeth. There is silly vanity in Eddie's cultivation of Anna, and silly vanity in Anna's patronage of him and in her whimsical enjoyment of his attentions. As her husband, Thomas, says, "If you were half as heartless as you make out, you would be an appallingly boring woman".

By the end of *The Death of the Heart* everyone—except Matchett, the maid—is either betrayed or betrayer. Eddie betrays Anna, perhaps with Portia, and Portia with Anna. But Eddie's private betrayal of Portia is worse, and it is here that Elizabeth used the essence of what had happened at Bowen's Court in the summer of 1936.

But it is unrecognisable. Portia is sent by Anna to stay at Seale-on-Sea with an ex-governess and her stepchildren. Seale is Hythe in every detail, and Waikiki, the villa by the sea where Portia stays, is an actual Hythe villa. In describing the Waikiki ménage Elizabeth achieves high burlesque, deadpan and wicked and very funny. Waikiki is the opposite of Windsor Terrace. Life at Waikiki is unedited, spontaneous— full of smells of cooking food and sweating people, full of noisy voices and banging doors and cascading plumbing. The controls, too, are different. In hyper-civilised sophisticated sterile Windsor Terrace, Anna Quayne can utter obscenities in times of stress without being unseemly: whereas the crude life of Waikiki is overlaid by a fatal refinement, a dogged gentility, an iron set of conventions (against which Portia, who can only be direct, is doomed to offend).

Eddie, visiting Portia during her stay in Seale/Hythe, betrays her casually with Daphne, the loud, aggressive daughter of the house, in a scene that combines the banality of adolescent experience with its unprecedented and unrepeatable anguish. A group of young people—Eddie, Portia, Daphne, Daphne's brother, and their friends—are sitting in a row in the cinema. Portia is next to her beloved Eddie. She feels a tension in him. "On her side, one of his hands, a cigarette between the two longest fingers, hung down slack; she saw only one hand. Hitching herself up on her seat, she looked at the screen, vowing not to wonder, never to look away". But one of the party lights up his lighter, and holds it down the row:

> The light, with malicious accuracy, ran round a rim of cuff, a steel bangle, and made a thumb-nail flash. Not deep enough in the cleft between their *fauteuils* Eddie and Daphne were, with emphasis, holding hands. Eddie's fingers kept up a kneading movement: her thumb alertly twitched at the joint.

End of chapter. Who holds whose hand in the cinema: it is the stuff of which teenage-girls' magazine stories are made. Elizabeth invests it with the incomprehensible world-shattering outrage that for the person concerned such things have. And poor Portia later digs the grave of her innocence by innocently asking "why" of both Eddie and Daphne, thus breaking all the world's rules. The intensity of this episode comes not only from imagination but from what Elizabeth inadvertently witnessed between Rosamond and Goronwy—but they were adults, and it was not in a cinema, and all is changed. The novelist has entirely taken over from the "wronged" woman. So far from revenging herself on Goronwy, Elizabeth put the experience towards making one of the most memorable and the most characteristic (in the confrontation between innocence and experience) of her novels, and the one that crowned a phase of concentrated fiction-writing that had lasted nearly twenty years. If she used Goronwy, it was to magnificent effect. And as Anna's friend St. Quentin Miller says to Portia in *The Death of the Heart*, "Nothing arrives on paper as it started, and so much arrives that never started at all. To write is always to rave a little. . . ."

The Death of the Heart is the novel of Elizabeth's that many people like the best. It was a Book Society Choice. It made her some money; and in the first autumn of the war she was doing some modernising of Bowen's Court, from where she wrote to William Plomer:

> This autumn is *most* lovely, with colours such as I've never seen, and the country round here melting in light. Noreen is here, keeping me company and doing the housekeeping beautifully. We now have the telephone [the number was Kildorrery 4] and Jim Gates (do you remember) is busy putting in electric light for me here.

As I am simply having old lamps wired for electricity, it does not change the effect of the lighting much. And it certainly is more cheerful, these long evenings, and easier to work by than candles jumping about.

William had visited Bowen's Court earlier, in the candlelight era, and wrote out his impressions of Ireland most lyrically, almost in a pastiche of the style of his "brilliant friend and hostess at Bowen's Court", in his autobiography.

If *The Death of the Heart* is the novel of Elizabeth's that many people like best, it was the one that she herself liked least. She said in a B.B.C. interview twenty years later that "it was really an inflated short story, that thing". She felt she could more profitably have crystallised the "struggle for ascendancy" (between Portia's values and the world's) into a story. Her friend Edward Sackville-West was one of the few critics who were equally unsure about it, but for another reason, the same reason that made him unsure about some of the stories in *Look at All Those Roses*. He wrote in *Inclinations* (1949) that Elizabeth's increased professionalism was sometimes "of the magazine order": ". . . the faint whiff of vulgarity which rises from the pages of a volume like *Look at All Those Roses* can also be discerned, as a disintegrating factor, in *The Death of the Heart*".

Elizabeth's vulgar streak has been conceded—the vulgarity of the perfect gentleman who has licence to break out. One cannot, after all, be abandoned unless one is essentially respectable. Nor was this precisely Sackville-West's meaning. One suspects that he deprecated her writing about vulgar people in banal situations—the Waikiki business, for example. Elizabeth's clever friends did not all encourage her in her burlesque, social-comedy manner; which is maybe why there is not nearly enough of it.

Some of the stories in *Look at All Those Roses*—which came out in the third year of the war—were written before, and some after, the novel. The collection includes yet another story of the parked-out, misfit little girl in the ever-so-kind household, "The Easter Egg Party". This story has a queer little echo in *The Death of the Heart*: the child in the Easter-egg story longs for "a green celluloid box to keep her toothbrush in", which she sees in a chemist's but doesn't have the money to buy. In *The Death of the Heart*, Portia, shopping in Seale/Hythe with Mrs. Heccomb, buys "a jade green box to keep a toothbrush in". When did Elizabeth long for, or buy, or see a child eyeing, that toothbrush-box?

What is true of *Look at All Those Roses* is that in several stories the characters, so far from being denizens of a Big House, are taken from a lower social stratum. "Attractive Modern Homes", about a couple who move into a new house on a half-finished estate on the outskirts of a strange town, is one of these: and the sympathetic magic with which Elizabeth entered into their alienation from each other, from their surroundings, is a far stronger indictment of what such an uprooting can do than any of the sociologists' subsequent analyses. Intuitively she picked on all the factors that have since become part of the accepted—if unacted-upon—wisdom. The story could be used as a social-planners' tract, were it not touched with a poetic battiness that rescues it for art.

Elizabeth also here transposed into a lower social class than her own a theme that she had had to think about in relation to her own experience: the mature woman in love with a man ten years younger, in "A Walk in the Woods". She is married; he is a neighbour's lodger. In a wood full of trippers, they look for somewhere to make love. "You're my only life", she tells him. "My only way out. Before you came, I was walled in alive. I didn't know where to turn. I was burning myself out. . . ."

But when they kiss it is he who pulls apart. And two giggly schoolgirls in the woods see her as "a haggard woman with dark red hair and a white face: something in her expression set them off giggling all the more". His self-consciousness makes him look even younger. He still needs her: "Passion broke down a wall in both their lives. But her spirit was stronger than his, and so he was frightened of her". At the end of the story she sees his life "curve off from hers, like one railway line from another, curve off to an utterly different and far-off destination". So experience is put at the service of imagination. In life, the ever-watchful story-maker in Elizabeth precluded any prolonged self-deception or self-pity, even as it provoked a normal amount of self-dramatisation.

Several stories in *Look at All Those Roses* are already about the war. The war, and London under the blitz, was the first of the experiences that irrevocably cracked the crust of life for Elizabeth, that made "life with the lid on" irrevocably untenable, as it did for so many other people. She said, for all that: "I would not have missed being in London throughout the war for anything: it was the most interesting period of my life".[9]

E B

CHAPTER VIII

Noon

Eᴌɪᴢᴀʙᴇᴛʜ ʙᴇᴄᴀᴍᴇ ᴀɴ A.R.P. ᴡᴀʀᴅᴇɴ—"air raids were much less trying if one had something to do". Alan joined the Home Guard, and was put in charge of the full defence of Broadcasting House during raids. "The man's a lion in an air raid", said a B.B.C. colleague. The Regent's Park area of London was badly bombed, both in 1941–42 and, even more seriously, in 1944, when a V-1, landing across the road, blew 2 Clarence Terrace hollow inside, wrecking every room. As a warden for her own district of Marylebone, Elizabeth was on a rota to attend the Warden's Post, to man the telephone and answer enquiries or calls for help; and to patrol in pairs, in tin helmet and boots, the local streets to see that the black-out was observed and, when the air-raid warning sounded, to see that the streets were cleared. Everyone had to be under cover, and those who were more than five minutes' walk away from their homes were directed to the shelters. "Walking in the darkness of the nights of six years", wrote Elizabeth "(darkness which transformed a capital city into a network of inscrutable canyons), one developed new bare alert senses, with their own savage warnings and notations".[1]

Elizabeth described herself to Virginia Woolf as being, in the first months of the war, in "a stupefied excited and I think rather vulgar state". During the blitz on London which began in August, 1940, Clarence Terrace suffered badly. On

September 24th, Elizabeth wrote to Noreen Colley (now Mrs. Gilbert Butler) in Ireland an account of what had happened, including some human details that the historians leave out: "I am getting quite nice and thin. Raids are slightly constipating", she told Noreen in a P.S. The letter also includes, straight from the horse's mouth as it were, those observations about the gallantry of Londoners that later became journalists' clichés. That September she and Alan were time-bombed out of Clarence Terrace at three minutes' notice, at four o'clock in the morning, and became refugees for a week. They went to the Mount Royal Hotel off Oxford Street, but then two nights later were bombed out of that "after as appalling a night as I ever wish to see". Alan came into his own, marshalling the mostly aged residents of the hotel to safety.

> Alan had really rather a nice time that night, as he first, with a boy friend he collected, took entire command of the hotel and issued orders in a military ringing voice, and then he was allowed to go and direct traffic—one of those main streams of early morning traffic that suddenly filtered roaring down a small bye street, all wiser normal channels having become closed. I stood two blocks off, at the mouth of the shelter, and watched the direction of traffic with admiration (he wore his tin hat and L.D.V. armlet)—he clicked his fingers, and at intervals pushed back his tin hat in order to twist his front hair.

Writing about this awful week in an essay called "London, 1940" (in *Collected Impressions*), she said that fear was not cumulative; each night, it started again from scratch. On the other hand, resistance became a habit, "and, better, it builds up a general fund". She told Noreen:

> I should never have conceived it possible that the ordinary London person was capable of having such

uncrackable self-control and such good nerves. Everyone that one sees in the streets looks dead tired, and at
at same time much more grown-up than usual. And
the good temper is phenomenal: one never hears people
being cross, even on buses and places where feeling
usually runs highest. I expect that when once this is
happily over everyone will have a terrific revulsion and
be as cross as cats for about a year.

One minor discomfort, by day, is the extreme dirt
— the air is full of queer greasy dust from the debris
of the demolished houses, and this settles in one's hair,
one's face, one's clothes and quite often makes one's
eyes sore. It's rather touching to see people—girls—
put on more and more lipstick, cheerful as ever, with
the rest of their faces grey and streaked. And turbans
are more worn than usual, in order to keep the dust out
of the hair. One has to walk almost everywhere, as
buses, etc., owing to bomb-craters or dormant time-
bombs, get "diverted" miles out of their normal courses,
so one never knows where to pick anything up. Entire
districts, because of the time-bombs, become enislanded
for a day or two, and cannot be got at by any means.

The weekend after their ejection from Clarence Terrace they
went to the Tweedsmuirs at Elsfield—"it was *heaven* to spend
two nights in a quiet country house"—and then on Monday
drove back to London, hoping to find their house still there,
which it was:

So yesterday afternoon A. and I crept back in here,
though it is still officially "closed", with barriers and
bomb-notices at every approach. The whole of the rest
of this terrace is still completely deserted: it looks like
a street in a city of the dead, with dead leaves and bits
of paper blowing about. The postman takes a flying run
down the terrace once a day, otherwise no one else

comes, and I ooze out through the officially shut park gates and buy loaves etc. and bottles of milk . . . largely, I may say, for Lawrence [the cat]. I am keeping the maids stored in a different part of London, till the house can be opened more properly, but they crept in today and did some tidying up.

Elizabeth has in *The Heat of the Day* a description of a frightened cat in an air raid: "its fur seemed to shrink and dampen as a stick of bombs fell diagonally across the middle distance". By the beginning of the next year, Elizabeth was telling Virginia Woolf that No. 2 was now the only house in the terrace still occupied, except for one other, "a house with a *reputation*, full of rather gaudy, silent young men who come out in the mornings and walk about two and two, like nuns". Elizabeth wrote about being in the house in the closed Park in "London, 1940":[2]

> Just inside the gates an unexploded bomb makes a boil in the tarmac road. Around three sides of the Park, the Regency terraces look like scenery in an empty theatre: in the silence under the shut façades a week's drift of leaves flitters up and down. At nights, at my end of the terrace, I feel as though I were sleeping in one corner of a deserted palace. I had always placed this Park among the most civilised scenes on earth; the Nash pillars look as brittle as sugar—actually, which is wonderful, they have not cracked; though several of the terraces are gutted—blown-in shutters swing loose, ceilings lie on floors and a premature decay-smell comes from the rooms. A pediment has fallen on to a lawn. Illicitly, leading the existence of ghosts, we overlook the locked Park.

"One feels this lovely batty unpractical Regency style will be utterly irreplaceable", she told Noreen. "It's a small thing, compared to vast troubles, but one would be inhuman if one didn't mind".

The immediate neighbourhood—Park Road, Baker Street —became important and beloved, and London a series of villages: "We all have new friends—our neighbours". Elizabeth's local cinema took a direct hit. London "contracted round her wounds". Amid the destruction, the late summer flowers in the Park seemed to be doing better than ever. "Through the railings I watch dahlias blaze out their colour". (Later in the war, the "beautiful spear-headed railings"[3] were taken away.) She put those dahlias into *The Heat of the Day*, in which they became "outsize dahlias, velvet and wine", beneath trees on which "each vein in each yellow leaf stretched out perfect against the sun blazoned out the idea of the finest hour." There were drifts of leaves, now, on the empty deck chairs; and that autumn of 1940, in the sweeping up of the leaves in the Park, there was always the tinkling of broken glass.

Personal belongings took on a special pathos—Elizabeth's typewriter, for example, left uncovered in the dust on the night they had to leave the house in a hurry. "Our own 'things'—tables, chairs, lamps", she wrote in the 1940 essay, ungrammatically, "give one a kind of confidence to us who stay in our own paper rooms". Elizabeth said that nobody who has not cleaned up a house in which every ceiling has come down and every window has been blown in knows what cleaning-up can be like. She wrote a story (in *Look at All Those Roses*) called "Oh, Madam", which is a monologue by a maid to her mistress, who returns to London to find her lovely house in ruins. The author's sympathy is with the maid, whose loyalty and concern and identification with the house are far nobler than her mistress's seemingly rather detached horror. ("Oh, Madam" was made into a stage monologue by John Perry and performed at a wartime charity theatrical by Mary Jerrold.) This feeling of the servant for the inanimate objects she cares for is something Elizabeth suggests elsewhere: Matchett in *The Death of the Heart* sees herself as the custodian and confidante of the Quaynes' family furniture, sometimes even in opposition to the Quaynes themselves. There is also a passage about "things" in *The Death of the Heart*, written before any bombs had fallen on London, which is painful in the light of what happened so soon after. Elizabeth had written that pictures would not be hung plumb over the centre of fireplaces, or wallpaper put up so very carefully, "if life were not really possible to adjudicate for". These things "are what we mean by civilisation":

> In this sense, the destruction of buildings and furniture is more palpably dreadful to the human spirit than the destruction of human life. . . . Only outside disaster is irreparable. At least, there would be dinner any minute; at least [Portia] could wash her hands in Vinolia soap.

Elizabeth knew better than most that life was not "possible to ajudicate for"; but, as she wrote to Virginia Woolf after hearing that the Woolfs' Mecklenburgh Square house had been destroyed, "All my life I have said, 'Whatever happens there will always be tables and chairs'—and what a mistake". But one had to carry on; gradually, even outrage becomes routine, and daily dread brings its own jokes—Elizabeth wrote to Noreen:

> The sound of the Boche bomber overhead is exactly like the enlarged sound of a wasp—it makes the same priggish and consequential noise. Do you remember that A. always used to call the particular wasp that annoyed him at B. Court "John Willy"? So now, when between eight and nine every evening we begin to hear over our roof our buzzing friend, A. says gloomily: "Here comes John Willy."

There was a sort of freemasonry among those who from choice or duty stayed on in London during the worst of the war. (Among the middle class, that is: few working-class adults who were not called up had much choice in the matter.) All involved in some sort of war-work, they spoke almost literally a different language, sometimes rather a silly and exclusive one, as Elizabeth was aware and showed in her story "Careless Talk", about the inability of someone up from the country to make any real contact with this inner circle. "Society became lovable", wrote Elizabeth in *The Heat of the Day*. "It could be established, roughly, that the wicked had stayed and the good had gone".

> This was the new society of one kind of wealth, resilience, living how it liked—people whom the climate of danger suited, who began, even, all to look a little alike, as they might in the sun, snows and altitude of the same sports station. . . . The very temper of pleasures lay in their chanciness, in the canvas-like impermanence of their settings, in their being off-time—to and fro between bars and grills, clubs and each other's places moved the little shoal through the noisy nights.

People flourished in London during the war who did not flourish in the peace, like the sinister Harrison in *The Heat of the Day* who feels "This is where I come in". Unlikely relationships briefly flowered: "There was a diffused gallantry in the atmosphere, an unmarriedness: it came to be rumoured about the country, among the self-banished, the uneasy, the put-upon and the safe, that everybody in London was in love". In London there was plenty of everything that mattered—"attention, drink, time, taxis, most of all space". Social life went on in pockets, in flats, houses, night-clubs, restaurants, provisional islands of light behind the rigidly blacked-out windows, behind the rackety unlit streets. In Clarence Terrace, Elizabeth served the coffee after a dinner party (the Spenders were there) on the balcony, during an air raid, the sky lit up by magnesium flares. "Not noticing", she made no reference to what was going on until they went in, and then: "I feel I should apologise for the noise". John Lehmann in his auto-biography[4] describes an imaginary party, typical of those he gave in the early years of the war, at which the guests were likely to include, he said, his sister Rosamond, Graham Greene, Cecil Day Lewis, Laurie Lee, William Plomer, Louis MacNeice, Henry Reed, Henry Yorke (Green), Rose Macaulay, Roger Senhouse, Raymond Mortimer, Veronica Wedgwood, and

> At the other end of the room Elizabeth Bowen, smartly turned out as ever in spite of wartime restrictions, is discussing novels with Philip Toynbee, lately released from the Army. Elizabeth is as usual in high spirits, radiating charm and vitality, the slight impediment in her speech giving an attractive touch of diffidence to her wide-ranging conversation: her stories of London in wartime . . . are just beginning to come out.

Such a cluster of literary names seems to require a proscenium arch around it, or a lions' cage. Elizabeth's best and most private life was always, as she said, "a non-literary life"; and she gives the lie to the apparent utter congeniality to her of such gatherings in a letter she wrote to Charles Ritchie, later in the war, about another literary party:

> I spent the only agreeable part of the evening with Peter Q[uennell] who was in a nice brisk well-fed mood. But the rest of the room (those crowds of *interesting* faces) gave me the creeps. The fact is, I am firmly and in-creasingly convinced that artists were intended to be an ornament to society. As a society in themselves they are unthinkable.

They were like vases of flowers or ornaments, she said, placed at random on the floor of an empty room, without the order or the proportion of larger pieces of furniture. Elizabeth met Charles Ritchie, a Canadian in his country's Foreign Service, based during most of the war in London, at the christening at Elsfield in February, 1941, of William Buchan's daughter Perdita, to whom she stood godmother. Charles recorded the meeting in his diary: "Well-dressed, intelligent handsome face, watchful eyes", he noted. "I had expected someone more Irish, more silent and brooding and at the same time more irresponsible. I was slightly surprised by her being so much 'on the spot'."[5] Half a year later he was writing: "The first time I saw Elizabeth Bowen I thought she looked more like a bridge-player than a poet. Yet without having read a word of her writing would not one have felt that something mysterious, passionate and poetic was behind that worldly exterior?"

Of course everyone, looking at Elizabeth, saw something a little different. A few months after that second entry in Charles's diary, James Lees-Milne met her for the first time:

> When she first came into the room I thought she was ugly with a prominent nose . . . then I decided that she was handsome, but not beautiful. She has a long face. A forward tuft of hair dances above a bandana tied round the forehead. When she smiles her charm is apparent. She speaks well and rapidly but speech is suddenly interrupted by an occasional stammer, not enough to embarrass one, because she has the mastery of it.[6]

(The charm of her smile was enhanced after 1941, when she had a lot of teeth removed—and replaced—in a nursing home in Mandeville Place. Undaunted, she received visitors in the interim between removal and replacement with her face swathed in clouds of chiffon.) On this occasion she and James Lees-Milne talked of the recent bombing, and confessed they had been terrified "last Sunday night". They were at lunch with Margaret Jourdain and Ivy Compton-Burnett in Cornwall Gardens. Elizabeth had great respect and admiration for Ivy, and wrote good critiques of her books, but never knew her really well; she was nervous before Ivy and Margaret came to Clarence Terrace for tea. The writer and journalist Nancy Spain was once at a publisher's party where she knew no one in the room but Elizabeth. Nancy overheard Elizabeth saying to some other woman writer, "It's really too bad of Cyril to say that Ivy is the only one of us all that will live".[7] (Nancy Spain had no idea who Cyril [Connolly] was, or who Ivy was. Ivy Compton-Burnett, who in turn had no idea who Nancy Spain was, was delighted when she was told this story.)

Charles Ritchie's diary
September 24, 1941:

> Dinner with Elizabeth Bowen and her husband Alan Cameron and a few critics and writers. So far in my excursions into High Bloomsbury I have not encountered, except for Elizabeth, any striking originality of thought, phrase or personality but rather a group of cultivated, agreeable people who think and feel very much alike.

December 21, 1941:

> Elizabeth came to tea in her smart black coat with a pink flower in her buttonhole. She lay on the sofa as she likes to do in an oddly elegant and relaxed pose. She never sprawls—mentally or physically. Her long, high-bred, handsome face was pink from the outside damp. She had on her gold chains and bangles.
>
> On the way home tonight Raymond Mortimer said to me, "Oh Elizabeth, she has such charm and is so kind and makes most of one's friends seem irremediably vulgar."

January 20, 1942:

> Elizabeth and I dined at Claridge's. She was in an easy and cheerful mood. She said, "I would like to put you

in a novel", looking at me through half-closed eyes in a sudden detached way like a painter looking at a model. "You probably would not recognise yourself." "I'm sure I wouldn't," I lied.

January 22, 1942:

Dined with Elizabeth at her house. She always manages to have unheard-of quantities of smoked salmon. The house was so cold that we put the electric heater on a chair so as to have it on a level with our bodies. Elizabeth was wearing a necklace and bracelet of gold and red of the kind of glass that Christmas tree ornaments are made of. . . . She had on a white silk jacket over a black dress. We sat on the sofa and talked.

April 13, 1942:

In the afternoon I went with Elizabeth to Hampstead. On the way back, walking through Keats Grove and the quiet French provincial streets full of flowering shrubs, Elizabeth talked about Virginia Woolf. . . . Elizabeth met a female admirer last night at dinner who said to her, "To meet you is like meeting Christ."

April 16, 1942:

David Cecil had dinner at Elizabeth's. I was charmed by him, his quick responsive flicks of attention, his irony and his wit, his contempt for the middle-brow, the snob and the inflated personality. At one point in talk he said, "One does not often have to put one's foot down, but I feel it is useful to have a Foot to Put Down." I like him and Cyril Connolly best of Elizabeth's literary friends.

(At another dinner with Elizabeth, two years later, Cyril Connolly appeared to be suffering from a sore throat, but said that "when he began to say critical things about his friends his voice came back to him".)

May 24, 1942:

A perfect May day. Elizabeth and I went to Kew. . . . It was a day like a page from one of her books, the involved relationship between the two people who are

wandering among the flower-beds. They sit together
on a bench to look across the narrow muddy Thames
at the set-piece of Syon House and discuss projects of
happiness, voyages they may never take, childhood, but
never Love. . . . At moments I could see Elizabeth
peering about her—her head a little back, her eyes
half-closed (how affected it sounds—how utterly unaffected the gesture was) focussing on the memories
of the place.

June 2, 1942:
Of what is her magic made? What is the spell that she
has cast on me? At first I was wary of her—*méfiant*—
I feared that I should expose my small shifts and
stratagems to her eye which misses nothing. Her uncanny intuitions, her flashes of insight like summer
lightning at once fascinated and disturbed me. Now day
by day I have been discovering more and more of her
generous nature, her wit and funniness, the stammering
flow of her enthralling talk, the idiosyncrasies, vagaries
of her temperament. I now know that this attachment
is nothing transient but will bind me as long as I live.

June 13, 1942:
Dined with Elizabeth. Drank a lot of red wine. Who
could help becoming attached to her?

Charles Almon Ritchie was about seven years younger than
Elizabeth, the son of a Nova Scotian barrister who had died
when Charles was ten. He had been at school in England as
a small boy, then to "an Anglican concentration camp of a
boarding-school" in Ontario; and then, after the University of
King's College in Halifax (his home city in Nova Scotia), to
Oxford, Harvard, and the École Libre des Sciences Politiques
in Paris. In London, at the office of the High Commissioner for
Canada during the war, he acted as Vincent Massey's private
secretary and rose to be First Secretary by 1943. No one's idea
of a Canadian, Charles was one of those North Americans to

whom background, education, travel, and elegant physical type give all the patina that the European upper middle class liked to claim as its own: learning easily worn, stylishness, *finesse*, *savoir-vivre*. In Europe by the time of the Second World War these attributes had already become associated with a concomitant distress, an aura of decline, of straitened circumstances, even at times a raunchy tattiness; cultivated North Americans, on the other hand, tend not to be too poor. When the Buchans—or Tweedsmuirs, as they by then had become —were in Canada, a friend asked if he could bring a clever young man to see them; this was Charles Ritchie, then a Third Secretary in Ottawa. He became a friend of the family; he was at Elsfield for the christening where he first saw Elizabeth, and at Alastair Buchan's wedding at Elsfield, in 1942 (where the Camerons also were, Elizabeth wearing a considerable hat), Charles was best man.

Charles was gregarious and he had charm; in his London posting he made quantities of friends, dined out and week-ended continuously, and generally had a good time. He liked women very much; before he knew Elizabeth, and during the time he was coming increasingly under her spell, he was veering between periods of sexual-social intensity and days when he felt (as he did on March 29, 1941): "I am sick of my present hectic life—the work, the miscellaneous loveless affairs and the mixed drinks. I wish I lived in a small provincial town and spent the evenings reading aloud the Victorian novelists to my wife and adoring daughters". He was curious about, attracted to, the more flamboyant elements in dislocated wartime London: "I suppose I ought to cultivate the society of solid civil servants instead of rococo Rumanian princesses and baroque dilettantes". Not a chance: the rococo and the baroque won every time. He was, while a shrewd, serious, and highly intelligent career diplomat on his way to the top, a romantic sensualist and, by his own admission, an aesthete. "Oh God", he wrote in his diary on December 17, 1941,

> let Cartiers and the Ritz be restored to their former glories. Let houseparties burgeon once more in the stately homes of England. Restore the vintage port to the clubs and the old brown sherry to the colleges. Let us have pomp and luxury, painted jezebels and scarlet guardsmen—rags and riches rubbing shoulders. Give us back our bad, old world.

Clever, gay, and gallant, with a love of talk and a "sensuous perception", he appealed and responded to these same things in Elizabeth. The relationship of each with London, with England, was not so very different either—he as an Anglo-Canadian, she as an Anglo-Irishwoman. Elizabeth's feelings for England were coloured always by the slightly romantic strangeness of its not being her native land; she could have used Charles's words about himself for herself—he saw, he said, things and people in England as "an outsider-insider—one immersed from boyhood in English life but not an Englishman".

They had both been brought up within tight social groups that looked to England as the source of what was best and right and worth fighting for. For even though Charles's family had been in Nova Scotia for four or five generations (Elizabeth's had been in County Cork for even longer), "the devotion to Crown and Empire was a romantic fidelity, quite different from the satisfied acceptance of the English by themselves as English". The Bowens' devotion to England had not in general been so intense or romantic; but the same condition prevailed for the Bowens, not belonging properly to the country of birth, separated by religion and interest and the walls of the demesne from the rest of Ireland. (When Elizabeth was taken by Terence de Vere White in 1947 to see the painter Jack Yeats in his studio, it was not a success, perhaps because the bringing together of two lions, especially in Ireland, is a tricky business; in any case, Yeats's comment was: "The English who settled in Cork remained English. They liked it because it seemed like a part of England. She was afraid I'd expect her to buy a picture". A strange thing to say of a member of a family who had owned land in Cork and lived continuously on it for three hundred years. But that is how it was.)

Both Charles and she owed their first allegiance to a "new" country looking for its identity, overshadowed in its history by the British connection. Even the way Charles in his diary characterised Canadians at a party is reminiscent of things said or felt about the Irish: "I do not think the English and Americans quite understand this sort of party. I sometimes think that the Canadians, who are at heart a sensitive, pugnacious, voluble and amorous race, are only released by whiskey". Elizabeth and Charles, both insiders-outsiders, "passed" in England on the very highest level; sometimes irritated by the English character, they were in a subtle sense secretly different, like spies. They were citizens of everywhere, and of nowhere—Elizabeth wrote to Charles:

> I think we are curiously self-made creatures, carrying our personal worlds around with us like snails their shells, and at the same time adapting to wherever we are. In a queer way I am strongly and idiosyncratically Irish in the same way that you are Canadian: cagey, recalcitrant, on the run, bristling with reservations and arrogances that one doesn't show.

Complex people, she had written in an essay on "Manners",[8] "are never certain that they are not crooks, never certain their passports are quite in order". Both, for all their style and panache, lived with insecurities and uncertainties; Charles described himself as a boy as a "vain, timid, harmless dreamer". With Elizabeth, Charles began to define himself; he wrote in December, 1942:

> Elizabeth has borne with all my attempts to play-act my life, although she has so little patience with histrionic characters, without ever making me feel a fool. She has shown me to myself—good money to some extent driving out bad.

While spending a lot of time with each other, they each spent a lot of time with other people as well, and both had work to do. In early 1943 Charles was wondering whether he should throw up his work as a diplomat and join the Army. Elizabeth thought that he might make "a useful soldier". She said that if he did, she would join the A.T.S. "I doubt if either of us will do either", wrote Charles. (He was right.) They talked about themselves. Charles asked her whether she thought it was possible to feel a "steady cold distaste" towards oneself; her answer was yes, if one had been over-praised for the wrong reasons. They talked about the intricate personal lives of women—a subject that interested Charles as much as Elizabeth—and the way in which women so often seem "to have the leisure to spin a cocoon of imaginings and questionings around their personal relationships", so that when a man blunders into this area he finds it "thoroughly mined beforehand". They shared, or Charles learnt to share with her, a distaste for that third-class emotion, guilt—a specifically middle-class complaint, Elizabeth told Charles. (Thirty-five years later, Charles was to say that, looking back on his life, what he chiefly regretted was the time spent anguishing over whether he ought to do something he knew he was going to do anyway.) Also, they found the same things funny.

From the loving grateful way Charles wrote in his diary about "dearest Elizabeth to whom I owe everything", it might seem that he was the chief beneficiary in the relationship.

But she no less than he had been restless, uncertain in her personal life over the past ten years. Charles for her became a "habitat", as Robert was for Stella in *The Heat of the Day*. Separated as they habitually were after the war by hundreds, or thousands, of miles, their life together was one of contrivance and provisionality; perhaps, in a way, this suited the people they were. Elizabeth settled, emotionally. Like Stella with Robert, in her novel: "To have turned away from everything to one face is to find oneself face to face with everything". Charles answered in her what Alan did not; but without Alan, Elizabeth would not have been the person capable of response. With both of them, sharing so much, she retained areas of reticence: "Every love has a poetic relevance of its own", she wrote in *The Heat of the Day*; "each love brings to light only what to it is relevant. Outside lies the junkyard of what does not matter".

Just before Christmas in 1942 Elizabeth and Charles went down to Wilsford, in Wiltshire, to stay the weekend with Stephen Tennant (the younger brother of Lord Glenconner), most of whose large house was now a Red Cross hospital; he had furnished a flat in it to suit his own extravagant taste.

> Such huge velvet sofas, piles of cushions and artificial
> flowers, chandeliers, such a disorder of perfumes, rouge
> pots and pomades, such orchid satin sheets and pink
> fur rugs, toy dogs and flounced silk curtains, mirrors
> at angles, shaded lights and scented fires.[9]

In the train on the way down, they found themselves sitting opposite Augustus John, wearing a tweed cap "which he removed to reveal that noble head of a moth-eaten lion". At Wilsford, they talked about writing, about how dialogue must always give clues, or counterpoints to clues; in that sense, Elizabeth said, every novel is a detective novel. They talked about sticky passages, and Elizabeth told them that when Virginia Woolf was writing her last book, *Between the Acts*,

she said, "For six weeks I have been trying to get the characters from the dining-room into the drawing-room and they are
still in the dining-room". Stephen Tennant before the war had
given legendary house-parties where the guests dressed up as
shepherds and shepherdesses, and were photographed by the
footman—all in the line of duty—as they postured and
gambolled. Elizabeth, who had been to Wilsford before (it
was there that she met E. M. Forster), was fond of Stephen,
who had a fine talent as an artist and longed, too, for literary
success. On one occasion, when Roger Senhouse, Raymond
Mortimer, and Stephen and Natasha Spender were there,
Stephen Tennant—all golden curls, ruffles, and bracelets—
read his own poetry aloud to the company after dinner. "That
is so beautiful I am going to read it again", he said. Only
kind Elizabeth remained totally patient and attentive during
the second reading. To Stephen, his "beloved Elizabeth
Bowen" seemed a calm, remote person: in comparison with
his own exuberance, and with that of some of his other friends,
she must have appeared so.

Christmas, 1943—a year later—Elizabeth and Charles
went together to the Christmas service at Westminster Abbey,
and both went back to join Alan for lunch at Clarence Terrace
—"cold duck and white Corton 1924". Elizabeth had been
to the Abbey on the morning of Christmas Day the previous
year as well, with a Colley cousin, and was moved to see the
place "packed with people from all over the Empire", as she
told Wingfield Colley—the Uncle Wink of her childhood. Her
identification with England in crisis was complete. Childlike,
she "revered and pored over" photographs of the Royal Family
that William Plomer sent her.

By mid-1944 Elizabeth and Charles had been close
enough for long enough for them to be conscious of their own
history: on May 7th they lunched at the Ritz, and "we talked
as we did when we first got to know each other. It was one
of those times which we shall both remember afterwards and

say to each other, 'That fine windy Sunday in spring when we lunched underground in the Ritz'." Always, she was conscious of being the same age as her century. In *A Time in Rome*, writing about Cellini, she said: "Twinship with one's century, as I know, somehow gives one the feeling of being hand-in-glove with it, which may make for unavowed extra confidence". During the war, this sense was accentuated; she says of Stella in *The Heat of the Day*, in a passage that reflects the title: "The fateful course of her fatalistic century seemed more and more her own; together had she and it arrived at the testing extremities of their noonday. Neither had lived before". The time in which they lived affected, determined, the nature of love:

> But they were not alone, nor had been from the start, from the start of love. Their time sat in the third place at their table. They were the creatures of history, whose coming together was of a nature possible in no other day—the day was inherent in the nature. Which must have always been true of lovers, if it had taken till now to be seen. . . . War at present worked at a thinning of the membrane between the this and the that, it was a becoming apparent—but then what else is love?

The war years were Elizabeth's noon, and *The Heat of the Day* the book that came out of it.

Psychologically, one of the results of the war for Elizabeth was the breaking down of boundaries and barriers. "It seems to me that during the war in England the overcharged subconsciousnesses of everybody overflowed and merged".[10] "Life with the lid on" was over for good, and a lifetime's policy of "not noticing" increasingly hard to maintain. It happened socially, as it did for all previously sheltered people, in a rather obvious way: in her neighbourhood, and in her work at the Warden's Post and on patrols, for example, she was brought into close contact with people she would not normally have become intimate with—girls like the butch Connie and feckless Louie in *The Heat of the Day*. But it goes further than this. She felt the "thinning of the membrane between the this and the that"; and wrote of the invisible presence—in mortuaries and under rubble—in bombed London of the unknown, uncounted dead, who "continued to move in shoals through the city day, pervading everything to be seen or heard or felt with their torn-off senses". The "wall between the living and the dead thinned", as did the wall between the living and the living, leading to an "instinctive movement to break down indifference while there was still time". Nearly all the short stories she wrote during the war (collected in *The Demon Lover*) have this element of time breaking down, a concept of London as a city of ghosts, as in "In the Square":

> Most of the glassless windows were shuttered or boarded up, but some framed hollow inside dark.
> The extinct scene had the appearance of belonging to some ages ago.

In "Pink May", a silly woman is haunted by what she thinks is a ghost, but sounds suspiciously like the voice of conscience —the faithless wife fumbling with a conflict that perhaps, under the circumstances, is not quite irrelevant:

> ". . . I mean, there are certain things that a woman who's being happy keeps putting out of her mind. (I mean, when she's being happy about a man.) And other things you keep putting out of your mind if your husband is *not* the man you are being happy about. There's a certain amount you don't ask yourself, and a certain amount that you might as well not remember. Now these were exactly the things [the ghost] kept bringing up. She liked to bring those up better than anything. . . ."

It is not only in London that the barriers of time and reality break down: in the stories "The Cheery Soul" and "Green Holly", ghosts walk in country houses used, or abused, for wartime purposes. Two major stories pit the pre-1914 distant past, with its spaciousness and grace and needle-sharp sensibilities, against the crude war-torn present. In "Ivy Gripped the Steps", a soldier revisits in requisitioned Folkestone (called, as usual, Southstone) a house where he used to stay as a young boy, his hostess a clever, charming widow; he had been half in love with her, half understanding her *amitié amoureuse* with a married man, and wholly manipulated by her. In "The Happy Autumn Fields", a girl in a bombed house dreams of—or dreams, simply—a family in the country, a large family of brothers and sisters and mama in the drawing-room and young love unacknowledged on an autumn afternoon half a century ago. The point about both these stories is that the memory, or the dream, has the texture and colour of actuality; it is the blasted present that is fragmentary, impossible, and therefore illusory. The realisation of the fragility of *things*—"tables and chairs"—made the whole city's fabric seem to Elizabeth like the gauzes of a stage-set; in "The Happy Autumn Fields" the dreamer awakes to the bombs:

> The house rocked: simultaneously the calico window split and more ceiling fell, though not on the bed. The enormous dull sound of the explosion died, leaving a minor trickle of dissolution still to be heard in parts of the house. . . .

The "calico" of the window may be the black-out curtain, but not solely; the same image comes again in *The Heat of the Day*, about the V-1 bombs—"droning *things*, mindlessly making for you, thick and fast, day and night, tore the calico of London, raising obscene dust out of the sullen bottom mind".

Where there are dreams there are also nightmares. In

the title story of the collection, "The Demon Lover", a woman checking up on her bombed house finds a message from a lover out of her distant past. He is coming to get her. Irrationally terrified, the woman, for whom this inexplicable message is like a message from hell, flees from the house into the empty scarred streets, the unoccupied houses meeting "her look with their damaged stare", and takes the first taxi she sees. As it careens off, she realises she hasn't "said where". She leans forward to knock on the glass panel separating her from the driver, and he turns to look at her:

> Mrs. Drover's mouth hung open for some seconds before she could issue her first scream. After that she continued to scream freely and to beat with her gloved hands on the glass all round as the taxi, accelerating without mercy, made off with her into the hinterland of deserted streets.

That is all. There is in that "screaming freely" the abandonment to terror that is the essence of every child's, and so every adult's, nightmare of someone "coming to get you". After the war, Iris Murdoch was sharing a taxi with Elizabeth, and when Elizabeth leant forward and knocked with her gloved hand on the glass partition to speak to the driver, Iris felt once again the atmosphere and the terror of "The Demon Lover". She said nothing of what she felt to Elizabeth, but held for a while in silence her gloved hand.

It is in the story "Mysterious Kôr" (which appeared first in John Lehmann's *New Writing*), harking back to the deserted city of Rider Haggard's *She*, that this conception of ghostly London is most striking, set in a night of full moon, in the light of which a pair of lovers walk, at the beginning, in empty Regent's Park:

> The futility of the black-out became laughable: from the sky, presumably, you could see every slate in the roofs, every whited kerb, every contour of the naked

winter flowerbeds in the park; and the lake, with its
shining twists and tree-darkened islands, would be a
landmark for miles, yes, miles, overhead.

But the Germans did not come now at the full moon; so to
the whiteness was added a total silence. The girl says:

"This war shows we've by no means come to the
end. If you can blow whole places out of existence, you
can blow whole places into it. I don't see why not.
They say we can't say what's come out since the bombing started. By the time we've come to the end, Kôr may
be the one city left: the abiding city. . . ."

Elizabeth was moving into a science fiction of the mind—as
the girl in the story, who has an "avid dream" in which Kôr
is more compelling than her lover; with him she looks down
the

wide, void, pure streets, between statues, pillars and
shadows, through archways and colonnades. With him
she went up the stairs down which nothing but moon
came; with him trod the ermine dust of the endless
halls, stood on terraces, mounted the extreme tower,
looked down on the statued squares, the wide, void,
pure streets. He was the password, but not the answer:
it was to Kôr's finality that she turned.

Till the proofs of *The Demon Lover* came and she reread all
the stories through together—"Mysterious Kôr" is placed last
—Elizabeth had not recognised that they had, as a collection,
"a rising tide of hallucination". She wrote about this in her
preface to the American edition; she said that the hallucinations in the stories were not a peril, nor were the stories studies
of mental peril. "The hallucinations are an unconscious, instinctive, saving resort on the part of the characters. . . . It is a
fact that in Britain, and especially in London, in wartime
many people had strange deep intense dreams". The fantasies,
and the dreams, of ordinary people were, she thought, con-

soling compensation for what she called the "desiccation" that war brought. Egotism had to go underground. The self-expression of every day was stopped—what to buy to eat, how to dress oneself, where to go—the choices were severely limited. "We all lived in a state of lucid abnormality", and Elizabeth's stories, though they deal with the particular and the personal, turn out to have expressed the experiences of many people. "Through the particular, in wartime, I felt the high-voltage current of the general pass".

She was functioning on a great many levels. There was this inner, imaginative world of her stories, and her novel. She wrote all through the war, and was a regular contributor to periodicals including *Horizon*, under the very personal editorship of Cyril Connolly, which ran for ten years from 1940. (*Horizon* seemed and seems a landmark of a periodical, perhaps because it was in its way and in its time fighting for beloved, threatened values; nothing, since its demise, has taken its place; the nearest contenders have been, in comparison, things without a voice, surviving not on hope but on subsidies.) There was the heightened social life of London and the occasional country visit away from the worst of the war; there was her life with Alan, and her life with Charles; there was fear and uncertainty, Virginia's death, the death of friends in the war, exhaustion, housekeeping difficulties, and the recurrent blasting of the house or its environs. Yet Edmund Wilson, in London at the end of the war, was impressed by the "good faith and sobriety" of the artistic and literary world, "dwindled and starved as it is":

> It was also reassuring and pleasant to hear Elizabeth Bowen say that, except for some disagreeable moments when "one of those humming things" had landed near her, she had enjoyed London during the war. "Everything is very quiet, the streets are never crowded, and the people one dislikes are out of town."[11]

Elizabeth, by staying in London and playing her part in the defence of London throughout the blitz, had earned the right to say she had enjoyed London during the war. She got off lightly only in that, unlike many women, she had no husband, brother, or son away fighting. Egalitarians might raise their eyebrows at Elizabeth's wartime existence as they might at Cynthia Asquith's, which Elizabeth characterized to Susan Tweedsmuir as being "an awful time with a household staff of semi-idiot refugees". The answer to this is that love, death, fear, and bombs are none of them respecters of persons. "Whatever you are these days", says the woman in "Pink May", "you are rather more so. That's one thing I've discovered in this war". Elizabeth—resilient, hard-working, and an enjoyer—was, in the war, "more so".

In the summer of 1944, 2 Clarence Terrace was hit by a series of blasts. On July 10th Elizabeth was wondering whether it was worth trying to put things straight again; but ten days later a last blast brought down all the ceilings and broke all the windows. She and Alan only escaped being killed by a chance. They moved out, at last. Charles wrote in his diary:

> It was the last house in London which still felt like a pre-war house. There was always good food, good talk and wine (as long as wine lasted) and a certain style. Then I liked the house itself with its tall airy rooms and good, rather sparse furniture. I suppose they will re-open it after the war if it is not hit again. Elizabeth's nerves have been under a terrible strain, but she is resilient and if she can get away and get some rest she will be all right. In the midst of it she is still frantically trying to write her novel.

She and Alan moved to a flat belonging to Clarissa Churchill (later Mrs. Anthony Eden) in a high modern block nearby. Almost at once, in the flat, Elizabeth began to write the short story "The Happy Autumn Fields", putting into it all her too recent knowledge of how it feels to have a house falling about your ears and, in the dreaming time-travel, escaping from it. "She told me about it", wrote Charles, "in an excited way while I lay on a sofa looking out at the sea of green tree tops with here and there an isolated high building". But by October Alan and she were back in Clarence Terrace, "so glad to be reinstated in what again seems a house", she told Susan Tweedsmuir a few months later, "that we have really nothing to grumble about".

The war in Europe was nearly over. The Home Guard had the order to "stand down"—Alan's part in the defence of London was done. At the beginning of 1945, Charles Ritchie, recalled to Ottawa, after a round of farewell parties, left London.

CHAPTER IX

After Noon

I n June, 1942, Charles Ritchie had written in his diary:

> I went to see Elizabeth this afternoon and found her
> standing on the balcony of her sitting-room that looks
> over Regent's Park. The tall, cool room is full of
> mirrors and flowers and books. She wants to dedicate
> her next novel to me. I hope she will, and that it will be
> her best. Later we walked out into Regent's Park. It was
> a blazing June day—we sat on the bank by the canal
> watching the swans "in slow indignation", as she says,
> go by.

The Heat of the Day is very much Charles Ritchie's novel, not
only because, as she had promised, Elizabeth dedicated it to
him. She put into it everything about London in wartime that
she had experienced at the time she first knew him; the involvement of the two main characters, Stella and Robert,
wartime lovers, made a parallel to their own attachment.

The Death of the Heart had opened with two people
walking in Regent's Park on an ice-bound winter's day. *The
Heat of the Day* also opens in the Park, but on a late September afternoon in 1942; there is a concert in the open-air
theatre that lies to one side of Queen Mary's rose gardens:
"Great globular roses, today at the height of their second
blooming, burned more as the sun descended, dazzling the

lake". At the entrance to these rose gardens there are—
still—high, beautiful, ornate wrought-iron gates; the couple
who met, in a desultory way, at the concert, drift together
out of "the lovely gate":

> Ahead one had still an illusion of wooded distance, out
> of whose blue and bronzy ethereality rose the tops of
> Regency terraces—these, in their semi-ruin, just less
> pale than the sky. They were shells; the indifference of
> their black vacant windows fell on the scene, the move-
> ment, the park, the evening they overlooked but did not
> seem to behold.

It was on a late September afternoon in 1941 that Elizabeth
and Charles looked at the rose gardens together. They had
been talking of those roses for days; then one perfect afternoon
she telephoned him to say that if they did not go that very
day it would be too late, the roses were almost over. Charles
put away the foreign office boxes in the safe, locked up, and
took a taxi to Regent's Park. Later he wrote:

> As we walked together I seemed to see the flowers
> through the lens of her sensibility. The whole scene,
> the misty river, the Regency villas with their walled
> gardens and damp lawns and the late September after-
> noon weather blended into a dream—a dream in which
> these were all symbols soaked with a mysterious associa-
> tive power—Regent's Park—a landscape of love. A
> black swan floating downstream in the evening light—
> the dark purplish-red roses whose petals already lay
> scattered—the deserted Nash house with its flaking
> stucco colonnade and overgrown gardens—all were
> symbols speaking a language which by some miracle
> we could understand together.

The Heat of the Day was a long time in the writing; it did not
finally come out until February, 1949, making a gap of eleven

years since the publication of her last full-length novel. The first five chapters had in fact been written by summer, 1944, and duplicates sent for safe keeping to Susan Tweedsmuir at Elsfield. But, as she told Lady Tweedsmuir, the protracted upsets of that V-1 summer made her feel that any work she did on the novel would probably not be of high quality, would betray the strain. So she concentrated on finishing the short stories for *The Demon Lover*, some of which had already appeared in periodicals, and that book was brought out—by Cape—in 1945. For Elizabeth did not stay with Gollancz; and after the war William Plomer returned to Cape as reader and editor, and looked after her interests there. It was thus the very subject of *The Heat of the Day*—the war—that held up the writing of it; and she did not really get down to finishing it until the war was over. She wrote to Charles in Canada in March, 1945, that she had thought it would only be necessary to glance through the early chapters, but she found in fact a fundamental necessity to rewrite. "I suddenly feel I know a lot more than I did. I have got the hang of what I meant":

> Any novel I have ever written has been difficult to write and this is being far the most difficult of all. . . . The thing revolves round and round in my brain like what you're at work at does in your brain. Almost anything that happens round me contributes to it.
>
> Sometimes I think this novel may be a point-blank failure but I shall still be glad to have tried. I would not in the least mind if this were my last shot, if I never wrote anything else again.
>
> It presents every possible problem in the world. In some parts of it even, it seems right to give an effect of garrulity or carelessness. A good deal is written already, much of what is still to be written must be point-blank melodrama. . . .

In a way the novel seems to have the same difficulties as making a film, if one were an ambitious
director; continuity, the to and fro between different
themes. . . . Some of it is quite funny. I don't mind
rather like broad Dickens-type burlesque funniness but
I do *loathe* and want to avoid a particular kind of
pursey irony—*coterie* irony.

The "Dickens-type burlesque funniness" that found its way
into *The Death of the Heart* in the Waikiki passages is indeed
also in this book, in the Connie-and-Louie routines and in the
Holme Dene sections, again here centering on a house and
its atmosphere, but a very different house. Waikiki was vulgar-
genteel, a house of noises and smells and spontaneous living;
Holme Dene is the very worst of English killjoy gentility, it is
"a man-eating house", "one of a monstrous hatch-out over
southern England in the 1900s", conceived to please and
appease middle-class ladies. It is a house of imitation old oak
and coffin-stools and screens and unopened bedrooms, with a
garden filled with gnomes and pergolas; a house where
sexuality is disallowed, where Muttikins, perpetually to be
appeased, sits in the vantage-point middle of the sitting-room,
knitting. It is a house of spiritual poverty: Anne, the little
girl parked out there, leads

> a pat little lifetime without moments, an existence
> among tables and chairs, without rapture or mystery,
> grace or danger. . . . Though she did not know it, she
> had never seen anyone being happy. . . . This was de-
> meaning poverty. Pity the children of the poor.

(Here "tables and chairs", the symbols of security, are presented as limitations in opposition to rapture, mystery, grace,
danger—but then the author knew that there are wilder and
wider things to be known once security has had to be abandoned.) Holme Dene is a house without privacy, where no

one can go and post a letter without a comment being made: a house of spies, a house to breed spies—Robert, the son of the house and a good man, is betraying his country.

Whereas Harrison—a bad man of no known abode—is on the track of Robert; Harrison, too, is a spy, but because he is on our side he is allowed to get away with it. Stella, to whose flat overlooking the Park both men come, learns only that for her personal loyalty overrides loyalty to country, and that one never knows the person one knows best. The character of Harrison, the counter-spy, fascinated Elizabeth most: "His vocabulary *and* his moral vocabulary keep presenting new possibilities and yet the other man, the heroine's lover, Robert, is still the problem character and the touchstone of the book".[1]

Others beside herself, when they read the novel, found Robert the "problem character". Tetchily, her friend Edward Sackville-West wrote that "it is difficult to see why Stella (whose attractiveness we never doubt) should have been drawn to so null a man. There are signs of fumbling here".[2] Even Alan, and his friend Eric Gillett, at dinner at Clarence Terrace, told her that Robert was unreal, a woman's idea of a man. Elizabeth was disappointed, tried to justify herself. "I can't agree with you", she said, and went off to bed early. Rosamond Lehmann wrote to Elizabeth:

> I *don't* agree with the critics who say Robert doesn't come off, doesn't live. To me he is absolutely solid: he had to be discovered through Stella, as we have to be kept guessing, in suspense. But I would feel happier if he had provided some more and more explicit, less abstract, self-documentation in their last scene. . . . What bothers me a little is that I cannot see why he shouldn't have been a Communist and therefore pro-Russian, pro-Ally, rather than pro-"enemy".

Rosamond Lehmann was moved to tears nevertheless by this novel; and she expressed the feelings of many of their generation when she told Elizabeth, "I suppose you must know, inside you, what you've done":

> The sustained excitement, the almost hyper-penetration, the pity and terror. It is a great *tragedy*. Oh, and the wild glorious comedy, the pictorial beauty, the unbearable re-creation of war and London and private lives and loves. You do, you really *do*, write about love. Who else does, today? . . . How proud Charles must be.

The Heat of the Day has its weaknesses: the character of Robert, and the introduction of "point-blank melodrama", which, much as Elizabeth hankered after it, was not a manner in which she wrote naturally—though in her later writing she had recourse to it—was seemingly forced into it, more and more. The war had made "mere" sensibility distasteful; she said that "these days one feels rather a revulsion against psychological intricacies for their own sakes". It was a fatal sign, she said, if one felt tempted to say to one's characters what used to be said to oneself during adolescence—"For heaven's sake stop fussing over yourself and try to get on with something more important!"[3] The blurring of the character of Robert is perhaps due to the fact that she had never before tried to portray an attractive man who was not something of a cad, or something of a cold fish, or a born uncle; Robert is in the genre of romantic anti-hero. Also, Robert must not "be" Charles, or be obviously based on Charles; and indeed the only ways in which, to the outsider, he seems to be Charles at all is in his height, his long elegant hands and head, the way he lies on a sofa in Stella's flat "extended at full length, narrow and Byzantine in the dressing-gown". Robert has the invisible qualities of both Charles and his creator, perhaps, in that he, too, is "cagey, recalcitrant, on the run, bristling with reservations and arrogances that one doesn't show". Elizabeth and Charles never actually discussed the resemblance or non-resemblance of Robert to Charles;

but they did have a good deal of talk together about the nature of treason and of the spy. Charles knew people who were working in M.I.6, several of them old friends of his. Elizabeth was fascinated by his accounts of their behaviour and personalities. There was one in particular—Elizabeth never actually met him—whose temperament and circumstances were not so different from those of Robert in the novel, although this particular man never in fact did anything treasonable.

As far as style is concerned in this most "narrative" of Elizabeth's novels to date, her contortionist manner of sentence construction is enough in evidence to be picked up by those who disapproved of it, as in the last sentence of a key chapter, where Stella is suddenly aware that Harrison is waiting outside her flat: "In the street below, not so much a step as the semi-stumble of someone after long standing shifting his position could be, for the first time by her, heard". Contorted, maybe, but effective: one hears that slight shifting of the feet on the pavement.

Daniel George, who read the novel in manuscript for Cape, wrote about her characteristic contortion—at its most noticeable in this novel—in his report. So far from seeing it as affected, or deliberately high-flown, he saw it as the extreme of colloquialism: she wrote so colloquially, he said, "that unless the reader is lucky enough to coincide with her in placing a stress on the key word of a sentence, he may be baffled completely".[4] (One is reminded here of Gerard Manley Hopkins and his "sprung rhythm", of which the same may be said.) In many instances it is just a matter of double negatives and of the habitual placing of the adverb before the verb on the "To whom do you beautifully belong?" model. This last was, perhaps, principally what made people continually compare her style with Henry James's. One sentence that Daniel George picked out for comment he called "almost more Jacobean than James". Elizabeth knew that in *The Heat of the Day* "his infection showed"; when questioned about it in the 1959 broadcast interview, she said that "you can't say it's like catching measles, because it's a splendid style, but it's a dangerous style". For all that, she could not read James's "more complicated" books: "I haven't ever read *The Ivory Tower*, he's quite beyond me there, I really belong to *Portrait of a Lady*".

Daniel George wrote four pages of notes on what he called "snags in the crystal stream" for her to think about, adding his own not unwitty comments. One sentence from the book—which she did not amend—was " 'Absolutely', he said with fervour, 'not'." His comment was "Far, I diffidently suggest, fetched".

She altered some but by no means all of the contortions he picked out. But she became sensitive to the problem. When she wrote her next novel, *A World of Love*, she asked Spencer Curtis Brown, the only person who had at that time read it, to make notes "on any of the inversions in sentences which struck you as overdone. I could alter them before the book goes to Cape. I *don't* want to develop stylistic tricks!" But Daniel George's criticism was all within the context of a reaction that was enthusiastic, eulogistic, and respectful: "She succeeds time and again in expressing what has hitherto been inexpressible. To read her novel . . . is to know that not all the rubbish one reads can finally corrupt one's taste".

The extreme emotion of Rosamond Lehmann's positive reaction to *The Heat of the Day*—too emotional, most of it, to be exposed to cold print—can only partly be explained by the kindly convention among this group of friends of writing long, rhapsodic letters to each other about each other's books (a convention counterbalanced by a quite uninhibited tendency to gossip about each other's personalities and private lives). Not only for Rosamond, the novel summed up and expressed the heightened emotions of those years of war; and for a later generation it is a time-defeating glimpse—even a "hallucination", in Elizabeth's terms—backwards into a London that is still the same London, however well the scars have healed, however spick the remaining Regency terraces now look. Elizabeth had told Charles, apropos of the Folkestone house she had used for "Ivy Gripped the Steps", that it always gave her "the oddest feeling to find anything *still* existing in real life after I have put it in a story". But she would see very little that has changed today, since the 1940s, in the rose gardens in Regent's Park. *The Heat of the Day* has become the classic novel of London in the war; perhaps only *Caught*, by her friend Henry Green, can be discussed on the same level.

Among the many shortages of the war, there was, for Elizabeth, a shortage of money. On two occasions she had to ask her agents, Curtis Brown, to guarantee her overdraft at the bank (she kept her account where she had first banked, as a girl living with Aunt Laura, in Harpenden) on the strength of royalties expected from Cape. Her bills included those for the repair of ravaged Clarence Terrace—no government compensation for war damage was paid until after the war. *The Heat of the Day* did very well; 45,000 copies were sold almost at once in England, and in the United States it did very well indeed—it was a choice of the Literary Guild, which assured Elizabeth of a sizeable lump-sum payment.

As a journalist, and reporting for the Ministry of Information, Elizabeth was more free to travel during the war than many people. She wrote about the Channel ports on the Kent coast of her childhood, about Folkestone where, after France fell, the residents moved out and the Army moved in. She wrote about Dover, in the days before the Allies invaded occupied France in 1944. She noticed that Dover people spoke of the opposite coastline as "the German coast": "When they once more speak of 'the French coast' that will

mean something." A month before V-E Day—the end of the
war in Europe—she was in Hythe, where she had lived with
her mother, and found it "its nice self", halfway between
front-line conditions and normal. She told Charles: ·

> Small shops gradually re-opening, residents creeping
> back to the rather pleasant villas clustered in gardens
> all the way up the hill. The sea front is "open" again;
> the miles of coils of rusty barbed wire snipped away and
> flung back. Soldiers about still, but not so many. I like
> the narrow, steep-roofed High Street, so quiet now that
> one hears nothing but rooks in the early morning. . . .

Britain was nearly ready to pick up her life again. The last
days before V-E Day were emotionally trying—the last days
before the outbreak of peace, as Elizabeth said, becoming
more and more like the days before the outbreak of war.
"A sort of general paralysis and apprehension, and everyone
wondering what they ought to *do*. It's a pity there's no reverse
equivalent of trying on gas-masks, which so pleasantly filled
so many hours in 1939". She was writing to Charles from
Faringdon, Lord Berners's country house; from her open
bedroom window she could hear the fountain playing in the
stone basin in the middle of the lawn. The fountain playing
was an event; it had been turned off all through the war.

> After lunch we all went out and stood on the terrace;
> Robert [Heber-Percy] did something to the fountain;
> there was a breathless pause, then a jet of water, at first
> a little rusty, hesitated up into the air, wobbled, then
> separated into four curved feathers of water. It was so
> beautiful and so sublimely symbolic—with the long
> view, the miles of England, stretching away behind it,
> that I found myself weeping. I think a fountain is much
> nicer than a bonfire; if less democratic.
>
> Afterwards we began talking about fountains—
> Versailles, and Rome, and the Villa d'Este fountains at

Tivoli. They run through all the happy Latin spectacular parts of one's life. May you and I, soon, look at a fountain together.

V-E Day, when it came that May of 1945, and the days following it, were for Elizabeth in London "great and beautiful".[5] The whole city seemed to leave the ground—"On a monster scale it was like an experience in love. Everything, physically—beginning and ending with the smell of sweat, so strong and so everywhere that it travelled all through this house by the open windows—was against exultation, and yet it happened". The night before, the nine o'clock B.B.C. news had announced that the next day was, definitely, V-E Day. It was a dark, gloomy Monday night with, by midnight, thunderstorms.

> I switched off the wireless and said to Alan, "Well, the war's over," and he said, "Yes, I know," and we gave short gloomy satirical laughs, went into the dining-room and sat on the window-sill for about an hour, quite unable to rally, he furious because he hadn't made any arrangements about his office, and I furious because I hadn't got any flags. The park looked as dark as a photograph and was quite empty; and I thought, well, I knew one would feel like this.

Later, following a white blaze in the sky, they went out and found Marylebone Town Hall floodlit, "looking so exactly like a building in heaven that I burst into tears". A few people were moving about, very silently, "like shoals of fish", slow and incredulous. (Elizabeth wept from exaltation; she rarely wept in adversity.)

On V-E Day itself, Elizabeth found some banners (with the wrong king's head on), finished writing a broadcast for the B.B.C. French service and a *Tatler* piece that were both due, and gave lunch to Hester Chapman and Clarissa Churchill, "who were coming to lunch anyway". It wasn't till evening that they went out to see the town. Elizabeth was determined to get to Westminster Abbey.

> Almost all the girls walked as though they were wear-ing new and much too tight Victory shoes, but were now exalted beyond minding; and aging unloved-looking groups of women drifted along smiling almost bridal smiles, with coquettish bows of tricolour ribbon or miniature Mad Hatter top hats on their hair. A very stout woman bursting out of a flowered silk dress stood by herself in the middle of Oxford Circus and beauti-fully swung a clapper round and round, undeterred by the fact that its noise could only be heard in the brief intervals between the disporting bombers. The pubs were not yet open and everybody was still strictly sober. . . . Almost everybody wore a curious limpidity of expression, like newborn babies or souls just after death. Dazed but curiously dignified. As you know, I do in general loathe Demos: I don't think anybody has less warm feelings or fewer illusions than I have. But after a *crise* (which happened quite early on) of hysterical revulsion and tiredness, I passed beyond, like the girls in the tight shoes, and became entered by a rather sublime feeling.

Neither the upper classes nor the intelligentsia were to be seen on the streets. "The intelligentsia, I learned later, remained in bed, drank and thought. I must say that I drank a good deal". The walk to the Abbey and back was exhausting: back in Clarence Terrace Elizabeth kicked off her shoes and "lay on the floor moaning". At the other end of the terrace there was a bonfire—nice to see the dilapidated façade blush "in flames that were *not* the flames of war". All the celebrations in fact struck Elizabeth as a "hilarious parody of war". Elizabeth's cook made her way all by herself to join the great crowd outside Buckingham Palace: "I shouldn't be surprised if a very large proportion of those crowds weren't composed of heroic solitary people . . . with a great capacity for being devout, a great power of exaltation, and perhaps not much private life". Her maid Nancy went round in a "gay and grand way" with an Irish-American cousin in the U.S. Army who turned up opportunely. "I was so glad; as she has really been an angel throughout the war".

The day after V-E Day, Elizabeth and Alan went to the wedding of one of her Warden's Post girl-friends; and it was that night that the best thing of all happened for Elizabeth. Coming back at midnight from a dinner party arranged some weeks before, she was walking home alone and "saw the searchlights": they were performing a sort of ballet in the sky, "each one staggered and whirled around the sky, scribbled, darted, and crashed into others". They whirled and twisted and then the tips would meet, as they used to on nights when they were pin-pointing an enemy plane, but this time it looked like "a drunken collapse against one another for support. They also managed to look extremely lewd". She had been standing in Grosvenor Square; now she began to walk on home. When she was halfway down Baker Street, the searchlights changed their pattern, each one sending up a vertical pillar of light, so that "the whole of the darkness above London became a Gothic cathedral". Finally they made their light drip downwards, like white rain, like icicles. Few people, tired out by the past two days' celebrations, were about to see it. The searchlights were Elizabeth's—and her Kôr's—personal celebration:

> I suppose that everyone, in those two days, found one thing that was in *their* own language, and seemed to be speaking to them, specially. The searchlights were mine. For me they were the music of the occasion.

Her sense of occasion moved her, in that week of victory, to write a grateful letter—almost amounting to a testimonial

—to Cyril Connolly. She had been asking herself, she told him, who apart from Churchill had been the people of stature during the war, the people to whom "one owes something better than mere survival", who made of that time a positive experience instead of "deteriorating dead loss":

> I thought, and think, of you: I know that many of us owe you a lot, and I do certainly. *Horizon* has been most valuable of all as evidence of continuity; and you've done so much for this continuity in your person. Your parties had something more than even your and Lys's beautiful hospitality can account for, and something without which even intellectual happiness would be desperate: real spirit. (I mean, obviously, not spirituality or spiritedness, but spirit.) But there's something beyond *Horizon* and the parties: it is reassuring even when one does not see you to know you are somewhere about the town. There has been no one else who, since 1939, has been, done and made just what, indefinably but outstandingly, you have. Yet, you *could* have been yourself and not done it.

And to William Plomer, who had spent the war years in naval intelligence at the Admiralty, she said:

> I know no one who has been more completely incarcerated and at the same time made less fuss. People who were never doing anything of the slightest importance, interest or value to themselves or anybody have been the ones who have gone on about "interrupted lives".

However, she said, criticism did not come well from her, who had had such a good war; "I cannot say I'm ashamed of the fact, as I don't think I had a good war at anybody else's expense". She was writing to William from Bowen's Court, at the end of that first post-war summer. In Ireland there were still no private cars on the road, owing to lack of petrol, and it was very quiet. She had come over in June, "feeling like death, full of visitations and repugnances": the arrival had been, as it often was, haunted; and it was raining. She wrote to Charles, the day after:

> The stillness and the silence for the first few hours are like something dripping on one's nerves, almost uncanny. And the strong, strange, indoor smell of the house. At first it never seems anything to do with *me*. More like something arrived at in the middle of a *bois dormant.* I should never be surprised as I first walk in to find ferns growing on the staircase or a mythical animal crouching outside my bedroom door. Considering how frightened I am in general of the supernatural, it's extraordinary that I am not very frightened; in fact never frightened here.

On the way she had stopped in Dublin, watched a cricket match at Trinity College between Trinity and Sir John Maffey's eleven, had gone to the sports and garden party next day: "Many beautiful elderly men in tops hats, a band playing Gilbert and Sullivan, and a great deal of charming, dowdy, feminine finery, sunshine, and large crowds filtering about under the College trees". It was the first "function", she realised, she had attended since 1939. Once at Bowen's Court, she and Alan had recovered strength working out of doors, clearing nettles and undergrowth. Elizabeth enjoyed this sort of thing; she felt she had the makings of a better forester than gardener—"plenty of brute strength and aggressive instinct, but the reverse of green fingers". Elizabeth and Alan stayed on at Bowen's Court, that first season of rest and freedom, until November.

In spite of Elizabeth's intense identification with London during the war, Ireland and Bowen's Court and her own Irish-

ness constantly counterpointed a life that was already complicated to pressure-point. At the very beginning of the war, she
was in her work searching into her family's past and into
Ireland's past in two books, both of which came out in 1942.
The lesser of these was *Seven Winters*, a forty-eight-page
evocation of the Dublin half of her childhood, published in
a limited edition by the Cuala Press, in Dublin, and by Longmans, in London, the following year. The memories recorded
in *Seven Winters* were a spin-off from the more important
book, *Bowen's Court*, a history of the Bowens in County Cork
from the arrival of Cromwell's colonel to the departure of
Elizabeth and her mother for England and, finally, the death
of her father. While the house, and the family in the house,
is the centre of the book, it necessarily encompasses the history
of Ireland, both on a local and a national scale, and is—on
the side, as it were—an extraordinarily fair account of England's dealings with Ireland and vice versa, and of her own
people, the Anglo-Irish, and of their relations with both the
English and the true Irish. "The stretches of the past I have
had to cover have been, on the whole, painful; my family
got their position and drew their power from a situation that
shows an inherent wrong".

She began writing *Bowen's Court* in the early summer of
1939, before war broke out; she finished it in December,
1941. The shattering change in the conditions in which she
wrote had its effect on what and how she wrote. When she
was describing ruined houses in County Cork, there were still
few ruins in England "other than those preserved in fences
and lawns". Later, she was writing about a home and a way
of life that seemed unchanging at a time when all homes and
all lives were threatened. The disparity between her subject
and the times in which she was writing focussed her vision.
Researching, intuiting, dreaming her ancestors' lives, she
stressed, she said in retrospect, those factors dominant in the

Bowens which seemed to her dominant in the world in which she wrote:

> For instance, subjection to fantasy and infatuation with the idea of power. While I was studying fantasy in the Bowens, we saw how it had impassioned race after race. Fantasy is toxic: the private cruelty and the world war both have their start in the human brain.[6]

But she keeps her balance; she does not fall into the trap of seeing "fairly ordinary Anglo-Irish gentry" as anything other than what they were. She wrote in an afterword to *Bowen's Court*, twenty years later, what may be the last adequate assessment of the old Anglo-Irish country gentry ever to be made by one of their number—for the reason that there are few left with the perception or the opportunity to make it except at second hand and by report. Elizabeth, looking at the Bowens from the vantage point of the 1960s, characterised her race and class and the society to which she had as a child belonged:

> If they formed a too grand idea of themselves, they did at least exert themselves to live up to this: even vanity involves one kind of discipline. If their difficulties were of their own making, they combatted these with an energy I must praise. They found no facile solutions; they were not guilty of cant. Isolation, egotism and, on the whole, lack of culture made in them for an independence one has to notice because it becomes, in these days, rare. . . . To live as though living gave them no trouble has been the first imperative of their make-up; to do this has taken a virtuosity into which courage enters more than has been allowed. In the last issue, they have lived at their own expense.

Stylishness, vanity, discipline, energy, lack of cant, independence, courage: these qualities were very much Elizabeth's own. The last sentence only gives one pause: psychologically, it may well be true of the Anglo-Irish; socially and economically, it is, to say the least, questionable.

She worked on the last chapter of *Bowen's Court* alone at Bowen's Court, in the quiet of the countryside, with only the wireless in the library to remind her that Europe was at war. It seemed very far away. The house and demesne were the very image of continuity: "I suppose that everyone, fighting or just enduring, carried within him one private image, one peaceful scene. Mine was Bowen's Court. War made me that image out of a house built of an anxious history".[7]

Elizabeth's duties as an air-raid warden were not the only work, apart from her writing, that she undertook during the war. She was involved, for example, in the P.E.N. conference of 1941 about helping writers in the Axis countries. And she was only able to get to Bowen's Court at all during the war —referred to in neutral Ireland as the "Emergency"—because of what she called her Activities. She had written in 1940 to the Ministry of Information to ask if she could be of any help with regard to Ireland: briefed by Harold Nicolson, she made her first "intelligence mission" that July. When it came to the point, she was nervous, and told Virginia Woolf:

> I hope I shall be some good: I do feel it's important. As far as my own feeling goes I feel low at going away. . . . It will all mean endless talk, but sorting out talk into shape might be interesting. I suppose I shall also finish my book [*Bowen's Court*]. But Ireland can be dementing, if one's Irish, and may well be so now. If there's to be an invasion of Ireland, I hope it may be while I'm there—which I don't mean frivolously, but if anything happens to England while I'm in Ireland I shall wish I'd never left, even for this short time. I

suppose the Ministry will give me a come-and-go permit.

After a couple of further Activities visits, by January, 1941, she knew what to expect:

In Dublin I get engaged in deep and rather futile talks; it is hard to remember the drift afterwards though I remember the words. I suppose that (smoke-screen use of words) is a trick of the Irish mind. They are very religious. It is the political people I see mostly: it seems a craggy dangerous miniature world.

She couldn't write about it all, she told Virginia, but would like to talk *"very much"*.

What she was chiefly engaged in was ascertaining Irish attitudes to the war, specifically in the question of the Treaty Ports in the south and west of Ireland, to which Churchill tried to persuade de Valera to allow Britain access. Elizabeth in her report about this stressed that any hint of violation of Ireland—that is, any attempt to take them by force, anything approximating an invasion—might well be used to reinforce enemy propaganda. Ireland, she said, was desperately afraid of becoming involved in the war:

That Ireland might lease her ports without being in-volved in war, is a notion that the popular mind here cannot grasp. I have spoken of the horrific view held here of the Nazi bombing of England. To the popular mind here "being involved in war" now conjures up only one picture, a bombing of Ireland. . . . One air raid on an Irish city would produce a chaos with which in the long run England would have to cope.[8]

In her report she castigated the Anglo-Irish for presenting themselves as England's stronghold in Ireland. If they merged their interests with the Irish people, she said, they could make Ireland a very much more solid and possible country with which to deal.

Lord Cranborne, who passed on Elizabeth's findings to Churchill, noted that her Ministry of Information reports had been "sensible and well balanced". Elizabeth saw Lord Cranborne at the Dominions Office in February, 1941; he listened to her with "sympathetic and charming Cecil politeness". (He was David Cecil's brother.) Getting into the Dominions Office was half the battle; she and her taxi-driver were challenged by bayonets while she stated her business. Once inside, "there were outer courts of rooms of gentlemen-secretaries and files, then his room, which was nice and long, with boarded-up windows, a stretch of Turkey carpet, a roaring fire". Just what she had imagined, in fact. At the War Office, however, also on an Irish errand, she had found everyone at eleven o'clock in the morning drinking glasses of milk, "which *was* something I had not imagined", she said (in what turned out to be the last letter she ever wrote to Virginia Woolf, the thank-you letter for her last visit to Rodmell).

There was, sadly, a gap, however lovingly bridged, between those "in the war" and those in Ireland leading relatively unchanged lives. "I loved hearing about your threshing", wrote Elizabeth to Noreen Butler, perfectly sincerely, in the letter in which she described the blitz of September, 1940; and she hoped that her husband Gilbert's gastric flu was better. These seem small dramas in comparison with fallen ceilings and Londoners' lives lost. Elizabeth told Noreen how glad she would be to be in Ireland for a little peace and quiet—"on the other hand I don't want to leave A. or anybody or anything for an indefinite period, with communications so bad and the Blitzkrieg on". Elizabeth wrote about the gap in "Sunday Afternoon", a story in *The Demon Lover*: a man, briefly visiting Ireland from London, is asked if he must go back there; he is having tea on the sunlit lawn of an Irish

TOP: *Florence Colley, Elizabeth's mother, around the time of her engagement to Henry Cole Bowen, Elizabeth's father, seen at right as a young man.* ABOVE: *Elizabeth (left) and her cousin Audrey Fiennes; at right, Elizabeth, six years old.*

TOP: *Florence Bowen, Elizabeth's mother, and Elizabeth, aged about three.* ABOVE: *Henry Cole Bowen at Bowen's Court, and at right, 15 Herbert Place, Dublin, where Elizabeth was born.*

TOP: *Meet of the Duhallow Hunt at Bowen's Court.* ABOVE: *The Pink Room, Bowen's Court, in the 1950s.*

Alan Charles Cameron, Elizabeth's husband, in middle age.

Elizabeth as a young woman.

TOP: *Sean O'Faolain and Elizabeth at Bowen's Court in the late 1930s.* ABOVE: *Elizabeth opening the door of 2 Clarence Terrace, 1946; at right: Charles Ritchie in the 1940s.*

ABOVE: *Alan Cameron studying the map.* TOP: *Elizabeth with Howard Moss at Bowen's Court.*

OPPOSITE, TOP: *Elizabeth in the kitchen at Bowen's Court with Molly O'Brien (right) and Mary.* OPPOSITE, BELOW: *With Mrs. Cleary of the village shop in Farahy; the annual settling of the Bowen's Court account was a matter of some ceremony.* ABOVE: *Elizabeth with gardener Eddie Flynn at Bowen's Court.*

ACROSS THE TOP: *Parties at Bowen's Court in the 1950s—from left, Lady Ursula Vernon, Jim Egan, Mary Delamere, Elizabeth, Stephen Vernon, Iris Murdoch. Opposite page—from left, Maurice Craig, Iris Murdoch, Eddy Sackville-West, Elizabeth, Hubert Butler.*

OPPOSITE, BELOW: *Formality—a studio portrait, 1950.* ABOVE: *Informality—in the country with a friend.*

TOP: *With Cyril Connolly outside Carbery, her last house, in Church Hill, Hythe.* ABOVE: *In Regent's Park, 1946.*

Elizabeth at Bowen's Court.

TOP: *Elizabeth at the home of Alfred and Blanche Knopf in Purchase, New York, 1950.* ABOVE: *In America in 1963.*

Elizabeth at 2 Clarence Terrace.

One of the last photographs of Elizabeth Bowen.

country house. He replies that this is only a holiday, and "anyway, one cannot stay long away". At once he realises "how subtly this offended his old friends. Their position was, he realised, more difficult than his own. . . ."

The difference between a country at war and a country out of the war, to a visitor from England, was immediately apparent, if only because of the absence of black-out. She wrote in her history of the Shelbourne Hotel about those memorable wartime arrivals on the mail-boat; the uniforms of belligerent nations were not permitted in Ireland, so soldiers had to do a quick change into mufti at Holyhead. Nearing harbour, the travellers crowded on deck to behold "the lights of Ireland under the fading outline of the hills"; and once at the Shelbourne itself, those travellers were treated with soothing, nursery solicitude by the hotel staff, it being "the rooted belief of all chambermaids that those arriving from London were to be treated as casualties from bomb-shock". Stella in *The Heat of the Day*, crossing the Irish Channel to visit her son's inherited house, Mount Morris, was greeted, like Elizabeth on her Activities trips, by the unaccustomed display of lights:

> The exciting sensation of being outside war had concentrated itself round those fearless lights—though actually, yesterday night as her ship drew in, the most strong impression had been of prodigality; around the harbour water, uphill behind it, the windows had not only showed and shone but blazed, seemed to blaze out phenomenally; while later, dazzling reflections in damp streets made Dublin seem to be in the throes of a carnival.

On an Activities trip to Dublin in 1942 ("Miss her even more than last time", noted Charles; "I am getting dependent on her"), Elizabeth was interviewed for *The Bell*, an Irish monthly founded by Sean O'Faolain two years earlier. She had contributed to the first number an essay called "The Big House", describing and defending the atmosphere and ethos of houses such as Bowen's Court; she was working on her Bowen's Court book when she wrote it, but it seems, too, like a continuation of the first topics that she and Sean had discussed. The interviewer was Larry Morrow—alias "the Bellman". He talked to her in the Shelbourne, and wrote up their conversation in an ironically sprightly manner. His description of her physical appearance is in keeping with his view of her as "primarily an aristocrat":

> If you know your Holbein even tolerably well, you will have seen Elizabeth Bowen many times—in a dozen or so of family portraits. Indeed, the only thing about her appearance not wholly Holbein is the colour of her eyes—which looks as if it had been scooped from the Irish sea on a stormy day. She is, in fact—if she will forgive me—the synthesis of all the Holbein family portraits, even to that delicate rose-pink of the cheeks and the upper lip that is not so much a colour as a tinted shadow or the bloom on some rare fruit out of season. Altogether, there is the flat delicacy of tone about her . . . the lines that are not so much painted as etched on the canvas; the long, heavily-knuckled fingers; the high, almost boyish cheekbones; the upper lip, rose-petal coloured, slightly curled, showing the velvet side; the ring, the bracelet, the ear-rings of whorled dulled gold, which in some curious way seem to be not so much ornaments as part of the wearer's body. Even about her clothes—the floppy hat of dark brown felt, the folds of biscuit-coloured linen dress—there is the same timelessness. Even about her endless cigarette-smoking.

It is hard to see anything very Tudor or timeless in "endless cigarette-smoking"; yet his reference to her Holbein look, whether or not it was the Bellman's own thought, is apt. Alan Cameron had chosen to hang reproductions of Holbein portraits in his rooms at Oxford, as an undergraduate; in marrying Elizabeth, he married a face whose configurations he already knew and admired.

The Bellman and Elizabeth talked about the as-yet-unwritten Great Irish Novel. (Thinking as they were in Balzacian terms, neither of them seems to have considered *Ulysses* as a contender.) There was material, Elizabeth said, for an Irish *comédie humaine* in almost every small Irish town. "When that really Great Irish Novel comes to be written, I fancy you'll find that it has been written by a Protestant who understands Catholicism and who, very probably, has made a mixed marriage". Inevitably, the Bellman brought up the question of whether she herself was really an *Irish* writer at all. "There are people in this town", he said, "who refuse to admit . . ." Elizabeth dealt with this one very firmly:

> I regard myself as an Irish novelist. As long as I can remember, I've been extremely conscious of being Irish —even when I was writing about very un-Irish things such as suburban life in Paris or the English seaside. All my life I've been going backwards and forwards between Ireland and England and the Continent, but that has never robbed me of the strong feeling of my nationality. I must say it's a highly disturbing emotion. It's not—I *must* emphasise—sentimentality.

She turned the question a little by emphasising that it was the French novelists and the French short-story writers who had, in any case, most influenced her, and not the English. The Bellman's time was up: "Miss Bowen caught me in her sea-green eye and I sank full fathom five. As I was going down for the third time, I caught sight of a page-boy stooping before her with a silver tray on which lay a visiting card. It was obviously the cue for my departure".[9]

As to her Irishness—would she have given the same answer to the same question in England? Most probably, even in that close wartime community. The very strength of her identification with London at war heightened the tension always latent in the Irish/English duality, dormant in peaceful times when she was free to take or leave either world. Her consciousness of being Irish could be, as she said at the Shelbourne, an "intensely disturbing emotion". Why it mattered so much where her loyalties lay, why it was so inevitable that Dublin should ask of a major novelist "But just how *Irish* is she?" is a function of the relation between the two nationalities: "a mixture of showing-off and suspicion, nearly as bad as sex", she called it in *The House in Paris*.

Already before the war ended, Elizabeth had said to Charles, about London: "It is no doubt an old and interesting city but to me it has come unstuck". Had it not been for the war, it might have happened earlier. After the war, and with Churchill—whom she admired enormously—out of office, the pull of Ireland was even stronger. In 1948 she said that she felt increasingly Irish—"I suppose as one grows older one reverts to type". But already in that first post-war summer at Bowen's Court in 1945, she had given her opinion of the new England to William Plomer with a trenchancy that defies comment:

Selfishly speaking, I'd much rather live my life here [i.e., at Bowen's Court]. I've been coming gradually unstuck from England for a long time. I have adored England since 1940 because of the stylishness Mr. Churchill gave it, but I've always felt, "when Mr. Churchill goes, I go". I can't stick all these little middle-class Labour wets with their Old London School of Economics ties and their women. Scratch any of those cuties and you find the governess. Or so I have always found.

Patrician hysteria over Atlee's victory had its unattractive side; also its romantic one. Elizabeth's sentiments find their counterparts at every crisis in recorded history; her feelings—if not her expression of them—are those of Edmund Burke, who wrote in the authentic rhetoric of reaction on the death of Marie Antoinette:

> But the age of chivalry has gone. That of sophisters, economists and calculators has succeeded; and the glory of Europe is extinguished for ever.[10]

E B

CHAPTER X

New Directions

A LAN'S DETERIORATING HEALTH was one reason why they planned to spend more time in Ireland. His eye trouble —dating from trench poisoning in the 1914–18 war—was getting worse. He had always had one good eye and one bad eye; the good eye was now affected by cataract, not yet by 1945 at the operable stage. He had to resign his post at the B.B.C. "He has had a terrific tribute", Elizabeth told William Plomer, "of not only affectionate but professionally appreciative letters from a lot of people in the educational world, since his retirement was announced. I'm glad, as he really has worked like a Trojan, and I don't think he ever realises how high people rate him". They planned to spend half the year at Bowen's Court, and half at Clarence Terrace, letting the two top floors.

Alan did not retire completely. During the following seven years, he returned to work as educational adviser for E.M.I.,* carrying through a scheme for educational gramophone records. He knew a lot about music, was one of the editors of the *Oxford History of Music on Record* and a governor of the British Institute of Recorded Sound. But his failing sight was a wretched handicap. And he was drinking too much, and was overweight; and his heart was not strong.

Elizabeth was not alone among her friends in finding

* Britain's giant entertainment conglomerate.

post-war London depressing. They were now middle-aged, and made a close, rather recessive group. Elizabeth wrote a funny, fantastic little story in 1946 (published in *The Listener*, and then in her collection *A Day in the Dark*) called "Gone Away", in which old-style English gentry—the vicar, and a collection of well-bred ladies—are kept in their "natural surroundings" in a Reserve, like Red Indians, as an amenity and an entertainment for the dwellers in the geometrical, glass-and-concrete new city.

They had survived the war, but now they had to survive the peace. Cyril Connolly expressed the impasse of this generation in an ironic piece in 1949 called "London Letter",[1] which begins, by the way, as a parody of one of Elizabeth's lyrical Regent's Park passages, with the park smelling of new grass, "the crocus carpets on display", and so on, and then:

> . . . while as night falls other cries mingle with those of the waterfowl, contraceptives reappear in the gutters, a body (making the third unsolved murder in Regent's Park) is found in the thirteen-acre garden of Barbara Hutton's featureless house. . . .

Connolly imagines that a keen young American novelist, "we will call him Harold Bisbee", in London for the first time, is ready to absorb the cultural scene. At his first literary cocktail party he will observe four facts about English writers: "They are not young, they are not rich, they are even positively shabby; on the other hand they seem kind and they look distinguished. . . . No one, certainly, can be in this for the money". And who, in 1949, *are* the English writers?

> The Sitwells are generally in the country but Mr. Eliot will probably be there accompanied by Mr. John Hayward (Dr. Johnson disguised as Boswell) and they already convey an atmosphere particularly English to the gathering (not angels but Anglicans, as Gregory said). Towering over the rest are Mr. Stephen Spender

and Mr. John Lehmann, two eagle heads in whose expressions amiability struggles with discrimination (Bisbee's European visit will largely depend on their summing-up). About nine inches below them come the rank and file, Mr. Roger Senhouse, Mr. Raymond Mortimer, Mr. V. S. Pritchett, Miss Rose Macaulay, Miss Elizabeth Bowen, Quennell, Pryce-Jones, Connolly, we are all there.[2]

But why, Bisbee will wonder, is Dylan Thomas the youngest person present? Where are the under-thirties?

There was no clear answer to what had gone wrong for "this trusting group of middle-aged friends". Was it the fault of their schools, the families, the war? "Is it taxation? Is it the Socialist Government? Is the Government not Socialist enough?" Or was it the uncertainty of living "*entre trois guerres*"? Whatever "it" was, it was apparent to all of them. Evelyn Waugh, after a dinner party at the Connollys in January, 1948, at which Elizabeth was a fellow guest, noted the good food but also a deterioration in Cyril: he saw *Horizon* failing (it in fact folded at Christmas, 1949—only contributions inexorably kept on coming in, "like suicide's milk", said its editor), and Cyril's increasing subjection to "inertia, luxury, and an insane longing to collect rare things".[3]

Evelyn Waugh himself was in the ascendant; *Brideshead Revisited*, which came out the year the war ended, was a critical and commercial success. Elizabeth adored it: she wrote to Charles Ritchie that "I haven't had such a reaction to any (contemporary) novel for a long time. . . . As a whole it did seem to me superbly and triumphantly romantic, with that sort of shimmer of the past (or rather, the shimmer one's own feeling can cast on the past) over it all". She thought it stirred up "overpowering sensuous emotion", like parts of Proust, and captured "the climate of love".

Brideshead was the last really prize-winning bloom that

the modern Mandarins produced. "Mandarin" here is a Connolly term, used of artists believing in the importance of their art, in grace and subtlety and sensuality and sensibility and romantic individualism: Proust, Henry James, Virginia Woolf, E. M. Forster, Elizabeth Bowen. At its worst it leads to inflation of language and of imagination, to affectation and to all manner of silliness. Proustians developed "a wool-winding technique in friendship, an indefatigable egotism in affairs of the heart, combined with a lively social ambition".[4] The mode could only flourish within an élite highly educated in a one-sided way. Snow's *Two Cultures* debate pin-pointed this one-sidedness.

The authentic "shimmer of the past" that Elizabeth caught in *Brideshead* had also something of the iridescence of decay. Irony, parody, nostalgia remained to the Mandarins. The modern world was inimical to writers who loved, "and ought to love", wrote E. M. Forster firmly, "beauty and charm and the passage of the seasons". (The very word "charm" has a period air; that quality became suspect.) The merits of the writers in English who overtook the Mandarins in the 1950s are not here at issue; nor were they a homogeneous group; and Mandarins are by no means extinct, nor ever will be. The crisis did not begin and end with the post-war period. E. M. Forster saw the books of the period between the two world wars—Elizabeth's own most prolific period—as those of a civilisation that felt itself insecure because of the change in society. He wrote of this change in *Two Cheers for Democracy*:

> It has meant the destruction of feudalism and relation-ships based on the land, it has meant the transference of power from the aristocrat to the bureaucrat and the manager and the technician. Perhaps it will mean democracy, but it has not meant it yet, and personally I hate it.

Forster's sentimentality with regard to the *ancien régime* does not bear examination. But the Mandarins were the clever children of that *régime* and at their best they were stylish in a way that their successors were not. They were also frivolous. Frivolousness is very important; it is part of Western humanism, it is play at its most evolved, and it is self-irony. It is under no circumstances to be confused with triviality. But the message of the 1940s, wrote Cyril Connolly in 1949, was this: "Nothing dreadful is ever done with, no bad thing gets any better; you can't be too serious". He was writing in the final number of *Horizon*, and ended his piece with a sentence that includes those elegiac, unforgettable, and characteristically overcharged words, "it is closing time in the gardens of the West. . . ."[5]

Not for Elizabeth, not altogether; she was courageous and adaptable. For her the post-war period turned out to be another opening time, into a rather more public life. The retired existence at Bowen's Court was a very part-time affair. She was by now very widely recognised as an established and major author. Her name went into *Who's Who*. In 1948 she was made a Companion of the British Empire as "novelist"— and told the Connollys: "It is particularly heartwarming that one's friends should be pleased. I must say that this is a most surprising thing to happen to *me*, of all people: I always feel so peculiar, if you know what I mean". For three successive years, from 1948 through 1950, she nobly acted as principal to the Kent Education Committee's summer school for teachers of English at Folkestone—"so distant in feeling from everywhere and everybody that I might be in Australia", as she told Veronica Wedgwood. (One of the organisers, Frank Jessup, was an old friend of Alan's.) Being principal did not involve much beyond being there and taking an interest; but the first year there was a project to bring out a commemorative magazine—one number only—called *Seahorse*, for which she wrote the editorial. The poet Francis Scarfe, who was also at the summer school and involved with *Seahorse*, dedicated a book of his poems, *Underworlds*, to Elizabeth a couple of years later. She also lectured at summer schools in Oxford for the Extension Lectures Committee.

For not only her writing but her thoughts about writing and writers were in demand. She was one of the authors chosen by Cyril Connolly in 1945 to answer a questionnaire in *Horizon* on "The Cost of Letters", beginning with a question about how much a writer needed to live on. ("I would like to have £3,500 a year net", said Elizabeth boldly; no one else seemed to require much over £1,000; John Betjeman, cagily, said only that he needed "as much as anyone else".)[6] In the same year she contributed over eleven pages of "Notes on Writing a Novel" to *Orion II*—a vintage volume edited by Rosamond Lehmann, Cecil Day Lewis, and others; and the *Partisan Review* in 1948 published the three-way exchange of letters between Elizabeth, V. S. Pritchett, and Graham Greene entitled *Why Do I Write?*, published as a book by Percival Marshall in the same year. Though revealing of Elizabeth's attitudes and approach, and full of insight into her own processes, there is, necessarily, a self-conscious air about the contributions to this book: "It is now for society to say what it thinks of us", wrote Elizabeth in her last letter of the series.

Society has and had on the whole a fine lack of concern with these matters; but one of the voices it heard was Elizabeth's. She began to broadcast; in the three years immediately after the war she did three literary pieces for the B.B.C.—on Jane Austen, on Fanny Burney, and on Trollope, this last in dialogue form; it was published as a pamphlet by the Oxford University Press, who in 1946 paid Elizabeth the compliment of sending it out in large numbers to friends and clients in America for Christmas. She also did "place" broadcasts, on the Kentish coast and on Bloomsbury. "Writing for the air frenzies me; it is such a new and different technique—all the same, its problems are fascinating". She went early into television as well, from 1947 taking part in a series called "Kaleidoscope".

She was now famous enough—and old enough—for some of her earlier writing to be reissued. In 1951 Knopf, in America, reprinted her two very first books of stories—*Encounters* and *Ann Lee's*—in one volume, with a retrospective introduction by Elizabeth. The previous year Longmans published her *Collected Impressions*—a selection of her essays, reviews, feature articles, and prefaces, including the Trollope dialogue and the "Notes on Writing a Novel". As paper gradually became less scarce in post-war Europe, her books began to be translated—into Rumanian, Danish, Norwegian, Swedish, Czech, Spanish, Italian, Japanese, Serbo-Croat, as well as French and German. There was an especially charming letter from her Japanese translator—"I am very happy in those warm summer days reading your masterpieces" —which ends with the P.S. "Is the pronunciation of Bowen, *bauin* or *bouin*?"[7]

She had become an industry, and organisation had never been her forte. Spencer Curtis Brown and his colleagues, as her agents, saw to the nuts and bolts of it but there was nevertheless a vast amount of correspondence about commissions, copyrights, contracts, fees, foreign rights, American rights, and so on. She began to employ a secretary. Sometimes she dictated the letters herself, sometimes Alan dictated them over her signature. He came into his own with her in these years. He had always done the Bowen's Court accounts and administered the practical side of their lives; now, working only part-time on his own account, he became virtually her manager. The letters composed by him have a brevity and firmness that bear the stamp of the professional administrator; Elizabeth herself, while always unwilling to write business letters, tended when she did so to write longer, less formal, and less decisive letters than Alan's. He was firmer than she about asking for top rates, and she deferred to him in all major decisions. "I will get Alan's views on this verbatim".

It is not always, however, quite clear whose voice is behind each opinion. Which of them, for example, dictated the letter of December, 1947, to Curtis Brown, putting Elizabeth's "excellent friend" Sean O'Faolain in his place?

> I have considered the matter of Sean O'Faolain's request to use my story "Her Table Spread" for the book on The Short Story he is preparing. On principle, and in spite of the fact that he is an excellent friend of mine, I should prefer you to hold out for an 8-guinea fee for the rights on this story. I think the principle of reduced rates, when Curtis Browns have been at pains for years to build me up to a certain price level, to be a bad one. I know that Mr. Sean O'Faolain is doing this book for Messrs. Collins, who are, as you know, a very well-to-do firm, and I think it is up to him as Editor to see that the authors receive the usual fees. If he does not feel able to meet this price, I am afraid he will have to omit the story from the collection.[8]

The extensive translating of Elizabeth's books was part of the movement among countries turned in on themselves by the disasters and austerities of war to cross frontiers freely again. French fashions took up where they had left off. "These Paris hats are more and more seeping into London", reported Elizabeth to Charles Ritchie in 1946, "disturbing us who have not yet got one." And not only French hats, but French intellectuals—"poets, publishers, pianists, everything". Elizabeth went to a party in the "glamorous Hollywood-like richness" of Lowndes House given by Mme. Massigli for the French Communist poet Louis Aragon, who was "looking rather strange in light-grey English tweed". She had met him a few days before more informally, at Cyril Connolly's, and described him to Charles as "a strange dynamic creature who seems to be made of colourless glass and fire; with a narrow, squeezed-in-a-door face, almost colourless large eyes with pin-point pupils, and colourless hair *en brosse*":

> I don't think anybody liked him particularly, but everybody was, literally, fascinated. Cyril had invited a ring of poets. Nancy [Mitford] Rodd distinguished herself by standing in the middle of the room and saying in her clear, high voice, "Of course, I think Aragon's marvellous—what a pity we haven't got any poets in this country!" Eliot and all the others merely lowered their heads like tortoises and blinked.

The traffic in cultural visits was two-way. Between 1948 and 1950 Elizabeth made several lecture tours for the British Council. The first, in February, 1948, was to Czechoslovakia and Austria. Elizabeth's schedule on these trips was packed with receptions, press conferences, broadcasts, and visits as well as her lectures. It was the sort of thing at which she excelled. Her repertoire consisted of a talk on "The Technique of the Novel", another on "The English Novel in the Twentieth Century", and another on "The Short Story". The British Council representative in Czechoslovakia reported back that "there was something of classic perfection in her lectures". Her last lecture in Prague drew the largest audience for an English speaker since the *Times* correspondent gave the first British lecture directly after the war in 1945. She went on to Vienna; Graham Greene, too, was in Vienna, researching the plot for *The Third Man*. He took Elizabeth out to dinner and then, with the help of a young friend in British Intelligence, he manufactured a happening for her. After dinner he took her to the Oriental:

> I don't think she had ever been in so seedy a night club before.
>
> I said, "I wanted to show you the International Police at work. They will be raiding this place at midnight."
>
> "How do you know?"
>
> "I have my contacts."
>
> Exactly at the stroke of twelve, as I had asked my friend to arrange, a British sergeant came clattering down the stairs, followed by a Russian, a French and an American policeman. The place was in half-darkness but without hesitation (I had described her with care) he strode across the cellar and demanded to see Elizabeth's passport.[9]

Elizabeth looked at him, Greene thought, with a new respect —"the British Council had not given her so dramatic an evening". But on her next lecture tour, to Hungary, in autumn, 1948, she was the subject of an un-manufactured incident.

On her arrival it was found that her visa was out of date. She duly presented herself at the Alien Police Headquarters two days later in order to put this right, but after nearly five hours of waiting and questioning she was told she must leave the country at once under guard. High-level intervention saved the day, though the aftermath had an operatic quality. The British Council officials were greatly relieved that Elizabeth did not make a fuss—"This affair has been extremely upsetting for Miss Bowen and it is greatly to her credit that she has taken it extremely well". (Her travel arrangements had all been made by the British Council in London.) The representatives on the spot, however, were concerned about the Council's "loss of face" and of carefully fostered goodwill. The treatment meted out by the Hungarian police was not the kind one was used to in Britain. Elizabeth's resilience and good humour was one thing. Alan's outrage was another. "I gather", noted a Council official, "that her husband may be expected to protest vigorously against the course of events". The employee who had made the travel arrangements offered her resignation. But her resignation was not accepted; Alan was smoothed down; Elizabeth called on the British Council chairman, who apologized; and all ended happily.

A final tailpiece to the Hungarian episode was an article on her in *Vilag*, the Hungarian Citizen Democratic daily, which, in the "official" translation in the British Council files, has charm of a surrealist nature. After saying, inaccurately, that "among her twelve books her favourite is 'The Death of Heart'" (*sic*), the writer goes on:

> Her house in Regent Park was destroyed by a V-2 and she now lives with her husband, who is an expert in English education, in one single room which has been repaired. Mme. Bowen is tall, interesting-looking, fair, she is like a figure stepping out of some English novel. Her hobby is cutting pictures from coloured paper and making surrealist boxes of them. She is engaged on writing a new novel which takes place during the war and deals with the problems of middle-aged people, as she puts it, "on whom the sun has already reached the top of head".

In 1949 Elizabeth became involved in a very responsible and unexpected aspect of public work. She was appointed a member of the Royal Commission on Capital Punishment, which met more or less monthly until it reported in 1953 (in favour of abolition). It was important and time-consuming, and she was one of only two women on the Commission;

the other was Miss (later Dame) Florence Hancock, a member of the Trades Union Council. The choice of Elizabeth was imaginative but somewhat arbitrary; some of the other members had initial doubts as to how she would manage. She managed well. Part of their work was to travel round visiting prisons—among them Wandsworth, Wakefield, and Broadmoor in Britain, and in East Coast cities in the United States, looking into the problems of long-term sentences and the treatment of prisoners. It was decided that it was not necessary for the members of the Commission actually to witness an execution, though they were prepared to; and, as Elizabeth said in her B.B.C. interview of 1959:

> We inspected the gallows arrangements and in America we saw what to me was the most horrifying thing, the execution place in Sing Sing; we saw how gallows work, we saw the traps, we saw the cells in which condemned people are confined, and we saw the whole circumstances and surroundings of an execution.

She did not find, however, that these horrors preyed on her mind. They remained compartmentalised, carved out of ordinary experience, with none of the "worked-up emotion" that she said as a reader of crime stories she was quite capable of summoning up. She was on a job, and an important one; emotion was readily withheld. In the final recommendations made by the Commission, Elizabeth's personal contributions—she had not been very vocal at earlier meetings—were twofold. In law, only physical provocation counted as provocation that could turn murder into manslaughter. On Elizabeth's suggestion, the Commission recommended the inclusion of verbal provocation. Some rather reserved point was also made about another thing about which Elizabeth felt strongly:

> I also objected to the thing by which clemency is more likely to be extended to a man who finds his wife has

been unfaithful to him, who finds her in the arms of somebody, whereas a man whose mistress distresses him in the same way is more likely to have the law against him. And I argued that in an irregular relationship passion and sexual feeling is nearer the surface, and if you were to allow for uncontrollable passion it is more likely, probably, to arise in what is described as a love relationship. . . .[10]

Thus speaks the experienced woman, the novelist, the lawyer's daughter.

The year the Commission reported was also Coronation Year. At the Coronation of Queen Elizabeth II, three women writers were invited by the B.B.C. to record their impressions —Elizabeth Bowen, C. V. Wedgwood, and Rose Macaulay. (Rose's was too mischievous to be used.) Elizabeth's broadcast was lyrical and romantic in the extreme. But that was the mood of the day. It was the first English show since the war, the very antithesis of austerity. It *was* a deeply romantic occasion for England. For colder, later days, however, it is the odd general observations that stand out in Elizabeth's broadcast: "Reigning should be enjoyable. Women, on the whole, show an aptitude for it; there are few who have not desired to try". (Elizabeth Bowen had great aptitude for it— though if she had been born to a throne it would have been Elizabeth I of England, not Elizabeth II, whom she would have more resembled.) Elizabeth also reported the Coronation for *Vogue*, both in England and America, the copy being handed in at noon on the day after the ceremony, which entailed sitting up most of the night—she had a very busy Coronation.

Elizabeth was not without honour now in her own country either. Trinity College, Dublin, gave her an Honorary D.Litt.

in the summer of 1949. Before this, during the year after the war ended, she had been very involved in the Swift bicentennial celebrations in Ireland. Elizabeth had been reading a lot of Swift and was "very much in the mood". The principal guest at one of the celebration lunches in Cork—at the "musty-looking but prosperous" Hotel Metropol—was Edith Œnone Somerville of the Somerville and Ross partnership, chiefly famous for their "Irish R.M." stories. Elizabeth described her to Charles Ritchie:

> She is said to be 87, is a little lame but holds herself very straight and has a blue-eyed, expressive, obstinate face. She wore a mannish coat and skirt and a bright green tie and a hat with dashing bright green plumes in front.

Since the death of "Ross", her beloved collaborator Violet Martin, Edith Somerville had occupied herself with bridge and spiritualism: by means of the latter the happy collaboration apparently continued uninterrupted. "Now that Virginia is dead", Elizabeth told Charles, "she and Colette and Edith Sitwell are the only living writers whom I really admire". (Somerville and Ross's *The Real Charlotte* was a novel that Elizabeth admired particularly; and indeed it is the nearest thing to the Balzacian Great Irish Novel that has ever been written.) Swift had stayed with Edith Somerville's forebears in West County Cork: "Nobody of any interest ever seems to have stayed with the poor Bowens, though to my certain knowledge they had just as nice a house".

"I did wish you were there", Elizabeth wrote to Charles of this celebration lunch:

> Monks with beards and those knotted ropes around their waist which always looks so stagey, gravely hanging up their umbrellas on the Hotel Metropol hat-stands and mingling with the Church of Ireland divines and

their wives. (Owing to the two Irish centenaries of this year being Swift and the Young Irelanders, many of whom are Protestants, Protestants are this year anyway rather a vogue. We are in constant demand.) I, as a comparatively junior Protestant writer, but still a Protestant, was second guest of honour. We had a very gay time at the top table.

Swift's "extraordinarily contemporary" political ideas excited her; and her reaction to his complex emotional life is expressive of her own extraordinarily direct approach to sexuality, at the polar extreme from the circuitous Proustian "wool-winding" processes of many of her fictional characters. Her directness is a cheerfully sophisticated version of the single-mindedness of her disastrously "innocent" girls-in-love like Emmeline and Portia:

> Swift's relations with Vanessa always interest me more than all the business with Stella: I can't get over, or past, the "little language", the baby-talk, which embarrasses me. All sublimations of physical love shock me. The scene in the garden with Vanessa, when they broke it off, both shrieked, and threw letters about always seems to me, though devastating, much healthier. She, poor girl, as I expect you know, as the result died.

There was a book about Swift that she found herself longing to write: " 'Swift in Ireland'—what a book it could be; and apparently it's never been written." But she heard someone else was working on it, and the moment passed, and she never did write it.

The only new full-length book that she did write between *The Heat of the Day* and *A World of Love*, which appeared six years later, was *The Shelbourne*, which Harrap brought out in 1951. This was a "popular" history of the Dublin hotel. Dublin's most prestigious hotels until recently have been the

Shelbourne, the Gresham, and the Royal Hibernian. The Shelbourne, splendidly sited in 1860s' comfort on St. Stephen's Green, retains much of its old atmosphere. There had been a hotel there since 1824, and it was not a bad idea to make this central city landmark the framework for a book incorporating Dublin social history, atmosphere, and anecdote in a way that would come naturally to Elizabeth. The idea was Cyril Connolly's: in her inscription in the copy she gave him, she called him the book's godfather. *The Shelbourne* came off, only just. She wrote it in the lively style she adopted for most of her journalistic feature-writing. It says much for her versatility and professionalism but adds nothing to her reputation. If she had been able at this time to have got involved in a novel, she would not have written *The Shelbourne*.

She was fond of the Shelbourne and of its denizens: one uses the word advisedly. The Shelbourne was and is a haunt. Elizabeth, when she stopped there as usual en route to County Cork, the month after the war ended, ran into "a most heavenly woman, the Dowager Lady Headfort, who used to be Rosie Boote, the most cracking Edwardian beauty", as she told Charles:

> She still wears her hair à la 1910 and wore the most nostalgically beautiful black hat trimmed with a wreath of flaming white marguerites. You know really what terrific *personalities* on the Proust scale those stars of the Gaiety and Daly's who married into the peerage were. They must have had something much subtler and less drearily biological than what is now called sex appeal.

Lady Headfort and Elizabeth proceeded to spend hours together in the corner of the Shelbourne bar, "the most charming *public* place to sit and drink in the world". These delights were more circumspectly presented in her book, the nearest we get to Rosie Boote's reminiscences being in a reference to the famous stage beauties who descended on Dublin: "The Irish Peerage, on more pages than one, records the happy end of that story".

The book catches fire when imagination is allowed some play: as when Elizabeth re-creates the view from the hotel windows during the Easter Rising of 1916, when Countess de Markievicz was to be seen marching up and down in the uniform of the Irish Volunteers, having "seized the Green" to no very clear purpose. The one true Bowen note is struck in a description of the nine weeks' strike that closed the hotel during the civil war: the assistant manager was alone in the place apart from the wild cats in the great kitchen—"leaping on and off the tables, glaring out from the cold blackness over the extinct ranges, these feline Maenads seemed to be chaos personified".

Though she preferred the cinema, because of the anonymous soothing darkness and because she could smoke throughout, Elizabeth loved the theatre, especially during and after the war. She was getting more and more addicted to both, and to detective stories, as she told Susan Tweedsmuir in 1945: "I suppose this is one of the worst symptoms of escapism". She used to go to the Noël Coward productions with Patience Erskine, her old Downe House friend, who now was Coward's gardener at Goldenhurst. (For a time, Elizabeth rented a London flat in the house of Gladys Calthrop, Noël Coward's stage designer.)

Elizabeth wrote a play herself. Called *Castle Anna*, it was written during the war, in collaboration with John Perry, whose collaboration with M. J. Farrell on *Spring Meeting* was enormously successful. "M. J. Farrell" was the pseudonym of Molly Keane, Anglo-Irish and a lifelong friend of Elizabeth's; John Perry, too, was from County Cork. After the war John Perry was running the Lyric, Hammersmith, and it was decided to put *Castle Anna* on.

The play was rather Chekhovian, about a spinster—played by Pauline Letts—in love with the family home—predictably, an Irish country house. The part of the wastrel gambling old land-owner—played by Arthur Sinclair—was written by John Perry, as he knew something about racing and Elizabeth didn't. The main weakness of the play was in its construction, which involved the passage of over twenty years between Acts I and II. It did not receive very good notices, though *The Times* printed a photograph of one of the scenes, and it did not run; it was a disappointment.

There is, however, one reason why it is worth rescuing from oblivion: *Castle Anna* was the first play in which Richard Burton appeared after being demobilised from the R.A.F. He was twenty-three. He went on after this to *The Lady's Not for Burning*, and never looked back. In *Castle Anna* he had a very small part; he played Mr. Hicks, a British officer stationed in the neighbourhood. He also understudied Philip Guard, who had the young male lead. Philip Guard was a conscientious objector and was inconveniently sent to prison for two weeks during the pre-run provincial tour. Richard Burton took over his part and was judged to be miscast. *Castle Anna* made no one's name.

Charles Ritchie had been in England to see *Castle Anna* in February, 1948; and in spite of being recalled to Ottawa before V-E Day he had been over in London again for an inter-governmental meeting the following spring, 1946, again to be recalled in a hurry. This time it was on account of the Gouzenko case: a cypher clerk in the Societ Embassy in Ottawa defected and revealed the existence of a Soviet spy-ring in Canada. The Canadian government started an investigation, which meant that the whole Canadian delegation had to return home earlier than planned. But later that same year he was in Paris for the Peace Conference; and Elizabeth, having got herself accredited as correspondent reporting the conference for the *Cork Examiner*, was there, too, staying at the Hotel Condé. In 1947 Charles was appointed to the Canadian Embassy in Paris as Counsellor, where he remained for three years, and where Elizabeth was able to visit him easily enough; in all their long friendship, and even when they were separated by the Atlantic and not the English Channel, no more than a few months at the most ever passed without their meeting. She entered with him into diplomatic circles, adding a new dimension to her acquaintanceship. Her cross-Channel conquests included the Duke of Windsor, who at one party, in communicative mood, spent a noticeably long time talking to her on a sofa.

Elizabeth in the years after the war had more concerns and more irons in the fire than ever before; and yet it was too intensive, too unsettled and hectic, for her to be writing much or easily. Although the idea had been to spend more time at Bowen's Court, her professional commitments in England meant that the peaceful life envisaged did not quickly become a reality. To the customary shuttling between England and Ireland was added the European lecture tours, journeys to meet Charles, and, by the beginning of the 1950s, trips to the United States. She was in perpetual motion. Living always in the assumption that her stamina was invincible, she began to find that it was not. After Charles went back to Ottawa in the spy-ring crisis of 1946, she got jaundice and felt, as she told William Plomer, "extremely ill, iller than I thought it possible to feel without actually dying".

The non-stop geographical dislocations were echoed by, or were echoes of, other dislocations. The strains and exaltations of the war gave place to anti-climax and a measure of disillusion. She was famous and loved, she was continually in demand, she was working, but her fertility was—in the nature of things, perhaps—not what it was. She loved Alan, whose health was giving anxiety. She loved Charles, who could not often be there. "No return can ever make restitution for the going away", she wrote in *The Heat of the Day*. "You may imitate but you cannot renew safety".

To none of these stresses did she give way, or even expression. She responded to all the stimuli that such a *mouvementé* life offered, and self-pity was not part of her armoury. Simply, one had to adjust, to all manner of things. In 1948, the year before *The Heat of the Day* was published, Charles Ritchie—now an established career diplomat—had married his cousin Sylvia Smellie.

CHAPTER XI

Dislocations

ALAN CAMERON DIED on August 26, 1952.
        In the spring of 1951 Elizabeth had returned from a
Capital Punishment Commission visit to the United States to
find him recovering from a bad heart attack. Later that year
she wrote to Hubert Butler—Noreen Butler's brother-in-law
and Elizabeth's cousin, at that time review editor of *The Bell*
—gracefully declining to review novels. She added:

> Alan has been told by the doctor he must retire this
> autumn—strain of work in London too much, given his
> bad heart-condition. Once out of it, no reason (D.V.)
> why he shouldn't have long and reasonably active life.
> So we are giving up this London house and moving all
> our stuff over to B. Court just before Christmas. We
> are both looking forward to a more regular and con-
> tinuous life there.

Elizabeth was lecturing in America in the autumn of 1951,
snatching a few days in Canada to see Charles, now back in
Ottawa as Assistant Under-Secretary of State for External
Affairs. So she and Alan moved over to Bowen's Court after
Christmas, full of hope, taking with them their secretary Mar-
jorie Frost. In April, 1952, she wrote to Blanche Knopf, "I feel
not a whiff of regret for London". Alan, though unable to do
physical work, was involved as always in the planning and organisation of Bowen's Court, especially with regard to the

planting of trees. Like Elizabeth's father, Alan loved trees. But he was not well. His temperament and his bad eyesight made him melancholy. When he could no longer read, Jim Gates's son Bill came up to the house to read to him. Diabetes and, latterly, dropsy, aggravated his other complaints. Eddy Sackville-West, asked at what time of day Alan's drinking began, said that it started, officially, at eleven: "But one hears the bottle and the glass soon after breakfast". Elizabeth never lifted an eyebrow over the drinking. She knew it could not at this stage be helped. In a letter to Alfred Knopf on August 11th, she said that Alan had had "a rather bad outbreak of the heart trouble, but he seems now to have turned the corner". William Buchan, at Bowen's Court on a visit, found Alan in bed and looking dreadful.

"I must always be glad that he went so peacefully, in a calm night's sleep, expecting to wake next day", she wrote again, afterwards, to Alfred Knopf. And to Veronica Wedgwood, who with Jacqueline Hope-Wallace had been at Bowen's Court only a few weeks before:

> It was a great thing that, as a crown to our life of nearly thirty years together, we should have had these months here in this house—as you know, the life we had just begun here was what we'd been looking forward to for so many years. We had such a lovely spring and summer, and everything.

To Audrey Fiennes—who had known Alan longer than Elizabeth had herself, who had been their companion in so many happy times, and Alan's companion so often when Elizabeth was away—she wrote, "Bless his heart. He was a happy man". He had been very much himself the evening before; and at the end, she said, he perhaps loved Audrey "best of all".

Aunt Edie came from Corkagh and took over, and Noreen and Gilbert Butler. "I'm sure Alan loved his funeral", Elizabeth told Audrey; the coffin was carried down the avenue from the house to Farahy church, as Henry Bowen's had been, with the family following on foot and neighbours from far and wide in crawling cars.

Elizabeth had thought it might feel impossible to stay on at Bowen's Court after the funeral, but found she had "an odd dread" of leaving. In her letter to Veronica Wedgwood she said she planned to go to the United States for a couple of months around Christmas: "In spite of the happiness that remains in this house, I think I'd be stupid to face mid-winter—or at any rate the first mid-winter—alone here. But in general I hope to be here, if I can".

There was every reason to be "in general" at Bowen's Court. It was her family home and now, Clarence Terrace being given up, her only existing home. She need be alone no more than she wished: visitors had always flocked to Bowen's Court and continued to do so. She was integrated with the life of the place in a way that was feudal, and familial. An English friend who came to stay during a year early in Elizabeth's widowhood was struck by the long, warm, and easy conversation Elizabeth entered into with a very raggedy local family they met on the road during a walk. This can only partially be explained by Elizabeth's sense of courtesy, curiosity, or obligation, or by the fact that one customarily passes no one on the road in the country in Ireland without exchanging, at the meagre least, a "Good evening".

Both Elizabeth and that family assumed that there was a relation between them, and an interest. When a local man was in trouble—he had been entrusted with someone's money, and had spent it—he came to the back door of Bowen's Court and asked Molly O'Brien in the kitchen if he could see Mrs. Cameron. He poured out his trouble to Elizabeth. She reassured him: she made some telephone calls to the relevant quarters; she sorted it all out. If feudalism leads to an abuse of power, that power is often abused to the benefit of the powerless—who know, in their turn, how to get what they can out of the system. For instance, the Bowen's Court garden provided flowers for the (Catholic) feast-days; people rang up saying, "It's for the altar", and flowers were sent in the belief that they were for the church, and then it turned out that they were all destined for the private altars in the houses, the village people vying with one another with chrysanthemums acquired from Elizabeth on false pretences—while an SOS was received from the church for its share, at the last moment. But it was all, as it were, in the family. "This place sustains me", she wrote two months after Alan's death, "and so do the people". And "she was a mother to us", said Molly O'Brien, who had worked for the Bowens since 1927.

Gerard Shiels was seventeen and working as a temporary postman when Elizabeth, who got a lot of letters, made his acquaintance. He was living, not happily, with foster-parents in a cottage between Farahy and Kildorrery, with no easy way to get out and make a life for himself. Elizabeth placed him with her friends the Vernons, whose prop and stay he became; she wrote to him, encouraged him to read and to educate himself, and took an interest in his life and activities as long as her own life lasted. Gerard was never "dropped" as some of her grander friends were. "She was a nice woman. That's all it was", said Gerard. She was not only a nice woman, she was a good woman.

This was a side of Elizabeth's life that her English and American friends knew little of. Veronica Wedgwood, staying at Bowen's Court in the winter of 1953, was more alive to the climate of Elizabeth's life there than many. They were both working hard—Elizabeth on *A World of Love* and Veronica Wedgwood on *The King's Peace*. As the generator that provided the electricity was giving trouble, the lights in the evenings grew dimmer and dimmer and they worked on by candlelight, without fuss. This was the occasion on which Veronica Wedgwood wrote home to England describing the new pink corset-satin drawing-room curtains; Alan's death did not stop Elizabeth from her continued commitment to make the house, now, a comfortable home. There was also new red upholstery on the sofa. Veronica Wedgwood slept and wrote in the room over the library, with "two windows on to the big paddock with its black Kerry cows and clumps of big bare trees, and one sideways on to the mountains, the overgrown rose-garden and the dovecot". They worked from ten till one-thirty, and again from two-thirty to eight. "A long day".

Characteristically, they fitted pleasures in as well. One evening they drove into Cork to hear a local orchestra. Veronica Wedgwood wrote home:

> Elizabeth—it turns out—is *more* tone deaf than I am.
> . . . We dined first with a wonderfully Irish set-up—a professor [Denis Gwynn], son of Stephen Gwynn [writer-brother of Henry Bowen's second wife, Mary], now aged 50 to 60, who lives in blameless devotion with a late-Victorian *femme fatale*, now nearly 80, and still incredibly the beauty and toast of Munster. She eloped from Church during Matins in about 1897, ran through an astonishing number of husbands on both sides of the Irish Channel, before settling to this charming and platonic attachment. The sort of face that Lavery painted.

(The lady was Mrs. Victor Rickard, formerly a Miss Moore.) They also went to lunch with Lord Donoughmore, where they met his countless dogs and heard his story "about his breeches splitting—in front—at the Coronation, which was all very well so long as he was swathed in robes but not so when the Peers proceeded to the banquet and were asked to leave their robes in the cloakroom".

Veronica Wedgwood appreciated fully on this visit the complexities of both Elizabeth's character and her position:

> One of the nice things about Elizabeth, as I'm only beginning to realise now, is that she's such a sane and

responsible citizen; sounds terrible—but you know what
I mean—not a wild irresponsible like darling Rose
[Macaulay] or a maniac always with her nose in the
Economist like . . . but a perfectly and unobtrusively
informed person, who sees and thinks about all the
snags without necessarily holding forth on them. It must
be odd and bewildering to be really and responsibly
devoted to this country (as she very much is) with the
complex background of divided loyalties and clashing
inheritances.

And in another letter on this visit Veronica Wedgwood paid
an even higher tribute to the quality of Elizabeth's sympathy:

If anything ever happened to a person you love
do remember that she would be the best in the world to
be helpful because she is really the only person of
our way of life and thinking who isn't always putting
sex first. She understands the intellectual quality of love
so well. I say this because the few people on whose
shoulders one might cry . . . are sometimes too
knowing about things that may well be of less importance. I say this of course only from watching her
with other people and what I have known and felt
about her.

Another visitor earlier that same year—1953—had been
John Lehmann, at that time planning the *London Magazine*;
the editorial board, of which Elizabeth was a member, first
met over lunch a year later. On this visit, "we talked without
stop, at meals, after dinner by the fire in the big drawing-
room, while she walked me round the old walled garden full
of dahlias and fruit bushes, and drove recklessly about the
countryside . . . and we came to a general agreement about
the kind of review we wanted the *London Magazine* to be".
In the autobiographical volume *The Ample Proposition* in
which John Lehmann described this visit, he wrote a pen-

portrait of Elizabeth, beginning with her "stylish, rather masculine carriage, as if about to settle on a shooting stick and lift binoculars". Elizabeth would have recognised this; she said herself that at country point-to-points she saw women, indeed settled on shooting sticks and lifting binoculars, who looked curiously like herself. John Lehmann wrote that he was

> captivated again by the quality she displays more abundantly than anyone else I know, of making one feel completely at ease, of immediately establishing rapport by a flow of uninhibited conversation which mingles sympathy, charm, wit, and shrewd intellectual comment.

It was her energy that struck him most forcibly of all— "She moved about the house like a young man setting out for a football match". She took him for "tireless, striding walks" and drove him around in the car "like one possessed, mainly on the wrong side of the road". On the first morning of his visit, a shortcoming on the part of the Irish airline Aer Lingus, with whom he had travelled, provoked her to write on his behalf an indignant four-page letter of protest to the management.

If this Elizabeth, in contrast to the more contemplative Elizabeth whom Veronica Wedgwood found, sounds rather too manic to suggest that she had achieved a working equilibrium, John Lehmann's picture of her in her early fifties is emphatically not the picture of a woman who had lost her appetite for life. But not all her visitors were so congenial, and it was with the trickier visitors that the cracks in the surface of life showed.

There had always been tricky visitors at Bowen's Court; one of them had been Carson McCullers, three years earlier. She began badly; wishing to confirm her plans, she put in a transatlantic telephone call to Bowen's Court, forgetting about the time-difference. As her biographer Virginia Spencer Carr tells it:

When a butler answered the telephone she said: "This is Carson McCullers calling from New York. I would like to speak to Miss Bowen."

The response was a dry "Madam, it is four o'clock in the morning. I suggest you call again later."

This incident struck Carson as being hilariously funny and became one of her favorite stories.[1]

There was no butler at Bowen's Court. The person who answered the telephone was most probably Alan, absolutely furious at being woken up.

Carson arrived in high ecstatic mood in May, 1950, planning to stay a month. She wrote home that she had made a "hit" at Bowen's Court in her jeans and "coat of many colors". Elizabeth took her round to see the local beauty spots, and then wanted, for part of each day, to get on with her work. Carson then found it rather too quiet—"She did not care to be left alone as much as she had been—almost ignored, she felt", is how her biographer put it. She did the unpardonable thing of breaking in on Elizabeth at her work. There were diversions—a visit from writer Frank O'Connor, interrupted by another from Noreen's brother Dudley Colley in his dashing Frazer Nash—but after a couple of weeks Carson "was intensely nervous and was making her hostess edgy too". Being bored, Carson consumed a great deal of whiskey.

She had been infatuated with Elizabeth, or with the idea of Elizabeth. Disillusioned, she went off to London, but reappeared a month later with her husband, Reeves, who also had a drinking problem; Rosamond Lehmann was staying at Bowen's Court, too, by this time, and Audrey Fiennes. The hostess's edginess needs no imagining. Elizabeth did feel affection towards Carson—but also that she was a "destroyer" with whom it would be a mistake to get involved. Audrey was deputed to take the McCullerses out in the car; a wretched commission, since they had to stop at every pub. This second disastrous visit was short-lived.

Another American visitor who ended up feeling thoroughly unwanted at Bowen's Court was May Sarton. Her story and her relation to Elizabeth is explicitly bound up with her lesbianism; and her final rejection by Elizabeth is a paradigm case for the fate of a great many women, not all of them lesbians, with whom Elizabeth formed a close friendship and who were, after a time, more or less dropped. Spencer Curtis Brown's sister "B" was one of them; and so, earlier, was Nancy Spain. (Nancy Spain's cultivation of Elizabeth had been intense. Neither Alan nor his friend Eric Gillett could stand her. They complained to Elizabeth about her apparently endless visits to Clarence Terrace. Suddenly Nancy's visits stopped. Why was that? asked Eric. The answer was that she had made a pass at Elizabeth; and that, in her case, was the end of that as far as Elizabeth was concerned.)

Enough lesbian sensibility has been discerned in Elizabeth's fiction for at least one critic to include her in a study of lesbian literature;[2] and enough in her manner for some people to have presumed that, however conventional her married life, it was towards women that her true inclinations lay. There was a good deal that was masculine both in Elizabeth's physical self and in her mentality: writers more than most people, if they are any good, are so because of an extended imaginative sympathy that can encompass more than one sexual, as well as social and historical, attitude. Elizabeth's code and her manner—in discussion, for example, or in "knocking back the drinks"—could be, and were, described as those of a "gentleman" as easily as those of a "lady". Her responsiveness to place, people, atmosphere, mood, on the other hand, was of the order that is pre-eminently considered feminine: it is inconceivable that any of her fiction could have been written by a man. Her fondness for cosmetics, her concern with her appearance were almost anxiously feminine. If, as a few of her friends thought, she was ever worried about herself as a woman, it was because she very much wanted to be one. She was a man's woman, not from fellow-feeling, but because she was very fond of men.

She loved her women friends, and with some of them the friendship was intense, if only because women's friendships lend themselves to exchanges of confidences, and "women's lives are sensational", as she said in *The Hotel*. She was not naïve about these things and was always, from a very young woman, acutely aware of the effect and power women can have over one another. She put these relationships into her books, from the first novel onwards. There was nothing "sensational", to use her word in the more vulgar sense, either in her manner of doing so or in putting them in at all: in the twenties and thirties lesbianism and homosexuality were novelists' topics. "If I write a story about 2 women called 'Barren Love' ", she wrote to A. E. Coppard in 1932, "shall I bring the G. Cockerel Press in for the tail end of the homosexuality ramp?"

For a heterosexual woman, a close friendship with another woman is precisely that, and no more. For a lesbian, nearly all relationships with women must be coloured by the possibility of love, just as for a heterosexual most encounters with the opposite sex have the sexual question built in, even if only to be roundly dismissed before it reaches consciousness. Elizabeth was very attractive to lesbians: women did on occasion fall in love with her. She had, like Davina in her story "The Disinherited", "just that touch of the sombre romantic that appeals to other women, even to relatives". She claimed to have felt a *"frisson"*—without specifying its nature—when hearing Vita Sackville-West's step on the path one night in the garden at Sissinghurst.

If Elizabeth on occasion connived in all this, it was as part and parcel of her fascination with other people's lives, of her ability to concentrate on another person of whatever age or sex, which made her what Julian Jebb called "a magic listener". She encouraged and enabled the other person to talk about himself or herself, without seeming inquisitive. Sometimes the release this afforded the other made him pour out to her things he had never told anyone. This intimacy could be, to use her own word, "unnerving". When the flood of self-revelation threatened to overwhelm them, when the boundaries were becoming dangerously low, Elizabeth could instinctively avert danger by some prosaic practical remark, which earthed the current, put a stop to the flow. This facility for cutting short a mood—or occasionally a relationship—could be disconcerting: chiefly, it was self-protective. Even her closest friends, of both sexes, had to accept that passages of closeness with Elizabeth might be suddenly interrupted by a display of queenly formality. Something untoward or impermissible, perhaps, had been touched on. One was not always sure.

The emotional women friends were particularly liable to be encouraged and then to be cut off in this way; Elizabeth was suddenly uninterested in going on with the friendship, and withdrew. She was capable of dropping people ruthlessly, men or women. "Take it from one of the best living novelists that people's personalities are not interesting", she told Charles Ritchie, "except when you are in love with them". She needed to be on the move emotionally and geographically. The ideal for a writer, she said in "Disloyalties" in *The New York Times Book Review* in 1950, is "to be at once disabused and susceptible, and for ever mobile".[3]

Even with friends she had no intention of dropping, her behaviour could be unpredictable. John Perry, with whom she collaborated on *Castle Anna*, and a regular visitor to Clarence Terrace, was in 1941 posted away with the R.A.F. "Will you write to me twice a week?" said Elizabeth. So he did. There was no answer. So he wrote once a week, and then once a month; she never answered at all. When in 1944 he came back to London, he ran into Elizabeth in the tube; she greeted him as if they had met the day before. "Oh, I never write letters to anyone". Blanche Knopf was another who never could come to terms with Elizabeth's frequent failure to answer her letters, whether personal or professional, and at times resorted to desperate telegrams soliciting instant communication. It is one of the unfair facts of life that people who are greatly loved and valued can afford to behave much more unpredictably than other people without in any way jeopardising their position: indeed it can even enhance their value. Elizabeth was very greatly loved by many people. Nor did her unpredictable behaviour imply a lack of affection in her own nature. William Maxwell of *The New Yorker* observed that she was at her best and most affectionate when she was with Blanche and Alfred Knopf—"I always felt that they must have played together as children"—and he remembered a dinner party with the Knopfs and Elizabeth as "a kind of blaze of happiness".

There were always women who loved Elizabeth, or pairs of women to whom she was an accepting, unquestioning friend. What irked her most about lesbian relationships, as about any relationships, was their characteristically "claggy" quality—"claggy" was her expression for anything over-analytical, sentimental, sublimated, mawkish, maudlin. She would discuss the troubles of lesbian lovers with a bracing, matter-of-fact, kindly exasperation, deploring "muffishness" and "squashiness". Once, staying in Kerry with Norah Preece, she heard the young girls of the house announce that they were having such trouble with their boy-friends that they had decided to be "toms". Elizabeth and Eddy Sackville-West told them that on no account must they be toms: "Always", said Elizabeth, "having terrible rows about bracelets".

Talking to Charles Ritchie about women's friendships—apropos of Virginia Woolf and her niece, and Jane Austen and her niece—she said that every young woman has such friendships and that "the older woman puts into them all the lyrical, poetic side of her nature and that she lives her youth again. The girl finds so much pleasure in being seen through the eyes of love and admiration that she may have a flirtation with a man simply for the pleasure of telling the other woman about it". This is all quite apart from lesbianism, Elizabeth said. She knew, in all these matters, what she was talking about.

Back in 1936, when May Sarton was very young and Elizabeth had had those late night talks with her in Clarence Terrace, May had fallen in love with Elizabeth. This was at the time when Elizabeth was at her most experimental, most un-poised, in her private life. From their confidential talks, May understood (as she told in her autobiography) "that earlier in her life [Elizabeth] had loved at least one woman, but I gathered this period was over. Now her love affairs were with men. She seemed to take it quite naturally that she could be in love and still very much married to Alan".[4] The following spring of 1937 Elizabeth went to stay a night with May at a house May had taken, with friends, in Rye. This one night together was for May Sarton "the climax of weeks of growing intensity". But she soon realised what it was for Elizabeth: "a moment of beauty, of release from tension, when she was herself in a state of emotional precipitation which had nothing to do with me". Elizabeth wrote to May explaining her state of mind and telling the truth. The episode at Rye was not repeated. The friendship had its ups and downs, but it persisted, with affection on both sides, until a visit of May's— not her first—to Bowen's Court in the mid-1950s. There are echoes of Carson McCullers's disappointment in May Sarton's account of it: "Elizabeth worked all morning of course, and I wandered about rather at a loose end". It was very cold, and "there was no Alan to spread his balm of kindness. There was in the house a feeling of pressures and anxiety and Elizabeth seemed more absent-minded than usual".

But there was worse to come: after a phone call from

London a charming young Californian called Miss Lovelace arrived "with all the flurry and excitement of the adorer who has found her way to the promised land". Elizabeth came to life; for May Sarton it was an ironic reminder of the days when she herself had been the welcome young adorer. (Rejection works wonders for May Sarton's rather saccharine style: in defeat she becomes a raconteur.)

> I stayed in my room as much as possible but had to go down at cocktail time when it was usual for guests to gather in the library. But there, so intense was the exchange going on that I felt like an intruder, treated with bare civility. It was as acute a case of psychological discomfort as I have ever experienced.

On the day both the lady visitors were to leave, Elizabeth broke the drive to Shannon at Spenser's castle, Kilcolman; May, "like an unwanted governess", sat in the back seat. It was pouring with rain, and the ruin is several hundred yards from the road. "Getting wetter, I followed youth and splendour across the uneven turf". While Elizabeth "spoke marvellously about Spenser, and Miss Lovelace glowed", May grew wetter and more miserable.

May Sarton bore no malice. She understood—rightly— the tensions in Elizabeth that made her so hard to fathom in spite of her surface accessibility, that "kept her every relationship in suspense except perhaps that with her husband. . . ."

Not that Elizabeth in her widowhood was dependent on visitors from outside Ireland. Besides neighbours and family friends in the "Big Houses" within a wide radius, and the Colleys at Corkagh, the Gwynn clan, and other relations, there were new friends—something she perpetually needed— in Ireland. The most important of these were there as a result of the "flight from Moscow": English people who saw in

Ireland, after the war, an answer to their distaste for high income tax, poor service in return for high wages—above all, for the Socialist government. In southern Ireland, land and country houses could be bought for relatively low prices and it was believed—not always correctly—that help in the house and garden could still be got cheaply and easily. It was a lost way of life that they came to find. Evelyn Waugh toyed with the idea, but abandoned it. Some who came were disillusioned, or lonely, and did not stay. Others found what they were looking for, or something quite different but sufficiently beguiling.

Jean and Barry Black bought Creagh Castle just outside Doneraile, only a few miles from Bowen's Court. Elizabeth, who knew the house of old, had used the view from its front steps in her description of Mount Morris in *The Heat of the Day*. In the mid-sixties, when Bowen's Court had gone, she told Jean Black that "there's *no* County Cork house . . . that I feel so attached to or love so much" as Creagh. The Blacks were not in the least literary. Barry was gentle and sympathetic; and Jean—an "unhaunted" person—had a hardy independence and enterprise that appealed to those qualities in Elizabeth. With the Blacks, Elizabeth went on holidays to France and Italy, in gaiety and—no less appreciated—comfort:

> I do thank you both, darlings, a thousand times. It seems to me that I have not, for ages, had such an absolute and utter sense of HOLIDAY, or such fun and so much hilarity. And really what a selfish pig I was, all our driving days, just sitting there in the beautiful Jaguar smugly, while everyone else did the work.

In the 1960s Jean Black worked on an archaeological dig in Jordan, where she took a house; here, too, Elizabeth went to see her, and saw "places of beauty and strangeness I would never, never otherwise have seen or even been able to believe had existed. Black irises and golden eagles. . . ."

Eddy Sackville-West was another who bought a house in Ireland, about eighteen miles from Bowen's Court, in County Tipperary. Partly he came to be near her; there was great affection between them. He had often stayed at Bowen's Court, and was there in April, 1955, to do "a little Gothic-castle house-hunting". He had his eye on Shanbally Castle; but in November that year Elizabeth wrote to Jean Black that he had bought Coolville, in Clogheen: "He's now in an awful state about having to buy all the pots and pans, but I feel this will be character-forming for him".

In *A World of Love*, the novel Elizabeth had begun when Alan died and published in 1955, she has a passage on the relation between the living and the dead. She told William Plomer that "Alan never seems dead, in the sense that he never seems gone; I suppose that if one has lived the greater part of one's life with a person he continues to accompany one through every moment". And in *A World of Love* a man long dead casts his loved shadow over the living. Yet the relation is an uncomfortable one:

> Life works to dispossess the dead, to dislodge and oust them. Their places fill themselves up; later people come in; all the room is wanted. Feeling alters its course, is drawn elsewhere or seeks renewal from other sources. When of love there is not enough to go round, it is the dead who must go without.

The most important to Elizabeth of the "later people" were Stephen and Lady Ursula Vernon, especially Ursula. Elizabeth was brought to them by Jim Egan, who was their agent and Eddy Sackville-West's; his father had kept a hotel in Killarney; he had the same kind of (reciprocated) devotion to Elizabeth as that of Jim Gates, in Kildorrery. Stephen Vernon was in a wheelchair. This meeting with Elizabeth recalled— to him—her own story "Look at All Those Roses", in which a woman whose car has broken down calls at a house where there is a crippled child: the garden at Bruree, the Vernons' home in County Limerick, was full of roses.

Lady Ursula Vernon was formerly Lady Ursula Grosvenor, daughter of the Duke of Westminster. She was the child of a broken marriage, as "displaced", as a little girl, as any in Elizabeth's stories. She grew up to be very beautiful— she was compared with Garbo—and her life as a young woman in the 1920s was glamorous and restless. When Elizabeth first knew her in the 1950s—and ever after, for those sorts of looks hardly change—she had still the small golden head and perfect profile of the twenties' beauty: exceedingly tall, exceedingly slender, with an unnerving adolescent edgy grace. She and Elizabeth, different as they may have appeared to outsiders, became very close. Ursula was as "haunted" as Jean Black was "unhaunted"; and this, too, answered a need in Elizabeth. They became conspirators. Elizabeth had taken to wearing dark glasses a good deal; it was also Ursula's custom. "Rioting around" (Elizabeth's expression) together, they looked, Stephen Vernon thought, like two *Tonton Macoutes*.

The Vernons had married in the war—it was Ursula's second marriage—and within a year Stephen, in North Africa with the Irish Guards, contracted polio, from which he made a long and painful recovery. Both he and Ursula knew about horses, and when Elizabeth met them they were running a stud at Bruree, where they had come after the war.

Elizabeth—who had hitherto avoided horses all her life— entered into the Vernons' world with enthusiasm. They had one racehorse that became a famous one, which they had bred originally for Ursula's father: this was Hugh Lupus. Elizabeth followed the fortunes of Hugh Lupus with the Vernons, going with them to race meetings at The Curragh and at Ascot. She met with them racing people who were totally ignorant, or confused, about her identity as a writer; one misinformed gentleman bore down upon her crying, "Ah, *The Viper of Milan*! What a book!"

Stephen Vernon had literary interests and (inadequately exercised) literary skills; Ursula did not. In any case, this was not the point. The Vernons provided Elizabeth with a much-needed emotional base in Ireland and an unfailing affection; and she, to them, was a miraculous addition to a life that was not without its complications and lonelinesses. Elizabeth, when in Ireland, became increasingly dependent on the Vernons.

Jocelyn Brooke wrote a short study of Elizabeth's work, which was published for the British Council in 1952. Elizabeth liked it: "I was not only impressed; I learnt a lot from it", she told him. "It gives me at once a base and a point of departure from which to go on". In his essay Brooke had written that *The Heat of the Day* was, if not the most successful, "one of the most interesting" of her novels. But, since it was specifically a war novel, he did not see that she could go much further in that direction. But in what direction could she now go?

> The earlier books . . . dealt with a world that has, for all practical purposes, ceased to exist: the crust of civilized life has been cracked in too many places, the abyss beneath our feet can no longer be ignored. . . . What will be Miss Bowen's approach, as a novelist, to the squalid, standardized and unhopeful world in which we are now living?

The answer is that she played her music once more, with feeling, positively for the last time. She was to write two more complete novels after *A World of Love*: but *A World of Love* marks the end of that ironic, atmospheric lyricism that for some readers means "Elizabeth Bowen". *A World of Love* is short; it is more plotless, more dependent on mood and atmosphere, than any of her others. There is an Irish country house, Montefort (based on a deserted farmhouse near Bowen's

Court). There is Jane, the young girl, the innocent. She is Portia from *The Death of the Heart*, only in that book Portia is plunged at once into the corrupting machinations of love. *A World of Love* is an overture: it takes as its epigraph Thomas Traherne's "There is in us a world of Love to somewhat, though we know not what in the world that should be. . . . Do you not feel yourself drawn by the expectation and desire of some Great Thing?" Jane is waiting for life to begin: "Like someone bidden to enter an already overcrowded and over-charged room, she paused for as long as possible on the threshold. . . ."

This is theatrical; and Jane's crossing of the threshold, metaphorically and actually, is the set-piece of the book. It is a dinner party in a neighbouring house now occupied by a Lady Latterly, a forty-year-old English sophisticate (part of the "flight from Moscow"), who invites Jane on a whim. She makes Jane go downstairs to the party alone; she herself, in yellow chiffon, is still completing her toilette:

> Jane entered a drawing-room black-and-white at the door end with standing men. As she advanced towards them the sound-track stopped. Bowers of flowers cascaded fern mist from the piano top; jaded late green heat came in at the open windows. . . . Brought to a standstill under all those eyes by the slight shock of her own beauty, Jane said, "Lady Latterly will be late," for the first time wondering why.

(The "sound-track" reference in fact makes it more cinematic than theatrical. In 1952 Elizabeth had written to her agents: "I always think my stories are more suitable for films (of the decorative rather than the box-office kind, I fear) than for plays. Do you know Carol Reed? I hear he often talks of my work, and I do wish someone would push him over the edge!")[5]

At the dinner party there is a spare place at the table; it

seems as if it is being kept for Guy, former owner of Monte-fort and frequent visitor here, now long dead. Jane has found love letters written by him in the attic at Montefort; in the absence, yet, of a real lover she has made him her own. The other guests are upper-class, middle-aged, a little depraved, a little shop-soiled. Jane's startling presence acts on their "bar-barian nerves". In the account of this dinner party, every petal that drops from the bowl of roses, every wineglass lifted from table to lips, every equivocal gesture or remark is charged with a significance that it seems reductionist, or superfluous, to call sexual. A rose lies on the empty place-setting. A moth (and moths were the only living creatures that frightened Elizabeth, unnerved her totally), singed by a candle-flame, falls on the rose. The eyes of a man guest consult Jane's; he pinches the moth to death:

> Everyone was aware of the old assassin wiping his fingers off on the sheeny napkin. The girl's odd bridal ascendancy over the dinner table, which had begun to be sensed since they sat down, declared itself—*she* was the authority for the slaying. Tolerating the tribute of the rose, she could not suffer dyingness to usurp: she let out a breath as the moth was brushed from the cloth. That done, she was withheld again.

Jane's story will begin only after the novel ends. One is left with a sick suspicion that Portia's story is indeed going to be repeated; that Lady Latterly may manipulate Jane as Anna Quayne manipulated Portia; and are we not given to under-stand that this young Richard, whom Jane is deputed to meet at Shannon airport, is one of Lady Latterly's admirers, with whom she is now perhaps a little bored? But the author leaves it all open, for there is eternally the "expectation and desire of some Great Thing". And in the last line of the novel, with the meeting of Richard and Jane, the curtain rises: like Oliver and Celia in *As You Like It*, "They no sooner looked but they loved". The perennial tension between hope and experience is exactly expressed in the letter Stephen Spender wrote to Elizabeth after he had read this novel: "The extraordinary thing is your attitude of believing and not believing, believing completely and not believing devastatingly, in ecstatic love of the kind with which your book ends".

There are echoes in *A World of Love* of other Bowen novels and stories, apart from the young-girl theme. There is the almost-ghost of Guy and the contemporaneity of past and present, which encapsulate Elizabeth's supposition that "obsessions stay in the air which knew them, as a corpse stays nailed down under a floor".[6] There are echoes of details: a shopping trip with the young to the local town—here, Clonmore—with a visit to the very amateurish local hairdressing salon, and the possibility of ice-cream, exactly as in *Friends and Relations*; and a railway-station goodbye involving three people, as in *The House in Paris*, in which the emotional tension is not between the man and his rightful fiancée but between the man and the second woman, with whom he has a strong unspoken understanding. *A World of Love* is a distillation not only of themes but of moments and moods that for Elizabeth, in over thirty years of writing, had come to have a mythical significance.

If it were only Jane's story—or the prelude to Jane's story—it would be a delicate but a minor thing. The novel gains weight from the adults at Montefort for whom this hot summer brings a wholly painful tension. They have to make sense of the past, for they have not much future. Middle-aged Antonia owns Montefort, though she is not often there. She has a career, and in the neighbourhood "plays her part of fame". Antonia is elusive, sometimes difficult. She is not unlike some aspects of her creator. She has a chronic smoker's cough, and a "restless mannishness"; in her untidy bedroom, on the bedside table are "a packet of Gold Flake, a Bible, a glass with dregs, matches, sunglasses, sleeping pills"; and on the dressing-table tangled pearls, spilt ash, and powder. This is pure Elizabeth. Antonia had loved Guy, as had Lilia, the other woman in the house. The love letters Jane finds may have been to one of them, or to neither. There is decay and anxiety at Montefort, its time is past. Jane is in the yard:

> Grass which had seeded between the cobbles parched and dying, deadened her steps: a visible silence filled the place—long it was since anyone had been there. Slime had greenly caked in the empty trough, and the unprecedented loneliness of the afternoon looked out, as through eyelets cut in a mask, from the archways of the forsaken dovecot. . . . Nothing more was to be known. One was on the verge, however, possibly, of more.

There is "more", however, only for the young, who have not had time to weave a web of ambiguous, stifling relationships. And at Montefort, there is no money for anything.

Rose Macaulay, who reviewed *A World of Love* in two columns of *The Times*, wrote in a letter that "it is rather fascinating, though not to everyone".[7] It is in fact so magnificently Bowenesque that it was after its publication that J. Maclaren-Ross chose Elizabeth as the subject of one of his parodies in *Punch*.[8] Making a *mélange*—as it is rather easy to do—of this new novel and *The Death of the Heart*, and sending up simultaneously Antonia in *A World of Love*, Elizabeth's style, and Elizabeth herself, he has an elderly Anna Quayne up in her bedroom: "She lit the sodden stub of last night's fag and took a sip of gin and meth to cut, as she'd have put it, the phlegm". Portia, thoroughly middle-aged now, is on a different floor busy typing her own novels. And Portia's pert daughter asks her mother, "And why the inverted syntax—this Welsh effect when Ireland your scene here, if anywhere, is?" It is fairly funny, but the only true parody of Elizabeth Bowen could only be written—and indeed perhaps sometimes was—by Elizabeth Bowen herself.

Elizabeth was happy about *A World of Love*. She wrote to May Sarton:

> You can see why it's deliberately such a short book. It's on the periphery of a passion—or, the intensified reflections of several passions in a darkened mirror. It was a joy to write—natural (because of the native naturalness of the setting) as no book of mine, I suppose for a long time, has ever been.[9]

But the run-down shabbiness of Montefort, the pathetic efforts of Lilia to keep up appearances in public, the mention, even, of problems with money, were reflections of a blacker reality. In this "darkened mirror" is to be seen Elizabeth's own predicament at Bowen's Court. She closed her eyes to financial worry as long as she could, even though sometimes, by herself at Bowen's Court, she felt desperately lonely. Writing to Alfred Knopf on the death of Blanche in 1966, she said, "I felt maimed when Alan died—after twenty-nine years together. That is the last thing he would have *wanted* me to feel; so I suppose it has been partly for his sake that I have tried to live my life well since". She did live her life well. The year that *A World of Love* came out she enjoyed writing a preface for an American edition of the stories of Katherine Mansfield, and the following happy summer of 1956 Charles Ritchie came to Bowen's Court—and, as always, the Cecils and Iris Murdoch; and that same summer she received an honorary doctorate from Oxford University. About this she wrote to Veronica Wedgwood:

> You I feel will understand almost more than anybody that it means the world to me—a very solemn and to me almost holy occasion, the conferring, which I shall

remember all my life. I nearly burst into tears, which I'm always liable to do when I feel strung up.

Isaiah Berlin, recently married to his beautiful wife, Aline, gave a big party to celebrate both his marriage and Elizabeth's doctorate, in the Codrington Library at All Souls. It was a great occasion. "I wonder how you feel in the 1950s?" Elizabeth asked William Plomer in 1958. "Personally I am enjoying the epoch—it is really the first one, it seems to me, in which I've enjoyed being 'grown-up' as much as I expected to do when I was a child".

In the same letter, however, she said that her reasons for not coming more often to London were "of the most banal kind: it's all so expensive". Her finances fell to such a low ebb that gradually she began to think the unthinkable: she would have to sell Bowen's Court. None of her friends had any idea of how serious she thought her predicament was, though they remarked upon her restlessness and unpredictability. She could not be still; she wanted endlessly to be with the Vernons, and took her visitors inexorably for wild car-rides over to Bruree, or to their holiday house in Kinsale. "Too much Vernons", muttered some of them, among them Eddy Sackville-West. But she did not take even the Vernons into her full confidence. In 1958 and 1959 she spent months abroad, working in Rome and New York (where in 1959 she had pneumonia), closing her mind as much as possible to the situation at home, leaving bills and rates unpaid, wages unarranged-for, servants confused. Friends and relations in England and Ireland were acutely distressed about her and the situation. But she answered none of their letters about what was going on.

Seeing Audrey Fiennes off at Fermoy station after Audrey's customary summer visit in 1959, Elizabeth walked up and down on the platform very hard and then came out with the whole sad story, and her decision to sell Bowen's Court, in the five minutes before the train went.

E B

CHAPTER XII

No Abiding City

ELIZABETH USED A LOT OF MONEY. Never, after the war, was she in one place for more than a few months at a time, and air travel is expensive. Hospitality at Bowen's Court was an imperative with her. (But not a totally unconscious one: just as she could cut people off emotionally without, as it were, a penny, so she was aware of the power of the host to withhold. One of the most socially terrifying scenes in her writing is that in *The Last September* where the officers' wives from the British garrison are vaguely but unmistakably frozen off on the steps of Danielstown.) Visitors to Bowen's Court ate and drank royally; she ran up large bills. No one was ever, when with Elizabeth, allowed to pay for anything. Not that everyone thought to offer: people who live in big houses are presumed by people who do not to be rich.

She was highly sensitive—sometimes over-sensitive—to the potential penury of other people. Francis Wyndham, travelling by train to stay with Leslie Hartley, saw Elizabeth in a first-class carriage; he went to sit with her. They did not talk much; she was reading the novels she had to review for *The Tatler*. Francis had to pay excess on his ticket, which embarrassed Elizabeth; and then at Leslie Hartley's the host told them about a novel he was writing, which began with a man travelling first-class on a third-class ticket. Money, and Francis Wyndham's possible impoverishment, silently dominated the weekend. On the return journey, Francis tipped Elizabeth's porter for her. She later wrote to him, sending stamps ("always useful") to pay him back.

This was excessive, but sometimes her sensitivity was very apropos. In the autumn of 1959, when she was writer in residence at the American Academy in Rome, at the time of her own confusion and distress over Bowen's Court, she ran into Julian Jebb, whom she had first met through Eddy Sackville-West. They lunched several times, and went to the movie *La Dolce Vita* together. Julian, trying without success to get into the film industry in Italy, was young and broke. He decided that the next time he saw Elizabeth he would have to ask her to lend him some money. She forestalled him. When he arrived to meet her at the restaurant, there was an envelope on his place. In it were two ten-thousand-lire notes—to him, then, a fortune. (He wrote her a poem, which he sent her when he left Rome. She never acknowledged it; until months later she sent him a collection of her stories, inscribed "For Rome and always".)

Elizabeth never had what Eddy Sackville-West called "proper money"; i.e., capital, unearned income. She and Alan had what they earned. Alan's pension could not sustain Bowen's Court. Bowen's Court now depended on what Elizabeth could earn, and now she had to manage, or mismanage, everything herself. Another death—Jim Gates's, in 1958—robbed her of the last source of support and practical advice at Bowen's Court. She was too proud and too habitually reticent to share the anxieties with outsiders. One summer she let the house, to make money; and she toyed with the idea of sharing the house with people who might carry half the expenses and half the responsibility—a solution she wished on Antonia at Montefort in *A World of Love*.

Elizabeth's courage was indomitable. All through the 1950s and 1960s she wrote hectically for magazines—mostly American magazines, since they paid so much better. She wrote for *Holiday, Parents', American Home, Glamour, Mademoi-*

selle, House & Garden, McCall's, as well as more serious pieces for *The New York Times Book Review* and the *Saturday Review*. Her feature articles ranged from "For the Feminine Shopper" for *Holiday* and "On Not Rising to the Occasion" and "How to Be Yourself but Not Eccentric" for *Vogue* to "The Case for Summer Romance" for *Glamour*. Feature-writing is as exact and exacting a skill as any other, and she had mastered it as many "serious" writers would not; but someone of Elizabeth's age and stature should by rights have been using her energy on the books that she still had in her. The articles paid, but they did not pay enough. It was a losing battle. She offered Bowen's Court to her nephew Charles, the only male Bowen of the next generation, who was farming in Africa; he could not take it on.

When she decided to sell, she sold brusquely. She put the affair into the hands of the family solicitor in Fermoy, and accepted the first firm offer he came up with; even though, to do him credit, he did suggest that she might do better to put the house into the hands of one of the big Dublin agents. The family felt that she could indeed have done better than she did. She did not consult them, or anybody.

Eddy Sackville-West was particularly hurt by all this. He had bought his house in Ireland partly to be near her; and now she upped and went and sold without telling him anything about it. Something curious passed between them before she came to her decision. Norah Preece, who was close to them both, was told by both Eddy and Elizabeth that the other had proposed marriage, and how embarrassing it had been.

Elizabeth was without the sort of person she had always needed, a loyal, loving, practical companion. (There was always Charles Ritchie, there would always be Charles Ritchie, but he was married, and far away.) Eddy, "small, elegant, gentle, exotic, acid", as Hubert Butler described him, frailer by far than she both in body and spirit, would be disastrously miscast in that role. No one could lean on Eddy. He himself, though chiefly attracted to his own sex, sometimes thought he ought to be married; but again, to someone who would look after him. Elizabeth could not do that.

Yet they were enormously fond of one another, and there they both were, and Elizabeth on the edge of crisis. There must have been some evening when the obvious, impossible idea was in both their minds, in their eyes, if not on their lips: an idea from which they both withdrew immediately, aware at once of aberration. They did not come quite so close ever again after this, nor after Elizabeth left Ireland, although they saw each other often. When Eddy died, in Ireland, in the summer of 1965, Elizabeth wrote to Jean Black asking her to take a "small and unostentatious bunch of flowers" to the funeral for her. "If I'd been still at Bowen's Court I'd have made [a wreath] myself, or tied up a bunch. It seems funny to be sending Eddy your flowers, from me; but after all it's all in the family".

The man who bought Bowen's Court was Cornelius O'Keefe, a County Cork man, who wanted it for the land and the timber. Elizabeth, determinedly optimistic, was persuaded or persuaded herself that he meant, however, to live in and care for the house. "It cheered me also to think that his handsome children would soon be running about the rooms".[1] She came back to Ireland for ten days at the beginning of January, 1960, to say goodbye to Bowen's Court. "Actually what I dread are not my own feelings but other people's", she wrote to Veronica Wedgwood. Ursula Vernon went with her, and Noreen Butler came to help her clear up and decide what she wanted to keep. Molly O'Brien closed the hall door behind Elizabeth for the last time and saw her drive away as if it were just an ordinary day—all emotion withstood, withheld, or by now simply over.

The contents of the house were auctioned in Cork later. The furniture did not fetch what it was worth. More people would have come to bid if it had been held in the house, for country-house auctions attract people from miles around. But it had been decreed that the floors could not stand it; there had been a recent local case of old floorboards giving way during a crowded auction. Soon after the auction, the house was demolished. "It was a clean end. Bowen's Court never lived to be a ruin".[2]

Elizabeth went straight back to America. She was expected at Vassar. ("Heavens, between ourselves, I am terrified of Vassar!" she wrote to Veronica Wedgwood.) Lecturing or being writer in residence at American universities was another source of income, another way of seeing something of Charles Ritchie, and in itself a source of pleasure and interest. She visited, many of them more than once, the University of Wisconsin, the University of Pennsylvania, Vassar, Bryn Mawr, Princeton, the University of California at Berkeley, the University of Oregon, the University of Washington at Seattle, Reed College, Amherst, Williams, the University of Chicago, Stanford. . . . From 1950 until her last illness there was no year in which she did not spend some time in the United States. It became as important to her as Ireland, England, France, or Italy. Now more than ever, she was dislocated, at home nowhere and so at home everywhere. As she said in *A Time in Rome*: "Anywhere, at any time, with anyone, one may be seized by the suspicion of being alien—ease is therefore to be found in a place which nominally *is* foreign: this shifts the weight".

America had attracted Elizabeth ever since her first visit to New York, in the early 1930s. "I was very happy there", she wrote to Lady Ottoline Morrell on her return:

> The height of the city, the air, the speed of everything are curiously exhilarating; the people I met had great charm, intelligence and variety; one seemed to live in a kind of snowstorm of impressions for all those

weeks; it was a very fine autumn and long theatrical American sunshine made everything unreal, or real, perhaps in an unusual way that got near one's nerves. It was not that it was all unlike England, but oneself seemed unlike oneself, which I always rather enjoy; it was like being disembodied.

Lady Ottoline replied that she longed to hear about it all. "It sounds to me as if you had fallen entirely under America's spell and lost not one heart but 6 hearts one inside another—but what really happened was that you 'won' so many hearts that you underwent a strange interchange of hearts! I shall never know—shall I?" (Probably she did—she went on to press Elizabeth to come round for a tête-à-tête.)

New York, however widely she travelled in the States, remained her favourite city. Nearly forty years after that visit she told her American ex-pupil Tom Hyde, "I find I always think of going 'back' to New York, rather than 'to' it—as though I'd been born there: perhaps some part of me was". In the winter of 1958 she wrote to Jean Black from "this darling city—I must say I do love it with passion". At that time of maximum uncertainty over Bowen's Court and her own future, she found ease in New York. She had a genius, wherever she was, for finding flats, often borrowed from friends. She now took an apartment in the East Sixties and, as she told Jean Black, "Charles very kindly provides a supply of Seagram's rye, which I do think is the nicest whiskey there is—this sounds as though I spent all my time supping it up; I don't".

Charles Ritchie, who had been in Bonn for four years, was from 1958 to 1962 the permanent representative of Canada at the United Nations, in New York. Elizabeth wrote to Jean Black:

I loyally wandered into the Security Council part of the U.N. to watch Charles in action. Nothing particular happened. It *is* a curious building, not unlike that penguin pool in the London Zoo which was considered so modern in the 1930s. . . . Charles is enjoying N.Y. with great enthusiasm, except for occasionally being slightly fussed by the U.N. . . . We had enchanted evenings, and odd hours by day, wandering round the city.

She was writing this from Wisconsin, where she was to be for four weeks: "I may as well get some fun out of it—also do as well and be as nice as I can, for these are most awfully nice people, though inevitably many of them are as odd as coots. . . . I must say that when I did first arrive here I looked out of my window and burst into tears, but that was partly spoilt-childishness, partly homesickness."

The most diplomatic and least hysterical of men, Charles Ritchie helped Elizabeth steer through this difficult patch. (He had visited Bowen's Court himself several times—and he did not encourage her to cling on to it.) Her uncertainty had made her vulnerable in other ways, and in her relation with Charles her widowhood had upset the balance. ("Why didn't he wait?") Once the sale of Bowen's Court was signed and sealed, she began to regain her poise. A friend seeing her in New York during her time at Vassar, just after the final visit to Bowen's Court, wrote home to England:

I think she is "through" her love affair. She gives me the impression of being—how shall one say—convalescent. Something is over and finished evidently. She wants company, isn't in that state that lovers are in of never wanting to fix a date because everything has to be kept clear in case the beloved turns up. Of course we just talked about books and her life at Vassar and about you, so what I said above is all guesswork.

The guesswork was right in spirit if not in fact. Elizabeth was, in a sense, convalescent, was through something, but not through with Charles.

The very regular visits to the United States had begun in early 1950. In anticipation of her first visit since before the war, she told Blanche Knopf that she would reserve the first day for shopping, "as I know how London clothes look in N.Y. I don't aim for a 'trousseau', but do need an evening dress, cocktail dress, wool suit for day, and some shoes". She wanted Blanche's advice on where to shop. (Blanche always delighted Elizabeth by being the only person she knew who was even more bedecked with junk jewellery than Elizabeth herself.) Blanche was out of New York during the visit, and wrote after Elizabeth's departure: "I am just back and find that you have thoroughly enchanted the town; the impact you made is almost a scandal because I think no one has ever come here on a flying trip such as you made and completely charmed everyone". In autumn, 1951, Elizabeth undertook her first American lecture tour, organised by an agency (later she did without) that she recommended to Veronica Wedgwood:

> They're highbrow—that's to say they don't send one to the wrong places; they are *not* too mercenary (I mean in the sense of pressing one to lecture to unsuitable audiences for what would be higher fees). . . . They work out one's itinerary and haggle for good fees on one's behalf. On the other hand, one does have to pay them 30%!

In America Elizabeth became very close to Catherine Collins, the wife of Alan Collins, who was president of Curtis Brown in New York. It was with "these angelic people", the Collinses, that she stayed the winter after Alan's death, at Hunt's House—an eighteenth-century house older even than Bowen's Court—at Hopewell, New Jersey. At Hunt's House she was able to get down to work again on *A World of Love* for the first time since Alan died, and in gratitude for this it was to Catherine Collins that Elizabeth dedicated the book. Hunt's House was a place to relax after the exhaustingly tight schedules of the yearly or sometimes twice-yearly lecture tours, as was the Knopfs' house at Purchase, with its beautiful garden.

Catherine Collins went with Elizabeth in January, 1960, on a journey to the Deep South—*Holiday* had commissioned an account of the trip, which was later reprinted in the collection of Elizabeth's pieces called *Afterthought*. There she met up with the writer Eudora Welty, "my beloved Eudora Welty". Elizabeth had met her first soon after the war, in Ireland. She came to Bowen's Court, and during her stay Elizabeth had written to Charles:

> You know my passion for her works. She had apparently drifted over to Dublin on her own. She sent me a telegraph from there and I asked her to come down and stay. . . . I take to her most immensely and I think you would. She's very un-writerish and *bien élevée*. A Southern girl from the State of Mississippi; quiet, self-contained, easy, outwardly old-fashioned, very funny indeed when she starts talking. . . . She's reserved (in itself, I think, a good point these days) so although we have chatted away a good deal, I really know little about her life, nor she about mine. I think she's like me in preferring places to people; and any unexpected sight or view while we are driving about the country makes her start up in the car with a smothered cry as though she had been stung by a wasp. . . . No one would pick her out on sight as "an interesting woman". Actually I think she's a genius rather than an interesting woman, which I am glad of as I prefer the former.

This description, while justly complimentary to Eudora Welty, who became her friend for life, is as revealing about Elizabeth as about its subject. In finding someone deeply compatible, someone "like me", one ascribes to him or recognises in him one's own qualities and characteristics. Eudora Welty was a most compatible companion, like Veronica Wedgwood and for some of the same reasons—as Elizabeth told Blanche Knopf during another of Eudora's visits, in spring, 1951:

> Eudora Welty is staying in the house—working away at one of her great short stories in another room. This is ideal: I'm so fond of her, and her preoccupation during the day with her own work gives me a freedom unknown when one has an ordinary "social" guest.

Elizabeth's activity during the 1950s, and only just less so in the 1960s, was so prodigious as to seem on paper impossible to sustain. To take just one year, 1953–54, the difficult first year after Alan died: she left the Collinses in January for New York—she had been in Princeton where, in Edmund Wilson's house, she had heard the tortured and half-incoherent John Berryman reading from his work in progress, and had taken in a flying visit to Memphis to give a lecture. In March she left New York for London, for the last meeting of the Royal Commission on Capital Punishment; in April she was in Rome, lecturing for the British Council and then staying on with friends; in May she was back in New York to give the Blaysfield Address at the American Academy of Arts and Letters; in England again in June, to report on the Coronation; the summer—with visitors—at Bowen's Court was interrupted by teaching in Oxford at the International Graduates Summer School; at the turn of the year she was in Rome again, then a two-week lecture tour in Germany in February, 1954, for the British Council and a stay in Bonn (where Charles Ritchie was from that year till 1958, as Canadian Ambassador to the Federal Republic), then America again . . . and so on, year in and year out, as well as producing her books and reviews and all the feature journalism.

In every house she stayed in, she shut herself up for part of the day with her writing, not only as an economic but as a psychological necessity. As May Sarton observed, "writing provided a continuity, a means towards self-integration. . . . That—and washing her white doeskin gloves, which were as much part of her style as the fact that she rarely wore a hat".[3] Descending on London, on New York, on Rome, she would have a session on the telephone, making arrangements for meetings with friends, fixing appointments. (Mornings were for writing; telephoning could only be begun after noon. Before that hour, the telephone paralysed her; after it, she became tremendous in her telephoning.) It is no wonder, however, that her reaction to the British Council's suggestion of a lecture tour in India, she told Reggie Ross-Williamson, was that it made her heart sink: "in fact I know that both physically and psychologically I just couldn't DO it!"

In 1956 she was awarded the Lucy Martin Donnelly Fellowship at Bryn Mawr for the autumn term, of which the best part, for her, as she told Bill Koshland of Knopf, was "the prospect of being in America a bit like a civilised human being, with time to live life and see my friends, and not to have to dash about giving lectures". Her duties at Bryn Mawr were not arduous: "I don't have to do anything", she wrote to Veronica Wedgwood, "except from time to time see any of the students who are interested in writing". She was very good with students, and they loved her. In personal contact with the young she had a graceful touch, a combination of respect for their values and curiosity about their lives. As writer in residence at the American Academy in Rome, she made friends with a pretty mixed bag of students and visitors. (The smaller the group, generally, the better she coped. Large gatherings of strangers could make her fall silent. She was not an indiscriminate "performer".) "What do the young *do* all day?" she asked Mrs. Laurance Roberts, wife of the director of the Academy; and by accompanying them on their sightseeing round Rome, she found out.

In America her friends were not all writers, publishers,

academics. She loved the shiny side of America—skyscrapers, jazz, strong drinks, the immediate hospitality and easy intimacy that was met halfway by her own un-British conviviality. She liked the rich worldly New York society of un-bookish people such as Kirk Askew—the art dealer—and his wife, who had an apartment on Park Avenue in whose comfort and welcome Elizabeth luxuriated.

For Elizabeth, though spending much time now in universities, was anything but an academic. Barely was she, nor did she aspire to be, a "lady of letters". "For a novelist it becomes easier, second nature, to imagine rather than to learn. Thousands of us would rather invent than study", she wrote in *A Time in Rome*. She had read and reread enormously, her judgements were astute and lucid. The short book *English Novelists*, which she wrote in the war, is clear and intelligent, an admirable survey. (Though she omits James Joyce entirely, and not because he was Irish, for Sterne and Goldsmith are in.) But some of her "literary" pieces have the dutiful air of the good Downe House person who has done her homework. She did not have that dubious asset "a trained mind", nor did she have the specialist's knowledge of English literature. In answer to an enquiry from her publisher at Longmans, John Guest, she said of James Hogg, "the Etterick [sic] Shepherd", "as a matter of fact I'd no idea he existed". She was highly intelligent but not intellectual; not by nature analytical. The impetus in her writing was to "make" or "do", rather than to "say". Her intelligence was intuitive, as was her talent. As she said in *Why Do I Write?*:

> I am fully intelligent only when I write. I have a certain amount of small-change intelligence, which I carry round with me as, at any rate in a town, one has to carry small money, for the needs of the day, the non-writing day. But it seems to me I seldom purely *think* ... if I thought more I might write less.

And though writing never came easily ("I'm a slow and fussy writer", she told Victor Gollancz, "but if I don't fuss I apparently can't write"), the pleasure of creative writing was for her "equalled elsewhere only in love".

Hostile to probing the sources of her inspiration, unversed in the technicalities of modern literary criticism, Elizabeth lectured mainly on the English novel and on novel-writing. Her lectures were best suited to smallish gatherings, whom her personality dominated and charmed. She became very professional, as royalty does. She turned up, for example, at the University of Virginia, to join a group of Irish literary visitors —Gogarty, Denis Johnston, Sean O'Faolain—at two o'clock in the morning, having dined and spoken elsewhere. A little fed up ("you hogs") that none of them had stayed up to meet her, she spoke the next morning "like an ambassadress", her theatrical dignity enhanced as always by the stammer, well under control. In *A Time in Rome*—written during these lecturing years—she said she found the lot of the vestal virgins enviable: "For what they forwent as women, they were compensated in the ways women most truly enjoy. An aura surrounded them. Limelit appearances, during which everything they said and did was above criticism, alternated with restful privacy". This was, more or less, her own situation in America.

In very high-powered academic gatherings, grandly produced—as at Princeton—what she actually had to say was sometimes inadequate. It did not very much matter. She was charming, and it was "a writer speaking", and "the writer", that fabulous beast, has an aura at least as bright as that of the vestal virgins for those who love or profess but cannot create literature. Not only was it "the writer", it was Elizabeth Bowen. Elizabeth's writing, esteemed as it was in Britain, was —and for the moment is—"bigger" in a commercial and a critical sense in the United States. In America she was a star both as a person and as a writer; and, for good and ill, her writing had been taken already into the machinery of university teaching programmes, with interpretive theses and dissertations emerging at the other end. In 1963, her publisher Blanche Knopf wanted to nominate Elizabeth for the Nobel Prize for Literature.

Elizabeth's visit to Rome for the British Council in 1953 was her first trip to Italy for seventeen years; before the war, she used to go practically every spring. Enamoured of Rome all over again, she planned, in that year after Alan's death, to write a book about Rome as therapy: something she could immerse herself in when anxieties made invention difficult. *A Time in Rome* reads as if it were the fruit of one single visit between February and Easter. In fact it was not published until 1960, seven years after its inception (and was dedicated to Kirk and Constance Askew, in whose New York apartment she finally completed it).

The most therapeutic part of it was the very many visits to Rome that the book necessitated. She had friends there; she worked in the day and spent "happy handsome evenings", as she said in the book, in varied company. In April, 1955, after reaching Rome via Paris, where she had seen Charles ("Paris was having a *faux* spring and was looking angelic"), she wrote to Jean Black, "Bif's party was a great success, and I enjoyed myself like anything. Douglas Fairbanks Junior and all sorts of stars".

Generally she stayed at the Albergo d'Inghilterra, Bocca di Leone 14, which she described in the first pages of the book. *A Time in Rome* is not a guide-book: it is a very personal account of Elizabeth's feelings about Rome—its atmosphere, its architecture, its history. It is full not only of sensation, but of deflected emotion. She did the groundwork intensively and thoroughly, walking the Roman streets day in and day out, exhausting any companion and sometimes even herself. As she wrote in the book:

> Knowledge of Rome must be physical, sweated into the system, worked up into the brain through the thinning shoe-leather. . . . When it comes to knowing, the senses are more honest than the intelligence. Nothing is more real than the first wall you lean up against sobbing with exhaustion.

If alone, she lunched slowly in quiet restaurants, and watched the waiters:

> No waiter hurries you; do not hurry him. Having set down your token basket of bread, he potters in figures of eight round his other tables, with extra solicitude for those empty, smoothing a cloth, cunningly changing the whereabouts of a salt cellar, or lifting a water carafe against the light as though to analyse its contents. Or he will pose for a minute or two in the street doorway.

She describes the waiter and not herself; but what one also sees is an un-Latin, distinguished foreign woman at her solitary table, smoking, with dusty shoes, and a tattered street-plan on the table beside her carafe of wine. One sees Elizabeth seeing the waiter.

She studied the city's moods, in its characteristic golden daylight and at night, recalling in her reaction to Rome under the moon the unearthly townscapes of her "Mysterious Kôr": the moon "gives texture in lieu of colour; masonry it reduces to chalk and ink. . . . I have never felt further from past people who, from where I am, have also looked at the moon: the moon is there, showing me that they are gone".

She speculated on Roman family life, on the personality of Livia, second wife of the Emperor Augustus, unable to bear him a child; on the sites of the ancient villas she invoked and evoked the bloody past, the ruins acting on her imagination as did the ruined houses at home in Ireland. The gardens of Rome especially enchanted her, and her lyrical rhythm of inversions make her descriptions of them unmistakably Bowen ("Private they formerly were. . . . Inky are the caverns of ilex shadow", and, of the Domus Aurea, "calcinated appear the alcoved chambers"). The cemeteries—places of "returned innocence" —caught her attention, and she wrote about them as she had in her very first novel, *The Hotel*; she found now "something approaching gaiety"

> in the jump of the little flames in the ruby glass lamps, the gestures of high-spirited marble angels, the positive glitter of so much whiteness, the prettiness of small children rendered in effigy down to the last lace frill on a little girl's dress or curl on the crest of a little boy's head.

She observed Roman cats and their ways (which Alan would have enjoyed, though she doesn't say this), and Roman citizens and their ways, not always gravely:

> Romans . . . never sneeze, and wonderfully seldom laugh. When *I* sneezed, it felt like some dreadful incontinence. The membrane inside their noses must be different. Laugh, I realise they do, but never nervously; it might be better to say they never titter.

A Time in Rome is filled with personal comment about life, religion, politics, love, and the politics of love. ("To love makes one less clever".) Nevertheless the last two sentences of the book, after describing the pain of departure, come as a slight shock. What she wrote, and what she had the panache to leave written, is the controlled, undirected cry of the displaced person:

My darling, my darling, my darling. Here we have no
abiding city.

When Elizabeth returned to Europe in the summer of 1960,
with no Bowen's Court to come home to, she went briefly to
ground in a borrowed flat in Stratford-on-Avon. "It struck me
this would be a good place to clear up work in—various
magazine commissions etc., I hadn't had time to cope with
before I left America".[4] "Convalescence" was not complete,
and coming back was an ordeal. Jean Black, visiting her at
Stratford, found her nervous and unsettled. Eddy Sackville-
West, when he saw her for the first time after the sale of
Bowen's Court, warned Molly Keane to expect an extraordinary change; she looked to him like someone who had
attended her own execution.

She had already arranged somewhere more permanent to
live, about which she had high hopes. She went back to
Oxford, to Old Headington. "I must say this flat is rather
nice", she wrote to Jean Black from there. "It has more of a
'house' than a 'flat' feeling". It could hardly have been in more
familiar territory. Isaiah—now Sir Isaiah—Berlin and his
wife Aline lived in the big house, Old Headington House.
White Lodge, also belonging to the Berlins, backed on to their
garden. Elizabeth's flat in White Lodge—at first-floor level,
with very fine windows—was approached from the back, near
where a door in the high wall of the Berlins' garden linked
the two houses. A flight of outside steps rose to the door of
Elizabeth's flat. When, going up these steps, she turned her
head to the right, she could see Waldencote, the little stone
house where she and Alan had lived for ten years. Elizabeth
was going back on her tracks.

At White Lodge she embarked on a new novel, and prepared the selection of essays, reviews, prefaces, and broadcasts
that was to appear in 1962 under the title *Afterthought*—in

the American edition the childhood memories *Seven Winters,* which had not been published in the United States before then, were included in order to make a more substantial volume. (Knopf were not keen on the project, but "I do not think we can stop her", wrote Blanche Knopf in an internal memo. "She wants Longmans to do it and if Longmans are going to do it we had better".) *Afterthought,* which *was* worth doing, was dedicated to Derek Hill, in gratitude for his painting of Bowen's Court. His house in County Donegal was one of those included in her annual summer tours of visits in Ireland; and for the rest of her life there was a ritual of Christmas with the Vernons followed by New Year with the Blacks. She could not consider buying a modest house in Ireland for herself. If there was no Bowen's Court, there would be no other Irish house.

The Oxford arrangement was a moderate success. Elizabeth loved Aline Berlin and saw a lot of her. Older friends were all around. She picked up the threads with Stuart Hampshire: he and she were closer in these years than ever before. But everyone was now older, tireder, grander, busier. Sir Maurice Bowra did not pay her quite the same attention that he had thirty years earlier. Sir Isaiah Berlin himself, though so near at hand and as fond of her as ever, was greatly occupied and in demand. He did not have so much time for the chats and dinners and expeditions that he and Elizabeth had shared in the past. Even with Lord David Cecil, her first and dearest Oxford friend, things were not always easy. The past cannot be repeated.

Elizabeth was every bit as distinguished and busy as any of them; but she was a woman on her own, and proud, and had perhaps hoped for the impossible. She was not reconciled to being older. She would have liked to deny both illness and aging. David Cecil had hoped she might take up the current generation of clever Oxford young, but she did not want to play that role, although individual chosen members of the younger generation she loved dearly. She was always out-standingly generous in giving her time and what practical help she could to young writers who interested her. She was a very kind person, and also she remembered what an enormous difference Rose Macaulay's support had made to her own career in early days. But if she could not mix with the young on terms of friendship and equality, she would rather keep away. Having no children of her own made her position harder. David Cecil, after going to a young people's dance at Peter Fleming's house, expatiated to Elizabeth on how pleasant it had been watching the children of one's friends; no, he hadn't danced, he just liked watching the young. "Don't say that again, David, you're sounding like Mr. Woodhouse in *Emma*", said Elizabeth sharply.

For all that, her own stamina was not what it was: she tended to go firmly to sleep at functions that bored her. She gave good parties at White Lodge, especially when Charles was staying. But some of her friends thought she could and should take a greater part in Oxford life. As Maurice Bowra said: "Elizabeth could have been the head of a women's college at Oxford or Cambridge. She had the right presence and authority for such a post and would have left a lasting im-pression".[5] It could have been arranged. But it was not what she wanted. She was a writer.

There had been no novel since 1955, and *A Time in Rome* had not convinced everyone. Evelyn Waugh, arch-gloomer, wrote in his diary on January 4, 1961:

> It has been a bad year for the old steeplechasers—Elizabeth Bowen, John Betjeman, Leslie Hartley down and out of the race; Nancy Mitford and Tony Powell just clinging to the saddle.[6]

This time Evelyn Waugh was not a reliable tipster.

Elizabeth was working on her new novel—*The Little Girls*. She was well into it by autumn, 1962, in Wisconsin.

She wrote to Sir Rupert Hart-Davis from there, sending her contribution for the seventieth-birthday party that had been given at the Garrick in London for Alfred Knopf and which she had attended in September ("Not only was he, bless him, clearly as happy as a bee and as proud as Punch, but I think all present had a splendid time"); at the same time she wrote that the pressure of university life "has *not* kept me from getting ahead with writing my novel". This Wisconsin stint found Elizabeth in an up mood: "I'm thoroughly enjoying myself here: love this great big teeming university and this pretty town", she told Veronica Wedgwood.

With *The Little Girls* Elizabeth tried to answer the question Jocelyn Brooke had asked in print ten years earlier about what her approach would be to what he saw as the "squalid, standardized and unhopeful" modern world, now that the world of her earlier novels had just about ceased to exist. She dispensed with the civilised surface of behaviour, to a large extent. She allowed the danger, despair, and passion that had always lain under the surface to be expressed. She admired the work of her friend Iris Murdoch, who, with a sensibility and a civilised approach to life like Elizabeth's own, was turning the structure upside down by allowing civilised middle-class characters to act out myth and nightmare and fantasy as characters in fairy stories do. Elizabeth also admired what Muriel Spark was doing (and persuaded Knopf that they should publish her in America). She felt that this was now the way to approach fiction, and that any resulting inverisimilitude was not important. She also decided to present the characters in *The Little Girls* entirely from the outside: no more descriptions of moods or "inner weather", no telling the reader what anyone was thinking or feeling. She remembered saying to Evelyn Waugh that he never told his characters' thoughts, and his reply: "I do not think I have any idea what they are thinking: I merely see them and show them".

None of this was easy. The ending especially caused her

problems. In May, 1963, she wrote to Charles from White Lodge:

> The chief thing is that I shall have *finished* "The Little Girls" three days hence. You may wonder why it has taken me so long. It's simply that I am ending it with a tremendously ambitious finale; in a way almost a novella in itself, but also like the finale of a musical: almost, one might say, like a comedy version of the mad scene in "The Duchess of Malfi". . . . Technically the thing is at once very tricky and very fascinating to write.

The room she worked in, she told him, was "a sea of undisturbed papers; dotty versions of various incidents in the final great scene, clipped together and stuffed under various pieces of furniture to prevent them blowing away". She had been working about fourteen hours a day.

But this ending was not right. In her last books particularly, Elizabeth relied greatly on the advice and support of Spencer Curtis Brown, whom she had known as both agent and friend for forty years, and who had often stayed at Bowen's Court; he was in a way the Jim Gates of her creative life, with an instinctive understanding of her intentions in her books. That summer she took the novel down to Monks Hall, his house in Suffolk, and in discussion with him worked out a different ending. Later, she wrote from Kinsale:

> Spencer, I can never say how deeply grateful I feel (and "grateful" is such a stale word) for the immense help and enlightenment you gave me, over what was necessary as to the final "signposting" of that story. . . . And what fun it was working at those extra scenes at Monks Hall, then bringing them down and talking them over. That was a wonderful week. I still miss working at that dear rocky table on the beautiful undulating vast floor of my room at Monks. Bless you.

Knopf already had the original version set in type; but Blanche Knopf agreed to substitute the new ending. "My goodness, yes, she HAS been nice about this", Elizabeth wrote to Spencer Curtis Brown. "I think the world of her. Really *handsome* about it, I mean".

Earlier in 1963, Elizabeth had been at the University of Pennsylvania, where a faculty member, Professor Theophilus E. M. Bell, finding her "jolly and easy to talk to", discussed with her *The Heat of the Day* and the fascination of military intelligence; he asked her what her next novel was about, and she told him that this new one, too, was about espionage and intelligence:

> Her lipstick was much too orange. . . . When she gave a formal lecture, she wore a drastically short dress, that made me feel she was thinking herself into the book she was working in, which turned out to be *The Little Girls*, and not the military intelligence novel she had hinted at.

But in a way *The Little Girls*—which she dedicated to Ursula Vernon, in whose house she wrote much of it—is a story of espionage into the past and into identity. It is written as comedy, but is full of "particles of sadness", as Dinah in the book says of *Macbeth*. It deals with three women in their fifties—three very competent witches—who had been at school together, and had performed a schoolgirl ritual of burying a coffer in which each had placed a secret object. Their ways in adult life have utterly parted. One of them, Dinah, searches out the other two to disinter what had happened between them, to discover whom they had become. "Those were the days before love. These are the days after. Nothing has gone for nothing but the days between". There is difficulty in finding the truth: "As we know, what anyone thinks they feel is sheer fabrication".

Dinah, the instigator of the enquiry, becomes direct in

her questioning: she asks Clare, "Are you a Lesbian?" Which provokes an attack from Clare on Dinah's self-protective detachment: "You are what you always were, and that's a cheat. A player-about. Never once have you played fair, all along the line". Dinah is "an enchantress's child". "I myself was not any one of those 3", Elizabeth told William Plomer, of *The Little Girls*. "But it is what Americans would call 'a recall of sensory experiences'. I've taken some liberties with the Folkestone landscape, but as it's called Southstone I suppose that doesn't matter". "The enchantress", Dinah's mother in the book —husbandless, vague, exquisite, socially ambiguous—has the personality and the mannerisms of Elizabeth's own mother. Dinah and her mother were not quite like the other Southstone families. They lived in a delicate limbo of their own rituals, unimpressed by the local variety. "They had no gong" expressed it, for Southstone, perfectly. And "they were none of them mental, by any chance?"

Elizabeth, because of her father, was more afraid than most people of mental illness. In the crisis over Bowen's Court she drew as near to it herself as she was ever to get. Dinah in *The Little Girls*, facing the past head on, has a kind of breakdown. She withdraws, takes to her bed, switches all her caring back into the past. But the human and spiritual links between childhood and age hold firm, across the no man's land of the years between. It is Clare who expresses in *The Little Girls* Elizabeth's faith in a kindly, continuous, if frighteningly arbitrary, pattern:

We were entrusted to each other in the days which mattered, Clare thought. Entrusted to one another by chance, not choice. Chance, and its agents time and place. Chance is better than choice; it is more lordly. In its carelessness it is more lordly. Chance is God, choice is man.

(Elizabeth could not at the end keep to her policy of not giving the characters' thoughts.) "Chance and choice"—the greater and the lesser power—were picked up by Elizabeth, consciously or not, from Yeats. In the poem "Solomon and the Witch", in the act of love between Solomon and Sheba there is hope of a return to the moment before the Fall—a return to Eden, "Chance being at one with Choice at last". And if not this time, then perhaps the next:

> "And the moon is wilder every minute.
> O! Solomon! let us try again."

The aging women who were the little girls see from a print of Southstone Old High Street how their childhood world is ruined. Dinah says: "It might be better to have no pictures of places that are gone. Let them go completely". But the three learn to attempt through kindness a synthesis between past and present, between innocence and experience.

Elizabeth attempted and achieved something like it. The year after *The Little Girls* was published, she bought a little house in Hythe on the Kent coast, where she had lived with her mother; she completed her return journey.

CHAPTER XIII

Coming Home

I T WAS NOT A SUDDEN IDEA. She had never ceased to think of Hythe; she and Alan had spent Christmas there in 1950. Twenty years before she finally returned, she had described it to Charles:

> It is a nice little town—reassuring and right-and-tight and sound. One of the few places that make me love England and Englishness. But I think that apart from Englishness there's a peculiar quality of Kentishness that I like. The Hythe people are flamboyant and hardy and unmawkish. The town has got the sort of density— in its life, I mean—that I associate with small towns in France. . . . Also I suppose I like Hythe out of a back-to-the-wombishness, having been there as a child in the most amusing years of one's childhood—8 to 13. But I can't see what's wrong with the womb if one's happy there, or comparatively happy there.

The house she bought, in a town of attractive houses, had no distinction at all. It was a small red brick box, built two years earlier, and called Wayside. She rechristened it Carbery, after the long-lost Colley property.

Carbery's great attraction was its position: it was on Church Hill, a footway, partly of steps, up a steep hill running inland. From the front, the house faced east over the church-yard and the church, and from the back, out over Romney

Marsh. Church Hill is picturesque in itself, and for Elizabeth it was full of memories. "I used to ply up it as a child", she told Charles Ritchie. "Always *eating* something, often sweets. How even a child could simultaneously ply *up* that hill *and* eat now beats me". Elizabeth loved Carbery. Also it was extremely cheap—£4,700—and even this was more than covered by the sale of some of her papers to the Humanities Research Center at the University of Texas in Austin. With her pictures and silver and books and furniture—the little that she had saved from Bowen's Court—she transformed the interior. There were only two bedrooms. "The west bedroom, which will be yours, is the larger of the two, and is over the living-room", she told Charles. "When you are not there I shall probably use it as a room to write in, as it's so pleasant".

Not that Elizabeth had entirely "settled". In the year she bought Carbery, she made two or three trips to America, one to Italy, and only cancelled an earlier Italian holiday because she was determined to go to Jerusalem with Jean Black:

> Wild *horses* wouldn't get me to put off our Jerusalem time, and there's not the slightest necessity for me to do so, but I think it would be foolish to spend 10 days flouncing about in Italy when I shall have such masses, still, to get straight here. Specially as Charles is hoping to arrive here, unless the world or anything blows up, on May 7.

The White Hart Hotel, in the High Street in Hythe, became her haunt; she and her visitors became almost family there. Elizabeth put her friends up at the White Hart, pre-paying their bills and leaving change for the meters in their rooms. The hotel people adored and indulged her, one member of staff recalling always the first time they saw her come in, in dark glasses and a leopard-skin headscarf, "a great lady".

Patience Erskine was living nearby at Aldington, in the

house Noël Coward had given her; Veronica—from 1968 Dame Veronica—Wedgwood and Jacqueline Hope-Wallace bought a country house near Polegate, over the border in Sussex and not far from William Plomer at Hassocks; Cyril and Deirdre Connolly went to live at Eastbourne. "B" Curtis Brown was in Lewes; and Charles, from 1967 to 1971, was in London as Canadian High Commissioner. Elizabeth's lifelong habit of visits and excursions was uninterrupted. With Audrey Fiennes she went to Suffolk, to Cumberland (they both loved Hadrian and wanted to see his wall), and to Ireland—tacitly avoiding the immediate Bowen's Court area. And the two went to Rome, using *A Time in Rome*, at Elizabeth's solemn suggestion, as a guide-book. These trips were illumined by Elizabeth's undimmed responsiveness, which made even the oddest errand, such as accompanying Norah Preece into Folkestone to buy a dressing-gown for a nun, a joke and an adventure.

She did not stop working. She wrote a preface for Sheridan Le Fanu's *The House by the Churchyard*, and contributed to a symposium to celebrate E. M. Forster's ninetieth birthday.[1] Cape brought out another collection of her previously published stories in 1965, *A Day in the Dark* (of which the title story, about an adolescent girl on the edge of understanding the adults' manipulation of her and of each other, is a Bowen classic), for which she wrote a preface. She appeared on television in a literary quiz series called "Take It or Leave It", proving a most professional and reliable trouper, anxious only—to the point of obsession—about her appearance: "Will I look a hag?" Lights and make-up had to be carefully arranged and, sometimes, rearranged. The concern about the way she would look was only an extension of what she had always felt about photographs of herself. She had made a "black list" from among those taken by Alfred Knopf, a keen amateur photographer. Often she refused requests from publicity people for a photograph; and the few "permitted" ones were used again and again. The worst thing that ever happened in this connection was when *The House in Paris* came out in America, and *Newsweek* published, alongside a very flattering review of it, a picture described by Elizabeth as "of a stout lady in riding breeches, a muffler and a 1917 hat examining a jar of newts (?) by a tombstone". Whoever it was, it wasn't Elizabeth and was, she told Blanche Knopf, "definitely damaging". A photograph of herself that she did like, taken by Alfred Knopf, and that Charles Ritchie liked and kept, was of her opening the door at Clarence Terrace with her latchkey, as he had seen her do so many times.

One of her television performances was a piece of imaginative creation outside the ordinary. In 1970 Julian Jebb devised a B.B.C. television programme called "An Imaginary Friend", in which various writers were interviewed about a non-existent John Woodby, presupposed to have recently died and to have exercised a marked but unspecified influence on all the interviewees. Elizabeth entered into the fantasy with ease. Her John Woodby was writing a book on "Reputation" —he was a sort of "secret agent to which so-called celebrities were being exposed". She had met him at a party just after the war, "in one of those sort of traffic blocks which occur in large crowded parties"; later he came to Clarence Terrace. She made him into an ambiguously sinister figure like Harrison in *The Heat of the Day*. She produced half a letter, purporting to be from Woodby and found in the lining of one of her old coats (so much more convincing, half a letter, than a whole one), which said: ". . . There is something slippery, on the run, about all you writers, how on guard you are, what do you believe you are defending, protecting, what holy of holies. . . ." Her Woodby story was an understated and characteristic bad dream: rather subtler, if less funny, than John Betjeman's, which injected a little melodrama by making

Woodby a fetishist with a room in Willesden full of boots and
shoes; he left John Betjeman his shoehorn when he died.

As soon as she moved to Carbery, Elizabeth with characteristic
courage and determination had started a new novel, which
came out in 1968 in America and in the following year in
England. *Eva Trout* was the last novel she completed. Its
eponymous heroine is the largest character Elizabeth created
—inexplicably large, and largely unexplained. She is an
orphaned heiress, unloved, clumsy, "left unfinished", innocent
with that damaging innocence so deep-lodged in Elizabeth's
mythology. Eva is on the loose, with money but little charm:
"I suspect victims; they win in the long run", says someone
else. "She went on wanting to move in; in she moved. . . . Those
consuming eyes and that shoving Jaguar". Her background is
disastrous, as her father's ex-lover says:

> "Eva's capacity for making trouble, attracting
> trouble, strewing trouble around her, is quite endless.
> She, er, begets trouble—a dreadful gift. And the more
> so for being inborn. . . . The Trouts have, one might
> say, a genius for unreality; even Willy was prone to
> morose distortions. Hysteria was, of course, the domain
> of Cissie . . . Eva is *tacitly* hysterical."

Eva is also chronically romantic. She lies ill in bed: "Supposing
somebody came in softly, saying 'How is my darling?' She *had*
heard somebody saying, 'How is my darling?'—but when?
where?" It was someone else's mother, to a child ill at school.
Eva's gender is ambiguous: " 'Girl' never fitted Eva. Her so-
called sex bored and mortified her; she dragged it about after
her like a ball and chain". To complete herself, Eva acquires
a child illegally, in America (this is the only one of her novels
in which Elizabeth—briefly and wittily—uses America as
a setting); the child turns out to be deaf and dumb. His

greater and even more dangerous innocence is her undoing. He shoots her dead.

In *Eva Trout* there is no longer a cracked crust over the surface of life. People say and do extreme things. There is one major conceptual shift in *Eva Trout*, and that is that instead of responding and reacting to situations, as most of Elizabeth's heroines do, Eva creates the situations herself. Elizabeth told her cousin Audrey that though she knew Eva as a result "had it coming to her", she only gradually knew, as she worked on the book, that it would be through the child. Yet the idea of the child with the gun—the supreme illustration of the lethal potential of innocence—had been there for a long time. In *The Little Girls* the secret thing that Dinah had buried in the coffer as a child was a gun she found hidden in her mother's bedroom: "Somebody's shooting someone else with it now, probably". Further back still, thirty years further back in *The House in Paris*, she had written of the illegitimate child Leopold (who of course had no actual gun):

> The child at the back of the gun accident—is he always so ignorant? I simply point this thing, it goes off: *sauve qui peut*. No one could be less merely impish than Leopold. Behind the childish *méchanceté* Ray saw grown-up avengingness pick up what arms it could. . . .

A psychoanalyst, in the unlikely event of his ever getting anywhere near Elizabeth, might have exposed, but perhaps not illuminated, the connections she preferred not to explore except obliquely and imaginatively in her writing: connections between her parents' history, her ambiguous situation as a child, her own childlessness and the child she might have had, her "dislocations"—and so on. The fact is that generally, in her early work, the child, however frighteningly candid, is the person one identifies with. We are on his—or more usually her—side. She wrote a book for children around the *Eva Trout* time called *The Good Tiger*, in which two children bring a little tiger home with them from the zoo. The tiger, misunderstood and feared for his innocent tigerishness, runs away. All ends happily, with the children and the tiger eating cake in a wood far from the adult world—a picnic-in-Eden story, in fact. There is throughout her work a tension between the benign and the malign in the child, as there is a tension between the clarity of innocence and its destructiveness. In her last two novels, children do seem to be more threatening, more likely to be vengeful "hostiles". Dinah's friend Frank in *The Little Girls* is "terrified of children", and Dinah regrets having lent him *The Midwich Cuckoos* (John Wyndham's novel about the beautiful children with paranormal powers who take over a country village).

The figure of Eva—who though she is not a child longs for the one person to whom she is "darling", and who though she is not a tiger affects an ocelot coat and fur gloves and drives a Jaguar—prowls through a novel that is full of jokes and social comedy. Mr. Denge, the Broadstairs estate agent, is like a character out of Dickens, as is the vicar with the perpetual cold. There is an important sequence set in the house in Broadstairs where Dickens wrote *Bleak House*. Elizabeth often went there from Hythe, and took her visitors there. The first time—in June, 1965—she wrote to Charles that the house was "a really very vulgar but enchanting stone house on a low promontory overhanging the sea", and she wondered how the great man had kept himself warm sitting in the big bay window at his desk, "the sea lashing about on three sides":

> As I told you, I am deep in "David Copperfield". It has given me an almost terrifying illumination about my own writing. Here really are the roots of so many things I have felt, or perhaps of my way of feeling things and seeing them.

These terrifying illuminations are implicit in *Eva Trout*, and give it its authenticity. As Roderick—Stella's son, and every woman's ideal son—says in *The Heat of the Day*, "art is the only thing that can go on mattering once it has stopped hurting". *Eva Trout* is a formidable novel, though a difficult one only for readers who longed for the old Elizabeth Bowen of *The Death of the Heart*. She herself was satisfied with it, and it won the James Tait Black Prize.

Elizabeth cared very much what her novels looked like. For *Eva Trout*, she wanted a jacket designed by Philippe Jullian, and wrote to William Plomer at Cape to ask for it:

> Now it's all over, between you and me and the doorpost I did loathe the jacket Capes gave *The Little Girls*. A young artist, I was told. I really don't want *Eva* to be used to break in any more young artists. Those 3 little arty monsters on *The Little Girls'* jacket couldn't have been worse. Neither do I want any more of Miss Joan Cassell.

(Elizabeth meant Miss Joan Hassall, who did woodcut frontispieces and embellishments for the Cape Uniform Edition of Elizabeth's fiction.) She duly got her Philippe Jullian jacket. Bob Wren Howard, the partner at Cape with whom she chiefly dealt, had died, and she now got to know Tom Maschler at Cape over the publication of *Eva Trout*. She reported to Spencer Curtis Brown that Tom Maschler was "not unlike a Byzantine representation of Our Lord, only without a beard and with (at first glance) a rather more ferocious expression". Spencer, now retiring himself, had helped and guided her over *Eva Trout*, especially in its final stage, as he had over *The Little Girls*: "I can't tell you what it means, your having this grip on and understanding of *Eva*. Talk about a miracle!" she wrote to him. (Spencer Curtis Brown's support was always practical as well as literary. It was he who, with Alfred Knopf, had negotiated the sale of her papers to Texas.)

In January, 1969, John Guest of Longmans gave a large party in the library of the Travellers' Club, a party "which coruscated", according to Raymond Mortimer in his thank-you letter. Elizabeth was magnificent in grey chiffon with rhinestones, and among friends—Raymond, and Elizabeth Jenkins, and Leslie Hartley—and admirers; among the latter the novelist Nina Bawden, confined to a sofa following an operation. She watched from afar her husband talking to Elizabeth, longing for him to bring her over. But he had no idea who Elizabeth was, and Elizabeth did not tell him; he said to his wife afterwards, "What a nice, amusing woman".

For Elizabeth had not changed. She could still charm the birds off the trees, still had a *farouche* diffidence, still cared deeply for "behaving properly", still defended fiercely her privacy and her inner self. Julian Jebb went to stay with her in Hythe soon after the publication of *Eva Trout*. They drank a lot of strong Martinis, chain-smoked, ate supper off a card-table "elevated neatly after strenuous stammering imprecations not to help".[2] They talked of Eddy Sackville-West, of Ireland, of Rome, of writing, love, and friendship; inevitably with Elizabeth, the guest talked more, revealed himself more, beguiled by the atmosphere she created.

She gave him the best front bedroom, and refused his offers to help with the washing-up. Julian went to bed; and then heard mysterious sounds from the kitchen below:

> The radio was tuned inaccurately to—I think—a piece by Handel. Above this sound—noise of music and dish-washing—I began to hear Elizabeth's voice in monologue. She sounded neither agitated nor calm, but she must have been speaking quite loudly for, although I couldn't hear a single word she said her voice, alone and unstammering, was unmistakable. I would estimate that this mysterious solitary conversation with herself lasted less than half an hour. She came upstairs, went

into her room, came out, went to the bathroom, returned to her room and, when I imagine she had got
into bed, briefly the monologue continued.

Julian Jebb's explanation to himself (for he never asked her
about it) was that the monologue was the necessary activity
of the artist, the writer who that day had done no writing:

> Perhaps that day . . . she had been robbed of her work,
> and so the subconscious took a lively leap as soon as
> she was alone. Words had to be said, even if they
> couldn't be written. Words of her own. For me, her
> solitary conversation had more to do with ritual, than
> exhaustion or alcohol or habit.

(Elizabeth's night-talking reminds one of Virginia Woolf, who
talked continuously and monotonously to herself in the bath,
to the consternation, at first, of the housekeeper at Rodmell.)

The next day Elizabeth took Julian to see Dickens's
house at Broadstairs. After that they were expected at Lord
Clark's house at Saltwood to watch an episode of his TV series
"Civilisation". Julian uninvitedly expressed his very mixed
feelings about this series and about Kenneth Clark's manner
of presenting it. "Then you don't want to dine with the
Clarks?" she asked. "Well, I'd better not, as I might say
something rude". "You might. I will say I am alone".

Julian had been guilty of imperfect manners: "A distinct,
though light change in tone ensued for the remaining hour
of my stay. She looked out of the window. We were both, in
our different ways, embarrassed. She dropped me at the
station, and I watched her juddering, wilful weave out of
sight".

In summer, 1969, Elizabeth began working on an autobiography to be called *Pictures and Conversations*. (The phrase is

adapted from the first page of *Alice in Wonderland*.) She was dubious, in general, about memories; as she wrote in *A Time in Rome*:

> Memory must be patchy; what is more alarming is its face-savingness. Something in one shrinks from catching it out—unique to oneself, one's own, one's claim to identity, it implicates one's identity in its fibbing. Proust remarks, creative wrong-memory is a source of art. Good: but when it deceives one about a city this trickiness is a plague and the very devil.

How much more so about the facts of a life. She told William Plomer that his autobiography was "the best account of your and my times" that she knew. "On the whole, I haven't cared much for most of my contemporaries' autobiographies such as (though don't tell them) Stephen's [Spender] and John Lehmann's. Most people do better to keep their traps shut".

Hers was to be no conventional autobiography. Indeed she said in a note to her publishers that it was not to be an autobiography at all in the accepted sense: it would not follow a time-sequence, and it would be "anything but all-inclusive". Its theme would be "the relationship between art and life". One of her reasons for writing it was the number of critical studies and theses being written about her, some of which had been found "wildly off the mark". "If anybody *must* write a book about Elizabeth Bowen, why should not Elizabeth Bowen?"

She took the beginnings of the book with her to Princeton in the autumn of 1969, where she taught for a term as part of the Creative Writing Program. Stuart Hampshire and his wife were in Princeton, and helped her settle into what she described to the poet Howard Moss as "the rather weird but endearing little duplex I am living in. Its environment looks like the ideal scene for a murder, and I'm so much hoping there won't be one". "It's very easy to run", she reported to Spencer Curtis

Brown, about 185 Nassau Street. And indeed Elizabeth loved the "convenience" of American homes and all American gadgetry: coffee-machines, matching towels, American cocktail apparatus, crush-proof everything were features of White Lodge and of Carbery—the polar extreme from the doubtful plumbing, ancient kitchen, and temperamental electric generator that had underpinned Bowen's Court.

America in 1969 was not at its happiest. Elizabeth wrote to Spencer Curtis Brown:

> No signs of Student Unrest *here*, so far. Indeed, such of the undergraduates as I've come across seem as mild as gazelles. (Passions may be seething in their breasts, but I doubt it.) All of them rather subdued—all, I think, overhung by the horrifying fear of having to go and fight in Vietnam if it does not stop *soon*.

A young Vietnam veteran brought her a "formidable short story" about his experience, which she was trying to help him with, "though I must say it's pretty good already".

Elizabeth's attitude to the Vietnam War was that it was harming America internally. She thought of America as a great nation; she could not bear America to be self-abasing, self-doubting, or, as she put it, "whining". She thought, too, that countries should restrict themselves to governing their own destinies—in the general as in the individual case, she was hostile to interferers. As she wrote in *A Time in Rome*:

> I am sick of the governessy attitude of our age, which is coming to be more genuinely presumptuous, nosier and more busybody than the Victorian. . . . Much about other peoples, nations who are our contemporaries, is a pity; but does it devolve upon us to tell them so, or say so in terms they can overhear?

Consistent with this, she was, she told Jean Black in 1965, "very pro-Rhodesian; I mean, Smith-Rhodesian. They may be foolhardy, but they're brave; and why *should* they be pushed around by people who don't understand their problems".

She was impatient with the Vietnam involvement. In safe company, in England, she voiced her unworthiest thoughts, watching the TV news: "I'm sick of seeing all those people in straw hats running about". In September, 1970, she wrote to Bill Koshland in New York:

> I can't bear the unhappiness this is causing you all. To tell you the truth, I don't care two hoots about the Vietnamese, Northern or Southern; what I can't stand is that America should suffer. What I do feel is that these insane protests and demonstrations can only be doing more harm than good.
>
> One immensely cheering-up factor in this country has been the change of government. I always have thought the world of Edward Heath. The idea (up to last June) of a possible *further* five years of that dreary Labour government had become a nightmare.

Like most people, Elizabeth moved further right as she got older. In her own person, she gave the lie to the total breakdown of the *ancien régime*. She was not formal towards those who served her—she sometimes confided more to cleaning-ladies, her own and her friends', than she did to friends. But they were impressed by her. She inspired in those who served her—waitresses, cleaning-ladies, shop people—the very opposite of class-resentment. They recognised and spoke of her without irony or embarrassment as "a lady", "a great lady", loved her, and would do anything for her. "An aristo-crat", thought Mrs. Chapple of Hythe, seeing her for the first time at the vicar's party in her dark glasses and a purple suit. Her evident superiority gave satisfaction. People like Elizabeth, people of quality with star-quality personalities, have special licence.

In Princeton, Elizabeth made the last of her close friendships with a much younger person. She described Tom Hyde, two years later, to Howard Moss: "He not only is nice, sweet-natured as well as intelligent, he looks nice, like one of those younger figures in a Mantegna background". (Unlike a Mantegna figure, he habitually wore an Oshkosh cap—he came from Oshkosh, Wisconsin, where the blue-and-white striped visored caps are made by Oshkosh B'Gosh, Inc.) Tom Hyde was an undergraduate, and attended her creative-writing seminar. After a single dinner together they were instant friends. When she left Princeton, she wrote to him, "I had an uncanny feeling of happiness, as though we were kindred spirits or something". She did not lose him when she left Princeton, as she encouraged him to go on to Oxford (and actively furthered his application to New College); once he was there, they met in London, in Hythe, in Oxford.

She took him to Ireland as well. He was one of the very few people with whom she revisited the site of Bowen's Court. In August, 1971, they drove from the Vernons in Kinsale to the Blacks in Doneraile, taking in Spenser's castle and the sights of County Cork. They approached Bowen's Court in Elizabeth's Triumph down the avenue furthest from Kildorrery: Elizabeth perhaps did not want the ordeal of being recognised and greeted.

> Elizabeth walked about in the opening where the drive ended and the house had been while I went over to investigate the walled garden. Several planks in the far corner, obviously engineered by local children, afforded an easy way over the wall. Inside the garden was like a fantasy world. All the trees were dreamy, overgrown and hung with a form of moss that looked like cotton. The pattern of the old garden survived in traces, and there was evidence of regular usage by children, which Elizabeth was glad to hear. The garden would have made a marvelous setting for a scene of a novel, perhaps something not unlike *A World of Love*.

We got our hands thoroughly purpled eating
blackberries or raspberries which grew on the outside
wall of the garden, and drove back to Creagh Castle
for tea.[3]

Elizabeth was not at all sentimental on this visit. Her career
of withheld emotion stood her in good stead. She showed a
party of children around on another occasion, explaining to
them where everything had been. But such exercises left her
exhausted.

Elizabeth's returns to Ireland were continuous—although, as
she told Jean Black, "relations, much as one does love them,
are for some reason more (psychologically) exhausting than
friends". The relations centred mainly on the Colleys—by
1971 "the colony that's the remains of Corkagh, ruled by
Aunt Edie (now ninety and a dynamo of energy)".

But her involvement with Ireland was increasingly a
matter of eternal returns to Kinsale, where the Vernons were
now living permanently in what had been their holiday house,
Fairyfield—"a rather charming little Victorian-gothic house,
with a terrace in front, perched up, looking across the
estuary", as she described it to Sir William and Lady
Hayter. Perched up it was, but also secluded, surrounded by
trees: a house full of strangeness, and of acceptance of strangeness, and of affection. Elizabeth's contact with Kinsale, south
of Cork city and on the sea, had not begun with the Vernons;
she and Alan had stayed there in the old days, and the incom-
parable Misses Acton, who ran Acton's Hotel, were her old
friends. Acton's Hotel, for Elizabeth and the Vernons in
Kinsale, played the same vital role as the White Hart in Hythe.

In 1965 Elizabeth had written the narrative for a pageant
on the history of Kinsale—which had been occupied by the
Spaniards in 1601, and where James II landed in 1689. It

was performed there at Charles Fort, which had more than once been under siege in the past. Her script was full of optimism about peace and progress in modern Ireland, written as it was three years before the renewal of sectarian horror in the North. Later a Nativity Play she wrote* was performed in Limerick Cathedral—though another performance has a greater historical significance. This was in the Protestant Cathedral in Derry, at Christmas, 1970, and something of a group effort between friends. Derek Hill produced it and designed and painted the sets. Jean Black and Stephen Vernon were the two narrators. The importance of it was that in troubled Derry the Protestant Cathedral was filled, for the first and possibly last time ever, with children and adults of all denominations. Anglicans, Presbyterians, and Roman Catholics all took part. Roman Catholics were among the congregation. (The brother of one of the Three Kings was later murdered by the I.R.A.) To Elizabeth, who of course was there in Derry for the performance, the whole thing was "an adventure and a great pleasure". It was also an extraordinary achievement. (The Nativity Play was included by Spencer Curtis Brown in his edition of the posthumous *Pictures and Conversations*.)

Elizabeth's religious beliefs were ethnic and social in origin, part of being Anglo-Irish. The Church of Ireland—the Anglican Church in Ireland—was as much part of her background, and as unquestioned, as Bowen's Court. Her attitude as an adult to Roman Catholicism was that it was a different, equally strong, and perhaps more dangerous magic. In 1946 she had written to Charles Ritchie from Bowen's Court:

> I have been very conscious of religion these last months here in this country. To be a Roman Catholic myself would be as unthinkable as ever. But I do see the

---

* An early version of the Nativity Play was produced around 1960 by Alan's cousin by marriage Celia Lanyon, in the village church at Hambledon in Hampshire.

efficacy and all-embracingness and sublimity of Catholicism in its effects on all the people's beings and lives around here. It seems to make them hard-boiled and spiritual at the same time. On Saints' Days, especially All Saints' Day yesterday, which they call "the day of the dead", one feels a sort of influence in the air like the flame of a candle burning.

Eddy Sackville-West had been a Catholic convert, and as fervent as converts must be. Elizabeth used to tell a story that once when Eddy accidentally dropped his rosary on the hearthrug, Desmond Shawe-Taylor picked up the fire-tongs, retrieved the rosary, and handed it back to Eddy on the end of the tongs. Desmond denied the story. It amused Elizabeth, however, even if it had its origins only in her imagination.

At Bowen's Court she used to go to the little church on Sundays, Alan accompanying her only on major festivals, when he would sing loudly. Her Anglicanism was more than merely social. She had a real knowledge of her Church's liturgy and a respect for its traditions, as for all traditions. She said of the ancient Romans: "Were they not the better for two things, devotion to ceremonial, faith in tradition? Once one breaks with either, endless unease begins".[4] In the late 1960s the Church of England introduced an "Alternative Service" to the familiar 1662 Communion Service in the *Book of Common Prayer*. Elizabeth's attention was drawn to an article, "The Destruction of Common Prayer", in the February, 1968, issue of *Theology* and wrote off to its author, Georgina Battiscombe, writer of many biographies including one of John Keble:

I am among the mutinous mutterers—and more, in not only a state of pain but (I suppose?) rather ungodly anger. I am appalled by the defeatism of so many of my fellow communicants, here in Hythe, on whom the Alternative Service has been imposed. *I* have taken my own course—left our parish church for a neighbouring village one where the 1662 service still goes on—for how long, though? Yet I feel this walk-out ought not to be the answer.

What can we DO? How are we to raise the shout? I move about a good deal, and see many people: I am a novelist, Elizabeth Bowen, though I am signing this with my married name, which I generally use. I long to know if any form of resistance *is* being organised? I would be glad to do anything I could. . . .

It was the only protest movement Elizabeth ever joined. She typed out a copy of the article and dropped it into the letter-box of Hythe's "excellent but deluded vicar". She met Georgina Battiscombe at the Guards' Club in London, a pleasant venue "appropriate or not to what we are wanting to talk about". They agreed that Elizabeth should write a letter to *The Times*. She would try and get Lord David Cecil's signature as well, and Georgina Battiscombe would try for John Betjeman's. But in the end Elizabeth backed out of the enterprise. She wrote and said she could not after all manage the letter to *The Times* and the matter was dropped by her.

She discussed a great many matters, including this one, with Oliver Peare, the "very nice, intelligent and conversible rector"[5] at Kinsale; but it was not a confessional relationship. She was one of those who disapproved at first of the post-humous publication of Rose Macaulay's *Letters to a Friend*, with their exposure of her spiritual life: she had always admired Rose's reticence. Her own concern with the formal side of religion, the outward and visible signs, was one thing. Her conception of the inward and invisible grace was another, her own, and very much more catholic.

She said in her Rome book that "Christianity is a revolutionary insistence upon seeing, seeing anew". She credited God with a godliness that many Christians deny Him; she assumed in Him an understanding of, if not a disregard for, the discreet breaking of society's rules, including its sexual rules, even when these are given the sanction of religion. "Religion one cannot be set against, if one has it in one, but forever I was set against propaganda. However noble the motive, secular or sacred, I will not have powder in the jam". Consequently, she lived without the guilt that consumes—not always disagreeably—so much of the nervous energy of most believers who are also rule-breakers. So far from God making man in His image, man makes God in his: Elizabeth's God disapproved of disapproval. "No, like you, I can't see (or feel) the conflict between love and religion", she said to Charles. "To me they're the same thing".

She believed quite simply in an afterlife, and a world elsewhere. She found atheism "claustrophobic". This was part of her feeling of the thinness of the barrier between the living and the dead; the ghosts in her stories may be sad, but they are rarely frightening. If one were to see a ghost, she said, it would not be in the grim dark but on a hot summer's afternoon. Her acceptance of and access to the paranormal had more to do with telepathy or a Celtic leaning towards the supernatural than with formal Christianity. One or two of her close friends were spiritualists. She wrote in *The Little Girls*: "Are not desires acts? One is where one would be. May we not, therefore, frequent each other, without the body, *not* only in dreams?" An unwritten section of her autobiography was to be on "Witchcraft: A Query. Is anything uncanny involved in the process of writing?" Elizabeth's writing was often sparked off by something momentarily glimpsed, half understood, which because it was only half understood was secreted, to flash into her conscious, writing mind when it was needed. Spencer Curtis Brown asked her in a letter whether the "apparently compulsive secreting and subsequent resurgence of the 'flash'" was to tie up with the witchcraft theme in her autobiography (which would be the rational expectation). She did not answer him, though she kept his letter among her notes. The last time William Maxwell ever saw her, at a lunch party in America, the conversation was about religion and the supernatural, and he said to her, "I don't believe in God and I do believe in ghosts". She replied severely, "I believe in God *and* ghosts".

However susceptible Elizabeth was to worlds elsewhere, she did not want to investigate them too deeply or consciously —that way lay "unease". She went with Rosamond Lehmann to a conference of the College of Psychic Studies, where she was asked to speak. She stood up and spoke as a staunch member of the Church of England. Her roots and her security were in simple, orthodox faith.

James Mossman, the television interviewer, obsessed by death and soon to die by his own hand, asked Elizabeth at the end of a television interview what her feelings were about aging—and, by implication, about death. Elizabeth replied, "I think the main thing, don't you, is to keep the show on the road".

Elizabeth kept the show on the road for as long as she could. She had had a chronic smoker's cough for years, and bronchitis recurred at shorter and shorter intervals. At Easter, 1970, in Kinsale, she had a "ghastly bout", and told Veronica Wedgwood that she felt "hazy and querulous". Better in the autumn, she stayed with the Hayters in Oxford, at New College, and managed to enjoy a party given by A. J. Ayer: "I thought we stayed just the ideal time—somehow at parties at which one stays standing up one seems to require to be more *concentratedly* intelligent than one does at those at which one can sit down". At another Oxford party, she relished "the high-powered inrush of Mr. Isherwood".[6] And that Christmas —1970—there was her Nativity Play in Derry.

In early 1971 she was in a nursing-home with pneumonia, and on recovery stabbed her foot with a pruning tool. The wound went septic. She had to cancel a pilgrimage to Rodmell with Howard Moss, but struggled determinedly off to Ireland with one shoe and one silver slipper. On her return she wrote to Howard Moss:

> I am so used to being well, as you have known me long enough to know. Eddy Sackville-West is said to have said of me, "Elizabeth is almost *rudely* strong". Anyway, I don't take reverses and disappointments well.

To escape the Hythe winter and its damp fogs, she went to the Bear Hotel in Woodstock for a couple of months in early 1972, where she occupied a warm, self-contained annexe in its old-fashioned yard. She asked Mrs. Chapple (who looked after her now in Hythe) to send her Scrabble from Carbery—"under the sofa in the sitting-room?" She tried to get on with her book, and saw all her Oxford friends—not Maurice Bowra now; he had died the summer before. No one realised how ill Elizabeth was. She went to see Susan Tweedsmuir at Burford, saw something of the novelist Elizabeth Taylor, whom she greatly liked and admired, invited all the world to the Bear, went to Charlecote, near Stratford, where Alice Buchan—now Lady Fairfax-Lucy—lived. Here she was in great form ("Just another inch of gin, duckie"). John Morley, a fellow guest at Charlecote, who was painting Lady Fairfax-Lucy's portrait, watched her drive away "in quite the dirtiest car I've ever seen, all windows closed, the engine screaming, her smoking a cigarette and, although amongst this we couldn't hear a single word, she was still talking".[7]

But three months later she had lost her voice, that deep, distinctive voice which was so much part of her personality. Charles was now back in Canada. Concerned, he flew over and sent her to a London specialist. The specialist sent her straight into University College Hospital for X-rays.

Elizabeth had written in *The House in Paris*: "But fate is not an eagle, it creeps like a rat". She had cancer of the lungs. In the hospital she watched the tennis at Wimbledon on television—"those duels"—and grappled with the novels entered for the Booker Prize. "How strange many of them are. I begin to fear that women have lost their genius", she wrote to Rosamond Lehmann. That summer she had a course of radium treatment, staying with Audrey at her flat outside Newbury and driven daily by Audrey to London for the treatment. She was optimistic. She was sure she was getting better. "*All* is now well", she wrote to Jean Black, "what might have been nasty taken in time". The radium treatment had made her skin red and raw. Continuing debility she put down to other side-effects of the treatment.

Her voice was the merest whisper. It was almost impossible to telephone. She had difficulty with breathing. She still went out and about, frustrated when waiters in restaurants could not hear her. She still insisted on going up to London from Hythe from time to time, even if she was so exhausted when she came home in the evening that she practically had to be carried down Church Hill from the taxi that met her at the station. At home she played Scrabble and smoked and drank with Patience Erskine, to whom she was still and always "Bitha". Mrs. Chapple looked after her. Small things brought back memories—a check scarf found in a cupboard that Mrs. Chapple was turning out. Charles had put it round her years ago after she had received a sharp knock from someone coming through a hotel door. Going back to Alan with a bruise under the scarf, she had said, "Charles hasn't been beating me." . . . With Patience she reread all the novels of Anthony Powell's *A Dance to the Music of Time*, and talked about them: she did not live to see the final volume. She read Dashiell Hammett and Raymond Chandler. She read all her own books over again. The last conversation she ever had with Patience was about punctuation—Somerset Maugham's, which she admired.

In December, 1972, very ill, she went as usual to

Kinsale. Gerard Shiels, shocked by her appearance when he
met her at Cork airport with the Vernons' car, pushed through
the customs to help her. She spent most of Christmas in bed,
through sheer force of will getting up to go to Communion
on Christmas Day.

On her return to Hythe it was obvious that she ought
to be in hospital. Before the ambulance men came, she said
to Mrs. Chapple, "Have you got anything to do at home?"
She wanted that hour alone in her own house. ("Someone
soon to start on a journey is always a little holy": *The House
in Paris*.) She took Cecil Woodham-Smith's *Queen Victoria*
in the ambulance with her. It was an entry for the Duff
Cooper Award, for which she was one of the judges. She had
worked her way faithfully through all the books entered. Too
ill now to go to the decisive meeting, she reported her own
first choice to fellow-judge Sir William Hayter—Quentin Bell's
Virginia Woolf, which turned out to be the decision of them
all.

In the hospital they came to see her—Isaiah Berlin, Cyril
Connolly, Ursula Vernon, Rosamond Lehmann. She was too
ill for all the people who would have liked to see her. Charles
came every day, and brought champagne; and Audrey. For
Audrey the visits were made more agonising because she and
Elizabeth could not easily communicate: Elizabeth had almost
no voice and Audrey was deaf.

Although Elizabeth spoke with such difficulty, at the end
her stammer disappeared completely. She asked for Spencer
Curtis Brown, who was her literary executor as well as her
friend. She was very weak. "Do you want the fragment of the
autobiography published?" he asked. "I want it published",
she said, twice. (When he did publish *Pictures and Conversations*, he included among other pieces to make up the volume
the fragment of a novel she was working on at the end. It is
only a chapter: a characteristic and suggestive fragment. An
arrival by car at a country house; the old, inside, looking out;

the young, outside, looking in—uninvited and unwanted guests, but clearly here to stay. It was called *The Move-In.*)

Audrey saw Elizabeth that day, too. Suddenly they were able to talk to each other. Audrey spoke to Elizabeth of the roses that had grown at each side of the steps at Bowen's Court. Their faint scent was always associated in Audrey's mind with Elizabeth's "Welcome home, darling" as they drew up inexpertly at the front door. Now she said, "Does the smell of those roses haunt you as it does me?" and Elizabeth's face came to life. They spoke of the two sisters who were their mothers; and they were close to one another. After that Elizabeth slept and only Charles was there. She died early on the morning of February 22, 1973.

Elizabeth Bowen was buried in Farahy churchyard near her husband and her father. It was a Sunday. All day and at the funeral the local people poured into the little churchyard bringing flowers. It was a very cold day, with snow falling.

NOTES

SELECT BIBLIOGRAPHY

BOOKS BY
ELIZABETH BOWEN

INDEX

Notes

UNLESS OTHERWISE INDICATED, all the correspondence between Elizabeth Bowen and Lady Ottoline Morrell, H. G. Wells, Rosamond Lehmann, A. E. Coppard, Blanche Knopf, Stephen Spender, Graham Greene, Sean O'Faolain, and Jocelyn Brooke from which quotation is made is in the Humanities Research Center at the University of Texas at Austin. The letters quoted from Elizabeth Bowen to Virginia Woolf are in the University Library of the University of Sussex, and those from Elizabeth Bowen to William Plomer in the University Library of the University of Durham. No further indication of these three sources will be given in the notes to chapters. In references for quotations from other letters in the Humanities Research Center, the abbreviation H.R.C. is used.

All other letters quoted, unless otherwise indicated, are in private hands; and where the name of any writer or recipient is not given either in the text or the notes, it is at the request of the writer, recipient, or owner.

Foreword (pages xv–xvii)
1. From Spencer Curtis Brown's foreword to E.B.'s *Pictures and Conversations.*

Chapter I: Bowen's Court (pages 3–19)
1. From E.B.'s *Bowen's Court.* Unless otherwise indicated in text or notes, all quotations from E.B. in this chapter are from *Bowen's Court.*
2. E.B. to John Hayward: from Rosamond Lehmann's papers in the library of Kings' College, Cambridge.
3. E.B.'s *Pictures and Conversations.*
4. *Ibid.*
5. Cyril Connolly, *Enemies of Promise.*

Chapter II: Bitha (pages 20–43)
1. E.B's *Seven Winters.* Unless otherwise indicated in text or notes, all quotations from E.B. in this chapter are from *Seven Winters.*
2. *Bowen's Court.*

Notes

3. *Ibid.*
4. *Ibid.*
5. *Pictures and Conversations.*
6. *Ibid.*
7. *Bowen's Court.*
8. *Pictures and Conversations.*
9. *Ibid.*
10. *Ibid.*
11. *Bowen's Court.*
12. *Ibid.*
13. *Pictures and Conversations.*
14. E.B.'s preface to reissue of *Encounters*, Ace Books, 1949.
15. "Out of a Book", in *Orion II*, 1946; reprinted in *Collected Impressions.*
16. B.B.C. talk of 1947, "She", included in E.B.'s *Afterthought.*
17. "Out of a Book".
18. *Ibid.*
19. "The Mulberry Tree", 1935; reprinted in *Collected Impressions.*
20. Priscilla (Hayter) Napier in *Downe House Scrapbook 1907–57.*
21. Felicity (Hurst) Elphinstone to V.G.
22. "The Mulberry Tree".
23. *Ibid.*
24. *Ibid.*

Chapter III: Encounters (pages 44–67)

1. Sean O'Faolain, *The Vanishing Hero.*
2. *Bowen's Court.*
3. E.B.'s preface to Knopf edition of *The Last September*, 1952.
4. Autobiographical note, circa 1949.
5. *Coming to London*, ed. John Lehmann.
6. E.B.'s preface to reissue of *Encounters.*
7. *Coming to London.*
8. *Ibid.*
9. "The Mulberry Tree".
10. E.B.'s preface to *The Early Stories.*
11. *Ibid.*
12. *Ibid.*
13. *Ibid.*

Chapter IV: The Oxford Connection (pages 68–89)

1. From "Elizabeth Bowen and Her Husband, Alan Cameron": unpublished essay by Susan, Lady Tweedsmuir (Susan Buchan).
2. Francis King to V.G.
3. C. M. Bowra, *Memories 1898–1939.*
4. *Ibid.*
5. E.B.'s preface to Knopf edition of *The Last September*, 1952.
6. *Bowen's Court.*
7. Norah Preece to V.G.

Chapter V: The Grand Chain (pages 90–112)

1. John Gross, *The Rise and Fall of the Man of Letters.*
2. Stephen Spender, *World Within World.*
3. John Gross, *The Rise and Fall of the Man of Letters.*
4. E.B. in *Why Do I Write?*, by E.B., V. S. Pritchett, and Graham Greene.
5. B.B.C. Third Programme interview with E.B., September 11, 1959.
6. Stephen Spender, *World Within World.*
7. E.B. to Lady Ottoline Morrell.

Chapter VI: The House in London (pages 113–134)

1. E.B.'s "Notes on Writing a Novel", published in *Orion II*, 1945, and reprinted in both *Collected Impressions* and *Pictures and Conversations*.
2. E.B.'s preface to *Stories by Elizabeth Bowen*; reprinted in *Afterthought*.
3. E.B. in *Why Do I Write?*
4. E.B. to Charles Ritchie.
5. *Recollections of Virginia Woolf*, ed. Joan Russell Noble: a book made from the edited transcripts of two B.B.C. television programmes on Virginia Woolf, in which E.B. took part.
6. Rupert Hart-Davis, *Hugh Walpole*.
7. Virginia Woolf, *A Writer's Diary*.
8. *Recollections of Virginia Woolf*.
9. *Ibid.*
10. Letter from E.B. in Rosamond Lehmann's papers in the Library of King's College, Cambridge.
11. *Ibid.*
12. Stephen Spender, *World Within World*.
13. May Sarton, *A World of Light: Portraits and Celebrations*.
14. Obituary of Alan Cameron in *The Listener*, September, 1952.
15. Obituary of Alan Cameron in *The Times*, September 4, 1952.
16. May Sarton, *A World of Light*.

Chapter VII: "People in Their Thirties" (pages 135–158)

1. Sean O'Faolain, *The Vanishing Hero*.
2. E.B.'s introduction to *The Faber Book of Modern Short Stories*.
3. Interview in *The Bell* (an Irish monthly founded by Sean O'Faolain in 1940), Vol. 4, No. 6.
4. E.B. to William Plomer.
5. Later Mrs. R. C. Chilver, and Principal of Lady Margaret Hall, Oxford.
6. E.B. to William Plomer.
7. E.B. to Jean Rowntree.
8. "Salzburg", reprinted in *Collected Impressions*.
9. Autobiographical note, *circa* 1947.

Chapter VIII: Noon (pages 159–184)

1. E.B.'s preface to Knopf edition of *Ivy Gripped the Steps and Other Stories*; reprinted in *Collected Impressions*.
2. In *Collected Impressions*.
3. From "I Hear You Say So", included in *A Day in the Dark and Other Stories*.
4. John Lehmann, *I Am My Brother*.
5. This and all other direct quotations from Charles Ritchie are from his *The Siren Years*.
6. James Lees-Milne, *Ancestral Voices*.
7. Cicely Greig, *Ivy Compton-Burnett: A Memoir*.
8. "Manners": a review of *Can I Help You?*, by Viola

Notes

Tree, 1937; reprinted in *Collected Impressions*.

9. Charles Ritchie, *The Siren Years*.
10. E.B.'s preface to Knopf edition of *Ivy Gripped the Steps and Other Stories*.
11. Edmund Wilson, *Europe Without Baedeker*.

Chapter IX: After Noon (pages 185–209)

1. E.B. to Charles Ritchie.
2. Edward Sackville-West, *Inclinations*.
3. Autobiographical material for *The Broadsheet*, n.d.
4. All Daniel George's comments are taken from Michael Howard's *Jonathan Cape, Publisher*.
5. This and the whole account of the victory celebrations which follows are taken from E.B.'s letters to Charles Ritchie.
6. Afterword to 1964 edition of *Bowen's Court*.
7. *Ibid.*
8. Quoted in *The Irish Times*, March 24, 1975.
9. *The Bell*, Vol. 4, No. 6.
10. Edmund Burke, *Reflections on the Revolution in France*, 1790.

Chapter X: New Directions (pages 210–229)

1. Cyril Connolly, "London Letter"; reprinted in his *Ideas and Places*.
2. *Ibid.*
3. *The Diaries of Evelyn Waugh*.
4. Cyril Connolly, *Enemies of Promise*.

5. Cyril Connolly, "Hail and Farewell II": reprinted in his *Ideas and Places*.
6. Cyril Connolly "The Cost of Letters"; reprinted in his *Ideas and Places*.
7. H.R.C.
8. *Ibid.*
9. Graham Greene in his preface to *The Third Man and Loser Takes All*.
10. B.B.C. Third Programme interview, 1959.

Chapter XI: Dislocations (pages 230–253)

1. Virginia Spencer Carr, *The Lonely Hunter*.
2. Jane Rule, *Lesbian Images*.
3. "Disloyalties"; reprinted in *Afterthought*.
4. This and the following quotations from May Sarton are from *A World of Light*.
5. H.R.C.
6. E.B.'s preface to Cynthia Asquith's *The Second Ghost Book*; reprinted in *Afterthought*.
7. Rose Macaulay, *Letters to a Friend 1952–8*, ed. Constance Babington Smith.
8. *Punch*, March 23, 1955.
9. Quoted in May Sarton, *A World of Light*.

Chapter XII: No Abiding City (pages 254–277)

1. *Bowen's Court*.
2. *Ibid.*
3. May Sarton, *A World of Light*.
4. E.B. to Jean Black.
5. C. M. Bowra, *Memories*.
6. *The Diaries of Evelyn Waugh*.

Notes

Chapter XIII: Coming Home (pages 278–301)

1. *Aspects of E. M. Forster,* ed. Oliver Stallybrass.
2. The account of Julian Jebb's visit to Hythe is from his unpublished essay "Memories of Elizabeth Bowen".
3. Thomas Hyde to V.G.
4. *A Time in Rome.*
5. E.B. to Georgina Battiscombe.
6. E.B. to Sir William and Lady Hayter.
7. John Morley to Lady Fairfax-Lucy, after E.B.'s death.

Select Bibliography

Elizabeth Bowen, V. S. Pritchett, Graham Greene: WHY DO I WRITE? London: Percival Marshall, 1948.

C. M. Bowra: MEMORIES 1898–1939. London: Weidenfeld & Nicolson, 1966. Cambridge: Harvard University Press, 1966.

Jocelyn Brooke: ELIZABETH BOWEN. London: The British Council, 1952. New York: British Book Centre, 1973.

Virginia Spencer Carr: THE LONELY HUNTER: A BIOGRAPHY OF CARSON MCCULLERS. Garden City, N.Y.: Doubleday, 1975.

Cyril Connolly: ENEMIES OF PROMISE. London: André Deutsch, 1948.

————: IDEAS AND PLACES. London: Weidenfeld & Nicolson, 1953.

A. E. Coppard (ed.): CONSEQUENCES. Waltham St. Lawrence, Berkshire: Golden Cockerel Press, 1932.

THE FABER BOOK OF MODERN SHORT STORIES (ed. and with an introduction by Elizabeth Bowen). London: Faber & Faber, 1937.

Graham Greene: THE THIRD MAN AND LOSER TAKES ALL. London: Heinemann & The Bodley Head, 1976. Published as THE THIRD MAN. New York: Pocket Books, 1974.

Cicely Greig: IVY COMPTON-BURNETT: A MEMOIR. London: Garnstone Press, 1972.

John Gross: THE RISE AND FALL OF THE MAN OF LETTERS. London: Weidenfeld & Nicolson, 1969. New York: Macmillan, 1969.

Rupert Hart-Davis: HUGH WALPOLE. London: Macmillan, 1952.

Michael S. Howard: JONATHAN CAPE, PUBLISHER. London: Cape, 1971.

Edwin J. Kenney: ELIZABETH BOWEN. Lewisburg, Pa.: Bucknell University Press, 1975.

James Lees-Milne: ANCESTRAL VOICES. London: Chatto & Windus, 1975.

John Lehmann: I AM MY BROTHER. London: Longmans, 1960.

————: THE AMPLE PROPOSITION. London: Longmans, 1966.

———— (ed.): COMING TO LONDON. London: Phoenix House, 1957.

Rosamond Lehmann: THE SWAN IN THE EVENING. London: Collins, 1967.

Rose Macaulay: LETTERS TO A FRIEND 1952–8 (ed. Constance Babington Smith). London: Collins, 1962. Westminster, Md.: Christian Classics, 1964.

Sean O'Faolain: THE VANISHING HERO. London: Eyre & Spottiswoode, 1956. Plainview, N.Y.: Books for Libraries, 1957.

William Plomer: AT HOME. London: Cape, 1958. Plainview, N.Y.: Books for Libraries, 1958.

Charles Ritchie: THE SIREN YEARS: UNDIPLOMATIC DIARIES 1937–1945. London: Macmillan, 1974.

Jane Rule: LESBIAN IMAGES. London: Peter Davies, 1976. Garden City, N.Y.: Doubleday, 1975.

Edward Sackville-West: INCLINATIONS. London: Secker & Warburg, 1949. Philadelphia: Richard West, 1949.

May Sarton: A WORLD OF LIGHT: PORTRAITS AND CELEBRATIONS. New York: Norton, 1976.

Hanna Sheehy Skeffington: BRITISH MILITARISM AS I HAVE KNOWN IT. New York: Donnelly Press, 1917.

Stephen Spender: WORLD WITHIN WORLD. London: Hamish Hamilton, 1951. Berkeley: University of California Press, 1951.

Oliver Stallybrass (ed.): ASPECTS OF E. M. FORSTER. London: Edward Arnold, 1969.

Susan Tweedsmuir: A WINTER BOUQUET. London: Duckworth, 1954.

THE DIARIES OF EVELYN WAUGH (ed. Michael Davie): London: Weidenfeld & Nicolson, 1976. Boston: Little, Brown, 1976.

Terence de Vere White: THE ANGLO-IRISH. London: Gollancz, 1972.

Edmund Wilson: EUROPE WITHOUT BAEDEKER. London: Secker & Warburg, 1948. Second revised edition, New York: Farrar, Straus & Giroux, 1966.

————: THE TWENTIES. London: Macmillan, 1975. New York: Farrar, Straus & Giroux, 1975.

Leonard Woolf: THE JOURNEY NOT THE ARRIVAL MATTERS: AN AUTOBIOGRAPHY OF THE YEARS 1939–1969. London: Hogarth Press, 1969. New York: Harcourt Brace Jovanovich, 1975.

Virginia Woolf: A WRITER'S DIARY (ed. Leonard Woolf). London: Hogarth Press, 1953. New York: Harcourt Brace Jovanovich, 1954, 1973.

Books by Elizabeth Bowen

ENCOUNTERS. *London: Sidgwick & Jackson, 1923. Published as part of* The Early Stories, *New York: Knopf, 1951.*

ANN LEE'S AND OTHER STORIES. *London: Sidgwick & Jackson, 1926. Published as part of* The Early Stories, *New York: Knopf, 1951.*

THE HOTEL. *London: Constable, 1927. New York: Dial, 1928.*

THE LAST SEPTEMBER. *London: Constable, 1929. New York: Dial, 1929. New York: Knopf, 1952.*

JOINING CHARLES. *London: Constable, 1929. New York: Dial, 1929.*

FRIENDS AND RELATIONS. *London: Constable, 1931. New York: Dial, 1931.*

TO THE NORTH. *London: Gollancz, 1932. New York: Knopf, 1935.*

THE CAT JUMPS. *London: Gollancz, 1934.*

THE HOUSE IN PARIS. *London: Gollancz, 1935. New York: Knopf, 1936.*

THE DEATH OF THE HEART. *London: Gollancz, 1938. New York: Knopf, 1939.*

LOOK AT ALL THOSE ROSES. *London: Gollancz, 1941. New York: Knopf, 1941.*

SEVEN WINTERS. *Dublin: Cuala Press, 1942 (limited edition of 450 copies). London: Longmans, 1943. Published as part of* Seven Winters and Afterthoughts, *New York: Knopf, 1962.*

BOWEN'S COURT. *London: Longmans, 1942. New York: Knopf, 1942; second revised edition, 1964.*

ENGLISH NOVELISTS. *London: Collins, 1942.*

THE DEMON LOVER. *London: Cape, 1945. Published as* Ivy Gripped the Steps and Other Stories. *New York: Knopf, 1946.*

THE HEAT OF THE DAY. *London: Cape, 1949. New York: Knopf, 1949.*

COLLECTED IMPRESSIONS. *London: Longmans, 1950. New York: Knopf, 1950.*

THE SHELBOURNE. *London: Harrap, 1951. Published as* The Shelbourne Hotel, *New York: Knopf, 1951.*

THE EARLY STORIES. *New York: Knopf, 1951.*

A WORLD OF LOVE. *London: Cape, 1955. New York: Knopf, 1955.*

STORIES BY ELIZABETH BOWEN. *New York: Vintage Books, 1959.*

A TIME IN ROME. *London: Longmans, 1960. New York: Knopf, 1960.*

AFTERTHOUGHT. *London: Longmans, 1962. Published as part of* Seven Winters and Afterthoughts, *New York: Knopf, 1962.*

THE LITTLE GIRLS. *London: Cape, 1964. New York: Knopf, 1964.*

THE GOOD TIGER. *New York: Knopf, 1965. London: Cape, 1970.*

A DAY IN THE DARK AND OTHER STORIES. *London: Cape, 1965.*

EVA TROUT. *New York: Knopf, 1968. London: Cape, 1969.*

PICTURES AND CONVERSATIONS. *London: Cape, 1975. New York: Knopf, 1975. (Posthumous: edited and with a foreword by Spencer Curtis Brown.)*

Readers who need a more detailed listing of works by and about Elizabeth Bowen, including her many articles for periodicals as well as critical books and articles on her work by others, are advised to consult J'nan M. Sellery's *Elizabeth Bowen: A Descriptive Bibliography*, University of Texas Press, 1977.

Index

Index

Index

Index

Bowen, Elizabeth—writing (*cont.*)
156, 188; influences on,
29, 36–7, 145–6, 207, 284;
"life with the lid on," 81,
82, 99, 137; male
characters, 103, 104, 120,
144, 151, 153, 155, 185,
189, 190, 191; "older
woman" as character, 74,
75, 80, 99, 117, 250–1;
theme of innocence, xiv,
38, 105, 152–3, 155, 248,
283; two dissimilar women
as characters, 80, 83,
104–5, 152; wartime
experiences, effect of, 160,
162, 163, 177–86 *passim*,
192, 193, 205
Bowen, Henry (fl. 1775), 4, 7–8
Bowen, Col. Henry, 6–7
Bowen, Mrs. Henry (Jane Cole),
7
Bowen, Henry Charles Cole, 4,
10–11, 12, 44, 231
and Alan Cameron, 79
and daughter (E.B.), 25, 26,
28, 30–1, 34, 46, 61, 64,
276
death and funeral, 84–5, 232
marriage to Florence Colley,
19, 20, 23, 24–5, 30, 31;
engagement, 18–19
mental illness, 24, 25, 26, 30,
84, 276
remarriage to Mary Gwynn,
45–6, 84
on the Troubles, 48, 83
as widower, 33
Bowen, Mrs. Henry Charles
Cole (Florence Colley),
17, 18
and daughter (E.B.), 23,
26–31 *passim*, 51, 52, 276;
effect of mother's death,
31, 32, 33, 52, 64

death and burial, 31
marriage, 19, 20, 23, 24–5,
30, 31; engagement, 18–19;
husband's mental illness,
24, 25, 26
Bowen, Mrs. Henry Charles
Cole (Mary Gwynn), 45–6,
84, 86
Bowen, John, 7
Bowen, Marjory: *Black Magic*,
34
Bowen, Robert Cole, 9, 10,
11–12, 86
Bowen, Mrs. Robert Cole (Elizabeth Clarke), 9, 10, 11
Bowen, Mrs. Robert Cole
(Georgina Mansergh), 11
Bowen, Sarah, 4, 11, 12, 20, 34
Bowen-Colthurst, Mrs.
Georgina, 44
Bowen-Colthurst, Capt. John,
44–5
Bowen's Court: building of, 4, 8
cost of upkeep, 86, 88–9, 253,
254
demolishment of, 3, 258
descriptions of, 5, 8, 9, 20,
85–6
E.B.: with Alan, 5–6, 79, 86,
87, 88–9, 97, 116, 136,
140, 155–6, 198–9, 202,
208, 210, 216, 228, 230;
after Alan's death, 232–8,
242–8, 252–60 *passim*, 263,
276; childhood and early
life, 20–1, 25, 31, 34–5,
45, 46, 48–50; decision to
sell and sale, 253, 256,
257, 259, 260, 276; final
leave-taking, 257; fondness
for and commitment to,
3, 88, 150, 206; history
of (*Bowen's Court*), 12,
22, 31, 115, 200–2, 206;
inheritance of, 5, 84; in

322

Index

Index